HOW TO STAY IN LONDON FOR LESS

HOW TO STAY IN LONDON FOR LESS

Short-Term Apartments Ideal for All Travelers

Diana and Ronald Jensen

Photographs by Clare Parmalee

CAPITAL
BOOKS, INC.
Sterling, Virginia

Cover photos: (upper left) Durley House, Knightsbridge; (upper right) Craven Garden Lodge, Baywater; (lower left) Lancaster House, Chelsea; (lower right) Draycott House, Chelsea

Capital Books, Inc.
P.O. Box 605
Herndon, Virginia 20172-0605

Library of Congress Cataloging-in-Publication Data

Jensen, Diana.
    How to stay in London for less : short-term apartments ideal for all travelers /
Diana and Ronald Jensen ; photographs by Clare Parmalee.
       p. cm.
    Includes bibliographical references.
    ISBN 1-892123-66-5 (alk. paper)
     1. Apartments—England—London—Guidebooks.   I. Jensen, Ronald.
    II. Title

   TX907.5.G7 J45 2002
   647.94421'01—dc21

                         2001037719

Printed in the United States of America on acid-free paper that meets the American National Standards Institute Z39-48 Standard.

Cover design by Kevin Chadwick
Text design by PEN & PALETTE Unlimited

First Edition

10 9 8 7 6 5 4 3 2 1

Contents

Acknowledgments

We wish to thank those who helped us through the ins and outs of writing this book. My sister and brother-in-law, Judy and Bill Clair, not only read the proposal as a family duty, but gave us the valuable insights of lifelong world travelers. Mike Kevany contributed the practical advice of a business expert and traveler. Jogues Prandoni spent hours introducing us to the quirky world of graphics and helped us tame rebellious icons (a struggle that continues to this day).

We are especially grateful to the apartment managers and their coworkers who welcomed us, and answered our unending questions before, during, and after our visits to their apartments—all without assurance that the book would be published.

Special thanks to our agent, Lynn Whittaker, for her enthusiasm for this project from day one and for knowing exactly the right publisher for us.

And thanks to our publisher, Kathleen Hughes, and editor, Noemi Taylor, for their faith in our manuscript, and to production editor Dorothy Smith for her guidance through the process of publication.

Chapter 1

Introduction to Short-Term Apartment Living

At two o'clock on a warm July afternoon in 1978, jet-lagged and bedraggled, we struggled up Egerton Gardens in Knightsbridge. We had been to London before, but this time we tried something new. We saw a tiny note for Lamb's Service Flats in a guidebook. Instead of a hotel room, we rented an apartment for our week's stay.

The residential neighborhood was beautiful, and the houses we passed grand indeed. Stately, white stone townhouses, just like the one in *Upstairs/Downstairs*. We matched the address on our confirmation letter to the one on the house before us and marched up the steps. Could this be Lamb's? There was no sign. Then we saw, nestled among the other nameplates by individual doorbells, our very own placard. Just like we lived there permanently.

Our entire experience with Lamb's was a delight. The inside of the house was as elegant as the outside. We had its smallest apartment but that was fine with us. The flat had built-in bookcases, antique knickknacks, a telephone, color television, and ample space for a sofa and chairs. The milkman delivered a pint each morning (milk on the bottom, cream on the top), and the housekeeper left a continental breakfast outside our door. It was a setting to match our fantasies. And Lamb's was only £13 per day (about $25).

We were hooked. We now can't recall the last time we stayed in a hotel. Today it is possible to rent an apartment or private house almost anywhere in the world. We have enjoyed apartment living in Bath, Stratford-upon-Avon, Cheltenham, Devon, and Cornwall; in Ireland, Dublin and Galway; in France, Paris and Brittany. We rented in New York City, San Francisco, Cape Cod, Toronto, Nova Scotia, and Prince Edward Island in the Americas. In each flat or house, we settled in, spread out, felt at home, and mingled with neighbors.

It is no longer possible, of course, to find a decent night's lodging in London for £13 — more like £130. London is the most expensive capital in Europe, the second most expensive city in the world. But choices for short-term apartment stays abound, partly because of the expanding global business economy. In gathering material for *How to Stay in London for Less,* we assessed more than 120 apartments/apartment complexes, representing more than 3,000 flats in central London. These apartments with all modern amenities are available, not just for the business person, but for all visitors. Take advantage of the London boom. We can assure you that there are more apartment options open to you now than ever before.

The Advantages of an Apartment Stay

Economy

According to the *London Financial Times,* the basic rent for a flat is generally 25 percent less than the cost of a comparable hotel room. These basic savings increase with each additional person in the flat. The savings are great because hotels must support restaurants, meeting rooms, expansive lobbies, and ballrooms in a city where real estate prices are exorbitant. Flats come without such extras, which most guests never use anyway.

In the British Tourist Authority's year 2000 listing of hotels in central London, the prices for a double room range from a low season cost of $119 per night for a room *without* private bath in Pimlico to $629 per night for a luxury hotel near Hyde Park. For a double room *with* private bath in a tourist class hotel, the range of prices in low season is from $130 per night in a hotel near Russell Square to $373 per night in Knightsbridge. According to the *New York Times* of July 29, 2001, the average cost of a hotel room for one person is $350.

By comparison, rental for a studio flat in central London can be as low as $65 per night, and a one-bedroom flat can be had for $79 per night. These are the least expensive flats we found, but they are all self-contained, clean, with linens supplied, and good cooking facilities. They are in neighborhoods that are both safe and convenient. In fact, for the price of a two-star double hotel room without a private bath, you can rent a two-bedroom apartment. (All prices in this book are converted into U.S. dollars at a rate of $1.62 to one English pound [£1] and include the value-added tax [VAT] of 17.5 percent.)

Economy need not sacrifice luxury or style. Many of the flats listed here are every bit as elegantly appointed as a luxury hotel and in the best neighborhoods. More than half have daily maid service and some offer shopping services. Luxury apartments are quite expensive but can also be a good value.

Beyond the basic cost savings in rent are the additional savings from meal preparation. Even if breakfast is excluded, sometimes a part of a hotel room rate, the savings on other meals are considerable. The U.S. government allows $105 per diem for meals in London, and that is not overly generous. A three-star restaurant dinner is considered modest at $70 per person. A pub lunch is between $10 and $15 (McDonalds, $7). Add a family with even one teenage appetite, and the savings become more remarkable. In fact, a family of four could rent a two-bedroom flat for the cost of one day's meals for four people. And we haven't even mentioned snacks, much cheaper from the corner grocery than a hotel coffee shop.

For those who want to minimize food preparation on holiday, as do working Londoners most days, many department stores have elaborate "food halls" with all manner of prepared or ready-to-fix meals, plus fruit and vegetables from around the world. What could be better after a hard day's touring than a game pie from Harrods and a glass of wine from your local Oddbins, followed by fruit and cheese with your feet up in front of the telly?

Space

Better living for less in a holiday flat also means more space than your average hotel room, especially in the lower price categories. There is room to unpack and stow your luggage out of sight. Even a studio flat is larger than most double hotel rooms, and the extra area becomes quite welcome after a stay longer than a day or two. The flats listed in *How to Stay in London for Less,* with the exception of two studios, have either a sofa or easy chairs, so that there is a comfortable place to sit and relax other than the bed.

A one-bedroom apartment has the added attraction of allowing a late read or TV show without bothering your traveling companions.

For the business traveler, an apartment offers a comfortable spot away from the sleeping area for an informal meeting with a client or colleagues. Often there is a computer connection with fax facilities available nearby, if not in the flat itself

Convenience

The number of short-term rental flats in London has increased remarkably in the last few years. Every neighborhood in central London has flats for rent. You need not find yourself on the outskirts but can be in the city center within walking distance or a short tube ride of most major attractions.

Familiarity

In addition to the practical considerations of cost, space, and convenience, a less tangible but priceless benefit of apartment living is that you are part of the neighborhood and can get to know London as few tourists can. Join Londoners as they shop for their dinner ingredients. After a purchase or two, the newsagent will share his worldview with you. Have a few pints at the corner pub and your face will soon become familiar to your local publican. As soon as we enter our "local," the Beehive, we are greeted by "Another year gone already?" and friendly waves.

Walk in nearby parks, explore alternate routes to the underground, and sample the restaurants around the corner and down the street. By the time you leave, you will be an expert on your neighborhood, ready to give advice and directions to "tourists" who wander by.

Disadvantages

Most apartment complexes do not have room service or on-site restaurants. They also do not have conference facilities for large groups, although some can provide meeting space for a small number of people. Some have on-site managers or 24-hour concierge services while some do not. In less expensive flats, towels provided are minimal, one bath and one hand towel per person. The same is true of china and cutlery, one of each item per person in the flat. A few apartments do not include private telephone service, but will add it on request with a deposit to British Telecom, the English telephone company.

It is important to know that very few London apartments and many hotels do not have central air conditioning. This is true of even the most expensive flats. Since London summer temperatures rarely rise into the 80s, air conditioning is desirable only during unusually hot spells. In our checklist, we have noted where central air conditioning is available. If you must have air conditioning for medical reasons, double-check with the manager at the time you make your booking

Many apartments, even very expensive ones, accept bookings only for a seven-night minimum. Some, on the other hand, will book you for as little as one night. We have included these minimums in our listing.

Our Goal

Our goal is to provide our readers with a full description of each flat. We want our readers to know exactly what is included in each apartment and what is not. If you rent a flat sight unseen without a recommendation, you could be in for an unpleasant surprise. You might find yourself in a dirty room with shabby furnishings in a marginal neighborhood.

The purpose of this book is to prevent such a disaster. We only include flats or flat complexes that we visited. We could not, of course, inspect each and every flat in large complexes. We did, however, view each type of apartment offered. Two Hyde Park Square, for example, has two types of studios (standard and superior) and two types of one-bedroom flats (superior and senior). We visited one of each. Since Two Hyde Park Square was built as an apartment block, "purpose built" as the English say, and each type of flat has the same floor plan, we feel confident that the quality of the flats we saw is typical of all of the flats in the building. Where each flat is individually owned and decorated, and management has less control, as is the case with Park West, we can be less certain of the quality of the furnishings. Since management does enforce standards for cleanliness, however, we know that each flat is clean and that it has the essential facilities.

Agencies that rent only individual properties of absent owners present the greatest challenge for us. Some of them represent very large numbers of flats. Barclay, one of the oldest and largest agencies, handles more than 3,500. We could not view all of them. The agency properties we did visit are described in the neighborhood listings. Agencies are listed in the appendix. Even if a particular agency has a flat of interest to you that is not included in our book, many agencies have photographs, or better yet, videos on their web page that present accurate portraits of their rental flats. If there is neither a photo nor video, be wary. Although most agencies are protective of their reputation and do not want to rent you something you would not be satisfied with, some agencies just want to rent flats.

If you hope to negotiate a lower price than the one listed (and some managers have told us that they do have flexibility), it is best to deal directly with the on-site reservation staff rather than an agency. Remember that the fee quoted you by an agency includes its commission as part of the rental price. On-site staff also are more familiar with each and every flat and can describe in detail exactly what is included. For each block of flats that we visited, we have the telephone number; fax, e-mail, and web site, if possible; and, when available, names of managers who can book your flat for you.

Our Ratings

Although we found the British Tourist Authority's (BTA's) rating system for flats helpful, it did not supply enough information to allow an informed decision in selecting an apartment. In addition, many facilities do not participate in the system. As a result, a large number of desirable flats are not rated and not known to visitors who rely on BTA for accommodation information.

Because of these limitations in BTA's program, we decided to construct our own rating system. Our system includes only properties that would be rated "standard" or above in other guidebooks. All apartments are self-contained with private baths, linens, appliances, customary household furnishings, and some extras. We chose the symbol of a castle 🏰 to represent quality. Our ratings range from three castles for "standard" to five for "deluxe." We add a plus, +, to the lower rating when a facility falls between two categories.

To make our system as objective as possible, we developed a checklist of amenities. Two raters completed a checklist for each flat.

Each three-castle flat is self-contained with private bath, linens, and an adequate supply of china, cooking utensils, and cutlery. All have a refrigerator, stove with cooktop (except for some studios that only have microwaves), microwave, electric kettle, teapot, toaster, color TV, and telephone.

In the four-castle category, all properties supply all of the above plus entry phone security or its equivalent, hair dryer, washer/dryer, full-sized refrigerator, and coffee maker. Five-castle properties contain all of the amenities of the lower categories but are the most luxurious and spacious with more gadgets or bigger appliances than other properties. Generally, they are in fancier neighborhoods.

We include two large mansion blocks, Chelsea Cloisters and Park West, that are unrated. The flats in these properties are owned by individuals, and the size and quality of your apartment depends on which one you get. We also include Ryder Street Chambers, the only complex in *How to Stay in London for Less* that does not have kitchen facilities. Due to fire regulations, you may brew tea or coffee but nothing else. The Chambers is charming, convenient, and good for those who want to eat out or have meals delivered.

In addition to the list of amenities, we also provide our readers with a lengthy description of the layout, style, adequacy, and quality of furnishings and decor in each flat.

Prices

As mentioned above, all of the prices reported in this book are in American dollars at a conversion rate of $1.62 to £1, and all include the VAT. (Although the pound was at a record low when we went to press, we chose a conversion rate of 1.62 to reflect the average rate over the last 10 years.) Some apartment complexes do not include the VAT in the price they quote you. Since the VAT has held steady at a hefty 17.5 percent for many years, unwary visitors may be in for a nasty shock when they hear the bottom line. While the VAT is recoverable for many items that are bought and

> **Prices:** All prices quoted were accurate at time of printing. All include VAT and are converted at a rate of $1.62 to £1. Always check at time of booking. Prices and rates fluctuate.

taken out of Britain, rental for short-term accommodations in flats or hotels usually is not. To save our readers the sticker shock of an unexpected VAT, we have included it in all of our prices, even when the leasing agency did not. If the rate quoted to you is lower than the one we have given, always double-check to make sure that the VAT has been included.

Hint: The exchange rate varies daily. To convert to current cost, divide the price by 1.62 and multiply by the rate in that day's financial section of your local paper.

If you are planning a longer stay, the VAT reduces to 3.5 percent after 28 days. Business-people who have an EU (European Union) VAT number may get the entire VAT refunded.

Travel Insurance

Apartment managers often require a large deposit or a week's rent at the time of booking. What happens if the unexpected happens and you have to cancel? If far enough in advance, you will get your deposit back. If not, you will forfeit your deposit and be held liable for the entire cost of your booked stay, if the apartment cannot be rerented. Travel insurance will help defer this expense.

According to the *Washington Post,* for complete travel insurance including trip interruption or cancellation, medical and emergency assistance, and lost luggage, the cost is 4 to 6 percent of the amount you want to cover. Components may be purchased separately, so if you have medical coverage, you can buy cancellation insurance alone.

A good resource for learning more about travel insurance is *www.WorldTravel Center.com.* It provides an explanation of travel insurance types and can direct you to underwriters.

How to Use This Book

Aside from the introductory and last chapter in *How to Stay in London for Less,* each chapter is organized in the same way, and deals with a specific neighborhood in central London. We have included those areas that are most likely to be visited by tourists, those that provide easy access to the rest of the city, and those areas with the most short-term apartments to let. The neighborhood chapters begin with Marylebone and move clockwise around inner London.

A brief description of the area and of the major attractions begins each chapter. So that you can see quickly what is available in each neighborhood, a table called "At a Glance" immediately follows. The table lists each apartment/apartment complex included in the chapter and the general types of apartments available. The range of prices for each type of flat in American dollars (including VAT), by night and by week, is in the square for that type of apartment. The prices reflect low and high season and variations in the quality of individual flats. Each chapter also has a map of all of the apartments included, so that you can see clearly where each is located.

We have also included photographs, one from each site that permitted pictures. Some were either occupied or undergoing renovation and could not be photographed.

Helpful Terms:

Bed-sit: Similar to a studio but often sharing a bath. Rarely used today.

English double bed: A bed as wide as a queen-size but shorter (5 by 6 feet).

Gastropub: Pub with restaurant-quality food and table service that provides dinner.

Listed and graded: Buildings registered as historic properties whose architectural integrity must be preserved.

Maisonette: Any apartment on two or more floors.

Zip-and-link: A king-size bed that can be separated into two single beds.

Detailed descriptions of all the apartments come after the table. Each description ends with detailed lists of amenities and information on reservations, prices, and so on. Those flats that are especially suited for business travelers and families are marked by the following symbols:

The chapters close with a history and fuller description of the attractions of the neighborhood, as well as notes on some of our favorite pubs, shops, markets, and restaurants near the apartments.

Chapter 11 describes flats that rent for longer short-term stays of from 22 to 90 days. These apartments are located throughout central London.

As mentioned above, the appendix contains a list of agencies that rent short-term apartments.

Helpful Hints

To and From the Airport

Over the past 25 years, we have probably tried every way to and from Heathrow except walking. On our first few trips we took the Airbus Heathrow Shuttle (020 722 1234; £7 [$11.34] one way or £12 [$19.44] there and back, called "return"), into the terminal near Victoria Station and then a taxi to our destination. When we became more familiar with London's underground, we took the tube into the city for £3.40 ($5.50) and walked to our flat. This was economical, but a royal pain during the morning rush hour carrying baggage for a three-week stay.

Change in London Area Codes: In April 2000, all of London's area codes changed. The old 171 code became 207. The old 181 code became 208. We included the new codes in all of our listings.

Now there is the new London-Heathrow Express, a rapid train direct from the four Heathrow terminals that will take you to Paddington Station in 20 minutes. Economy fare is £12 ($19.44). The trip is swift and comfortable, and there is plenty of space for luggage.

In the past few years, several shuttle services have sprung up that specialize in trips to and from London's airports. They advertise one-way fares of £17 ($27.54) to and from Heathrow. (Regular black cab fare to central London is about £45, or $73.) With three of us and a large amount of luggage, our fare to Heathrow was £25 ($40.50), cheaper than three express train tickets. Since the shuttle dropped us right at our terminal, it also saved us any hassle with our luggage. Although you travel by surface with the car service and could be delayed by traffic, our trip to Heathrow during rush hour took only 45 minutes. It was our easiest trip yet.

Some say that only black cabs are safe and reliable. Check with your landlord at time of booking for the airport service he or she recommends. If it's not a savings, make your own arrangements.

At Gatwick Airport, the Gatwick Express train to Victoria Station leaves every 15 minutes during the day and every hour at night. Fare is £10.20 ($16.52). Between 5 A.M. and 11 P.M., the Jetlink 777 bus (0208-668-7261; £8, or $12.96) leaves every hour or two for Victoria Station.

At the Airport

Since most flats do not allow occupancy until the afternoon and most flights, from the United States at least, arrive at Heathrow in the very early morning, there is no need to rush into the city. We always use this time to purchase seven-day Travelcards for travel by both tube and bus (valid each day after 9:30 A.M.). We buy the cards from London Transport at the ticket office near Heathrow's tube entrance. The cards can be purchased by zones. A card that allows travel in zone one, most of the places you will want to go, costs £15.90 ($25.76). Not only is the Travelcard a great savings, it is also a great convenience. You do not need to stop to purchase a fare for each trip, but just insert your card at the gate, retrieve it as it comes out the other side, and you are on your way. The Travelcard is also honored on city buses within the zones. Hop on at any bus stop.

> **Extra Photos:** Remember, if you have an extra passport photo, bring it with you. You will need it to purchase a Travelcard.

You are required to have a photo to buy a Travelcard. If you have an extra passport photo, bring it along. If not, there are photo booths at the airports. You will then be issued the photocard with your Travelcard. We used the same photocard for several years.

If you are too tired or jet-lagged to bother with all of this, Travelcards can be purchased at any tube station ticket kiosk or at major post offices.

Although the London underground system is a most convenient way of traveling around, do your very best to avoid it during rush hours. The trains are packed and uncomfortable, and even standing room is scarce.

Check-in Time

Just as for most hotels, the check-in time for flats and apartments is 2 P.M. If you arrive as early as most do, this makes for a very long waiting time, especially after a long flight and, for most of us, a lost night's sleep. Almost every apartment manager we spoke with said that he or she would be happy to let a visitor into the flat early if the other occupants had departed in time for the flat to be clean and ready. They cannot guarantee this, however, and at the height of the tourist season, the chances for early check-in are slim. The only way to guarantee an early check-in is to rent the flat from the night before.

Even if you cannot get in on arrival, most managers will check you in as soon as possible. All said that you are welcome to leave your luggage with them, so that you can at least go out and explore unencumbered. We use this time for grocery shopping—about all we are capable of after an all-night flight.

Off-Season Travel

Our academic work schedule lets us take winter vacations. London in the off season has many advantages. Air fares and apartments are cheaper. The theater season is in full swing. There are fewer tourists, and it is usually warmer in London than in Maryland. We know that it may rain or be chilly, but we come prepared for it, and London can be bleak and damp at any time of the year. The major disadvantage is that it grows dark at 4 P.M. For us this is not a big problem. After being out all day, we are tired and content to sit with our feet up and sip a cup of tea or a glass of wine.

If you are retired, take advantage of the savings from off-season travel. All flats included are suitable for older travelers, and most have an elevator, if one is needed. Check the listing.

On our last few January visits, London has surprised us. We have had many sunny days and only a few rainy, blustery ones. The parks are always green, and hyacinths blossom along the pathways. Only once did it snow, such a rare phenomenon that the city was in shock. It was the only topic of conversation for days.

And then, of course, there are the sales. Since most goods in London are more expensive than they are in the States, this is the only time of the year that we find real bargains. Laura Ashley's sales are terrific. Harrods is a mob scene.

Don't forget flowers. Even in winter, a large selection is available for your flat from all over Europe.

What to Bring for Apartment Living

London is one of the world's most cosmopolitan cities. You can find and buy anything you could possibly think of. You might not want to purchase it in great quantity, however, especially if waste bothers you. Since the place we usually stay does not offer a "welcome pack," there are a few items we bring from home—less now than we did on our earlier visits. We like to cook with Kosher salt, so we tuck a few weeks' supply into a plastic sandwich bag. The same with cornstarch or arrowroot to thicken sauces. Paper napkins are expensive and hard to find. We slip some into the bottom of a suitcase. Large and small freezer bags are useful for treats brought home from the bakery and for storing other items. On the trip over, you can put underwear, pajamas, or whatever in them, force the air out, and you have shrink-wrapped your clothes. They take up less space and the bags are very handy after you unpack. While flats provide towels, most do not supply face cloths.

It's up to you, of course, what you choose to bring. Whatever makes you feel at home.

Cooking in a London Flat

What could be simpler? It's just the same as cooking at home, isn't it?

But wait, what temperature exactly is Gas Mark Four? Is the gauge in centigrade? Is this a convection oven? How much is 258 grams? I only want four ounces of pâté.

It can be confusing. For this reason, we have included a conversion chart. Your flat will have an instruction manual that will tell you how to use your convection oven.

Conversion Chart

Ounces to Grams (multiply ounces by 30)			Oven Temperatures		
			Fahrenheit	Centigrade	Gas Mark
1 oz.	$\frac{1}{16}$ lb.	30 grams	32°	0°	
4 oz	$\frac{1}{4}$ lb.	120 grams	68°	20°	
8 oz.	$\frac{1}{2}$ lb.	240 grams	212°	100°	
12 oz.	$\frac{3}{4}$ lb.	360 grams	325°	160°	3
16 oz.	1 lb.	480 grams	350°	180°	4
			375°	190°	5
			400°	200°	6
			425°	220°	7
			450°	230°	8
			Broil		Grill

Remember that London cooks on a more powerful current. The electric kettle will boil quickly. Pans on your electric stove will heat up rapidly. The higher current is great for sautéing, just be aware that things will cook faster

> **Cooking "words to the wise":** Mince is ground beef, and salted beef is corned. A jacket potato is for baking. Courgettes are zucchini, aubergines are eggplant, mange tout are snow peas. Puddings are desserts. Biscuits are crackers and cookies. Baps are hamburger buns. Caster sugar is granulated, but icing sugar is confectioner's. Creams come single (18% butter fat), double (48% butter fat), and clotted (the real thing from Cornwall, Devon, or Dorset is 60% butter fat). Greek-style yogurt is an excellent substitute for sour cream.

Pubs and Beer

The pub is one of the unique pleasures of London and the United Kingdom. The neighborhood local is more personal and congenial than a bar or cafe—at least it can be after a few visits—and we have mentioned some of our favorites in each area.

English beer is also a bit different and one of the best reasons for visiting. Traditional English beer is actually ale. It is distinguished from American beer (usually lager) by the use of ale yeast. Most pubs serve several types and brands of ale varying in style and strength from light ales (light in alcohol, not necessarily color or taste) to "bitter" (which it is not), the standard ale. Pale ale is lightest in color and strongest. Brown ale is darker and weaker. Porters are dark and a bit sweet, and stout black and usually dry. All traditional ales or "real ales" are cask-conditioned, which means they are not pasteurized or artificially carbonated. The head is natural carbonation from the living yeast, not fizz; and the flavor, the natural blend of malt, hops, and yeast. It is served fresh from a handpump

> **Hint:** There is no table service in most pubs. You must order your beer and lunch from the bar.

that draws the ale by vacuum from the keg. The pump handle at the bar also carries a label naming the beer and its alcohol content, which is sometimes lower than American beers. To my mind, a good pint of bitter is almost worth the trip by itself.

There is another advantage to English pubs—no tipping.

A Note on Terms

When the English say a bathroom is *en suite,* they mean that it is in the bedroom. Most of the included flats have "power showers" to correct the very low water pressure that many Americans complained about. Satellite television is equivalent to U.S. cable television. A "welcome pack" is provided by many facilities. Usually it contains tea, coffee, sweets of some kind, and other things. Be sure to ask what comes in the welcome pack in your flat and make sure it is complimentary. English clothes dryers are much less efficient than U.S. ones. Don't think that yours is broken if it takes three times longer to dry clothes than you're used to.

We hope that you find *How to Stay in London for Less* useful and valuable in planning this and future visits to London. If you discover an apartment complex that is not included and you think it should be, please let us know. If you disagree with our assessment of a flat, please let us know that also or anything else you want to tell us. Please contact us through our web site, www.londonforlessflats.com, or through our publisher, Capital Books, Inc., 22841 Quicksilver Drive, Dulles, Virginia 20166. We want to hear from you.

Above all else, enjoy being at home in London!

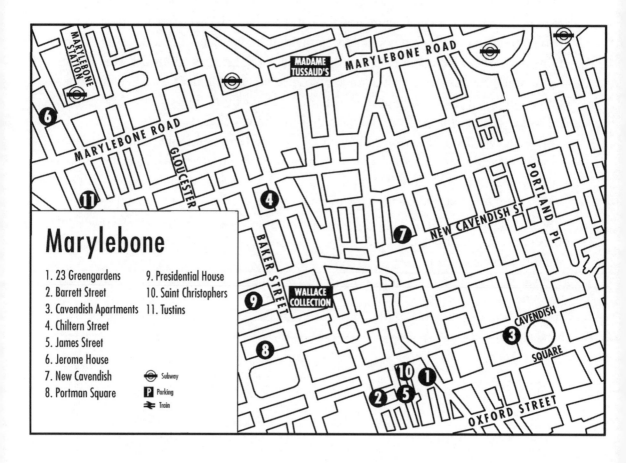

Marylebone

1. 23 Greengardens
2. Barrett Street
3. Cavendish Apartments
4. Chiltern Street
5. James Street
6. Jerome House
7. New Cavendish
8. Portman Square

9. Presidential House
10. Saint Christophers
11. Tustins

Subway
Parking
Train

Chapter 2

❦

Marylebone

Marylebone, "The Great City North of Oxford Street,"* may be central London's best-kept secret. It began as a village built beside a tiny riverside church, St. Mary-by-the-Bourne. Proximity to London attracted prominent Georgian families to turn its fields into grand housing estates grouped around squares that still bear their names—Portman, Cavendish, Montagu, and others.

Location is still a key attraction of the area. Its southern edge reaches Oxford Street and the great department stores—Selfridges and Marks and Spencer, while a 15-minute walk north brings you to Regent's Park: 400 acres of gardens, ponds, playing fields, and the London Zoo. Subways, buses, and trains intersect the area, providing quick access to all of London.

This modest, respectable district includes a number of treasures: Madame Tussaud's Waxworks on Marylebone Road; the Sherlock Holmes Museum around the corner on Baker Street; and the Wallace Collection on Manchester Square, one of the city's finest, and least-well-known, museums.

---

* Thomas Macaulay, 1831.

Marylebone at a Glance

Apartment	Studio	1-Bedroom	2-Bedroom	3-Bedroom	Other
23 Greengarden House No minimum stay		$314–$371 n $2,198–$2,598 w	$419–$496 n $2,495–$2,948 w		
Barrett Street Apts. 1-week minimum		$150 n $1,053 w			*Penthouse* $231 n $1,620 w (2 baths)
Cavendish Apts. No minimum stay refurbished nonrefurbished		$177–$286 n $1,237–$1,808 w	$163–$352 n $1,142–$2,284 w (1 or 2 baths)	$247–$590 n $1,713–$3,426 w (2 or 3 baths)	
Chiltern Street Apts. 1-week minimum		$127 n $890 w			
James Street Apts. 1-week minimum (flex.)	$93 n $648 w	$104 n $729 w	$162 n $1,134 w		
Jerome House No minimum stay	$175–$178 n $1,225–$1,247 w	$271–$275 n $1,897–$1,928 w	$339–$345 n $2,327–$2,415 w (2 baths)		
New Cavendish Street 1-week minimum					*Maisonette* $209 n $1,458 w
Portman Square Apts. No minimum stay		$227 n $1,377 w	$389–$551 n $2,592–$3,645 w (2 baths)	$503–$648 n $3,240–$4,374 w (2 baths)	

Apartment	Studio	1-Bedroom	2-Bedroom	3-Bedroom	Other
Presidential Apts. 1-week minimum (flex.) 	$105–$170 n $737–$1,183 w	$130–$194 n $907–$1,361 w			
St. Christopher's Place 1-week minimum (flex.) 		$116 n $810 w			
Tustin's Holiday Flats 1-week minimum 		$79–$102 n $551–$713 w	$143–$145 n $996–$1,013 w	$149–$152 n $1,045–$1,061 w	

NOTES: (1) All prices are in American dollars converted at $1.62 to £1 and include VAT. To convert to the current rate, divide the dollar amount by 1.62 and multiply by the rate listed in today's local paper. (2) n=night; w=week.

Marylebone Apartments in Detail

23 Greengarden House, St. Christopher's Place, London W1M 5HD

photo p. A

Tucked into St. Christopher's Place, a pedestrian mall of boutiques and restaurants behind Oxford Street, 23 Greengarden House's 23 apartments are intimate, luxurious, and homey. You enter the blue brick, two-building complex through large, elegant doors on the mall. The apartments are on the four upper levels, with one lift for each of the buildings. You exit the lift onto an outdoor balcony/hallway. The entrances to the individual apartments are off this hallway. Each flat has its own window box with real flowers. When we visited on a mild January day, primroses and ornamental cherries bloomed in all of the boxes. The external entrances give each flat a feeling of privacy and individuality. The location is convenient not only for the executive with business in the city, but also for the tourist. In addition to the boutiques in the mall, it is only steps from Selfridges and the shops and restaurants of Oxford Street.

There are 15 one-bedroom and 8 two-bedroom apartments. Both types range from small (style C), to medium (style B), to large (style A). The prices reflect the sizes of the flats.

Each flat opens into a small foyer. Immediately to the left is a compact but fully functional kitchen with convection oven and stove top, dishwasher, and microwave. The washer/dryer is down the hall in its own compartment.

Beyond the foyer and kitchen is a sitting room with fireplace, two comfortable sofas (or one sofa and an easy chair), end tables, and a TV with satellite and movie reception. In a corner is a dining table with chairs. Most also have a desk.

The bedroom is down a hallway in the one-bedroom flat with the bath opposite. Each two-bedroom flat has two baths, one *en suite*. All baths have tubs and power showers. In all of the bedrooms, there are either twin or queen-size beds with two bedside tables, lamps, an additional TV, and an easy chair or two. Drapes, wall coverings, and comforters are color-coordinated. Furnishings throughout are traditional, fine quality, and, at the same time, comfortable.

Each apartment is equipped with an entry phone; safe; fax facilities; and two direct-dial phones, one with voice mail and one with a built-in U.S. modem with ISDN line for digital data transfer. There is a small meeting room; laundry, dry cleaning, and babysitting services are available at cost. Guests are welcome to use the health club and gym at Greengarden's sister property, the Atheneum Hotel, on Piccadilly.

Nikki Pybus, the cordial and dedicated manager, has been with Greengarden House for the last 14 years. Including her, there is a five-person full-time staff committed solely to the care of the 23 apartments and the guests. Maid service is provided Monday through Friday. The staff will even shop for groceries with no additional charge beyond that of the purchases. Service is of primary importance to Ms. Pybus. She and her staff are delighted to do their best to provide whatever guests might want, if they only ask for it.

AMENITIES—Elevator, telephone (2 lines), color TV with satellite, radio, computer connection (U.S. modem, ISDN line), fax in flat, maid service (5 days), concierge (manager and staff), refrigerator, freezer (small), stove, toaster, tea kettle, teapot, coffee maker, iron, microwave, dishwasher, washer/dryer, hair dryer, toiletries, welcome pack.

RESERVATIONS/PRICES/MISC.—Minimum stay: 1 night. **Reservations:** Nikki Pybus. **Telephone:** 0207-935-9191. **Fax:** 0207-935-8858. **E-mail:** *info@greengardenhouse. com.* **Web site:** *www.greengardenhouse.com.* **Prices per night from:** 1 bdrm (A)-$371, 1 bdrm (B)-$343, 1 bdrm (C)-$314 (max. occupancy, 2); 2 bdrm (A)-$496, 2 bdrm (B)-$457, 2 bdrm (C)-$419 (max. occupancy, 4). **Negotiate price?** no. **Deposit?** all prepaid 14 days prior to arrival. **Check in:** 2 P.M. **Check out:** 12 noon. **Credit cards?** yes. **Tube stop:** Bond Street.

Barrett Street Apartments, Barrett Street, London, W1M 5HS

photo p. A

The eight Globe-managed apartments on Barrett Street are just around the corner from the Globe office in a very convenient and lively location. They are just behind Self-ridges, steps from the Bond Street tube and the bustle of Oxford Street. Barrett Street enters St. Christopher's Place, which is full of restaurants, boutiques, and pubs.

The flats are housed in a small, modern redbrick building with white trim. Shops and cafes are on either side. With the exception of the two-bedroom penthouse, all of the apartments are one-bedroom. They are all equipped to the same standard but some are larger than others, mainly in the living room or "lounge." All have the same basic floor plan. The flat entrance is into a short L-shaped hallway. At the short end of the L, the bedroom opens to the left, the small bathroom is on the right, and the living/dining area is ahead. The open-plan kitchen is at the far right end.

In the larger apartments, the living area has an upholstered sofa with a large easy chair and matching hassock. Floor-to-ceiling drapes along wide windows are in a complementary shade. There are a white wooden coffee table, white end tables with lamps, an additional chair, and a TV with VCR. The floor is pine. A wooden dining table with four matching chairs is close to the open kitchen. The kitchen is up-to-date with blond wooden cabinets, glass burners on the full-size stove, an under-counter refrigerator, a microwave, and a washer/dryer behind a cabinet front. There are good-quality pots, pans, and china with an ample supply of wine glasses. The bathroom, small but comfortable, has a tub/shower. Towels are changed three times a week; maid service is on Monday, Wednesday, and Friday. The bedroom has a double bed with bedside tables and lamps. A closet runs the length of one wall.

The living area in the smaller flats is more simply furnished. There are blinds but no drapes, an upholstered sofa with chair in the same fabric, a small sideboard with a drawer, and end tables with lamps. The dining table seats four and is less elaborate than in the larger apartment. The kitchens are the same and stand out because of the attractive cabinetry and clever use of space.

These apartments are compact, pretty, reasonably priced, and in a popular area. Since Barrett Street can be busy, be sure to ask for a flat above the side street if you want quiet.

AMENITIES—Elevator, telephone, color TV with VCR, computer connection through telephone, fax in office, maid service (Monday, Wednesday, Friday), refrigerator/freezer (small), stove with oven, toaster, tea kettle, teapot, coffee maker, iron, microwave, washer/dryer, welcome pack (extra charge).

RESERVATIONS/PRICES/MISC.—**Minimum stay:** 1 week. **Reservations:** Kiri Ballard. **Telephone:** 0207-935-9512. **Fax:** 0207-935-7531. **E-mail:** *lettings@globeapt.com*. **Web site:** *www.globeapt.com*. **Prices per week from:** 1 bdrm-$1,053; penthouse 2 bdrm, 2 bath-$1,620. **Negotiate price?** yes. **Deposit?** yes. **Check in:** 2 P.M. **Check out:** 12 P.M. **Credit cards?** yes, but at a 4.5% surcharge. **Tube stop:** Bond Street.

Cavendish Apartments, 65 and 62 Harley Street, London W1N 1DD

 refurbished, nonrefurbished

photo p. A

At 65 and 62 Harley Street, at the corner of New Cavendish Street, are two large, listed, Edwardian buildings that were once private residences. The buildings were modernized and internally reconstructed as one-, two-, or three-bedroom apartments. During the renovations the architect took care to protect the period details of the structures, and they retain the large rooms, tall windows, high ceilings, intricate plasterwork, and ornate chandeliers of the era.

The flats at 65 Harley Street are in the process of further refurbishment, and those not completed (five apartments) rent at a lower rate. If you are in search of a bargain, those not completed are a good buy ($1,142 per week for a two-bedroom with minor flaws, such as a small tear in the wallpaper). A central hall runs through these apartments, with the two bedrooms off it near the door. The living/dining area is at the end with the kitchen beside it. The bath is across the hall from the bedrooms, the master with a king bed and the second bedroom with a single. Both have end tables with lamps, high ceilings, and decorative moldings. The living room holds two sofas in a floral blue fabric, a coffee table, and a chair in front of a wall shelf system. There is a marble fireplace and a round dining table with four chairs. Colors are not coordinated (walls are pink; carpet, brown; drapes, a muted multicolor stripe), but this will be corrected on refurbishment. The walk-in kitchen has plenty of white metal cabinets, good counter space, under-counter refrigerator/freezer, stove, and microwave. A washer/dryer for tenant use is in the basement. The bath has a tub/shower, white tiled walls with blue trim, and white cabinet with sink. If the decor is a bit tired and out of date, the flat is comfortable, spacious, and homey.

The eight refurbished flats, on the other hand, are the epitome of Edwardian style in size and design detail. The one-bedroom retains the central hall with living room and bedroom on one side and kitchen and bath on the other. The bedroom has a zip-and-link king-size bed, a side table with lamp, and a TV. Matching blue sofas and plush blue carpeting dominate the living room and contrast strikingly with the white wainscoted walls. Three large windows provide ample light even in January. Guests dine off a square glass table in an alcove at the end of the room. The kitchen features a floor-to-ceiling window, white wooden cabinets, a tiled floor, white tiled walls, a full-size refrigerator/freezer, a stove, a microwave, plenty of new pots and pans, and a good supply of china.

All of the apartments at 62 Harley Street are redone, and they all have huge rooms. One has a dining room so big that it is sometimes rented out for parties. The living rooms of these flats all have matching sofa and easy chairs, marble fireplaces, large mirrors, chandeliers, very tall windows with deep-red velvet curtains, and formal dining areas, if they do not have formal dining rooms. On the ground and first floors, the ceilings are high and the plasterwork intricate. Master bedrooms have zip-and-link beds, side tables with lamps, closets, dressers, easy chairs, and velvet drapes. Kitchens have wall-to-wall white wooden cabinets, full-size refrigerator/freezer, stove, and microwave.

If you want to experience the feeling of life in a turn-of-the-century Edwardian mansion, then Cavendish Apartments are for you. For what they offer, they are reasonably priced. For a taste of grand city life at an affordable price, try 62 Harley Street.

AMENITIES—Elevator, telephone, color TV, computer connection in telephone, fax in office, maid service (Monday–Friday), concierge/housekeeper (9 A.M.–5 P.M., Monday–Friday), refrigerator, freezer, stove with oven, toaster, tea kettle, teapot, coffee maker, iron, microwave, washer/dryer (in basement for tenant use), hair dryer (on request), welcome pack (on request at extra charge).

RESERVATIONS/PRICES/MISC.—**Minimum stay:** 1 night. **Reservations:** Susan. **Telephone:** 0207-436-9981. **Fax:** 0207-636-1368. **E-mail:** *cavendish@ukonline.co.uk.* **Web site:** *www.apartmentsw1.com.* **Prices from:** *At 65 Harley* (refurbished)—1 bdrm-$177 per night, $1,237 per week; 2 bdrm, 1 bath-$204 per night, $1,428 per week; (not refurbished)—2 bdrm, 1 bath-$163 per night, $1,142 per week. *At 62 Harley* (all refurbished)—1 bdrm-$190 per night, $1,237 per week; 2 bdrm, 2 bath-$247 per night, $1,713 per week; 3 bdrm, 2 bath-$247 per night, $1,713 per week; 3 bdrm, 3 bath-$381 per night, $2,527 per week. **Negotiate price?** yes. **Deposit?** yes. **Check in:** by arrangement. **Check out:** by arrangement. **Credit cards?** all major. **Tube stop:** Baker Street.

Chiltern Street Apartments, 43a Chiltern Street, London W1

photo p. A

The 12 one-bedroom apartments on Chiltern Street are another of Globe Apartments' small wonders. "Small" because the rooms are tiny and "wonders" because of the starting price of $890 per week in a central and convenient area. Although on the rental market for more than 20 years, the flats were recently refurbished, modernized, and redesigned to fit a lot of comfort into a compact space.

The entry into the deep-lavender brick building (a perfectly acceptable color in a Victorian structure) is marked by a small white and lavender awning. Press the video entry phone to gain entrance. The flats start on the first floor (second for Americans); there is an elevator to the upper levels. While the apartments are basically similar, some do offer additional amenities, such as washer/dryers. Make your preference known at time of booking.

Each apartment opens into a hallway. Off to the right through glass French doors are the living room and kitchen. At the far end of the room on a slightly raised platform is a small yellow sofa that opens into a double bed. The heating system is cleverly tucked out of the way behind the sofa. A large mirror above the sofa creates an impression of space. Recessed lighting also saves room. In addition to the sofa, there are a matching easy chair, a cabinet holding TV and lamp, a side table, and either a dining table or a breakfast bar. The open kitchen alcove is to the left of the French doors and is equipped with white cabinets, an under-counter refrigerator, stove, two burners, microwave, and sometimes a washer/dryer. There is an ample supply of better-quality pots and pans and sufficient china, glassware, and utensils for six people.

Even though these apartments are small, they provide good storage space with mirrored closets along the hallway. A bath with a tub/shower, large towels, and a hair dryer is off the left of the hall, and the bedroom is at the end. The bedroom, very small, contains a double bed with blond wooden cabinets on either side. The cabinets have two drawers below and glass shelves above. There are two reading lights over the bed. Headboard, bedcovers, and drapes are in a matching blue and yellow fabric. The bedroom is carpeted; in other parts of the flat, the floors are polished pine. Mirrors are everywhere—essential in such a compact space.

A further economy in these flats is that they could sleep three people since each has a sofa bed. Two single travelers, on the other hand, could use the living area as a second bedroom.

Chiltern Street is a short walk to Regent's Park and the Baker Street tube station, two blocks to the Wallace Collection, three blocks to the shops of Marylebone High Street, and 15 minutes to the Oxford and Bond Streets tube. If you are comfortable with compactness, these flats are an excellent buy.

AMENITIES—Elevator, telephone, color TV, computer connection through telephone, fax (on request), maid service (once a week), concierge/housekeeper (manager on premises), refrigerator, freezer, stove with oven, toaster, tea kettle, teapot, coffee maker, iron, microwave, washer/dryer (in some), hair dryer, toiletries, welcome pack (on request for extra charge).

RESERVATIONS/PRICES/MISC.—Minimum stay: 1 week. Reservations: Kiri Ballard. Telephone: 0207-935-9512. Fax: 0207-935-7531. E-mail: *lettings@gloveapt.com*. Web site: *www.globeapt.com*. Prices per night from: 1 bdrm-$127, $890 per week. Negotiate price? yes. Deposit? yes. Check in: 2 P.M. Check out: 12 P.M. Credit cards? yes, but at a 4.5% surcharge. Tube stop: Baker Street.

James Street Apartments, James Street, London W1M 5HS

The 16 James Street studios and one- and two-bedroom apartments could not be in a more enticing location—smack in the middle of things: behind Selfridges Department Store, steps from the Bond Street tube and all of Oxford Street. Two blocks north is Marylebone High Street with its boutiques, full-service Waitrose grocery, pubs, restaurants, and, most important, Biggles Sausage Shop. Mayfair and its elegant residences are within an easy stroll, and Hyde Park is five blocks away.

While these apartments are in a hub of activity, they are surprisingly quiet. Another surprise is their price. For their location, they are a real bargain. A studio starts at $648 per week, inclusive of VAT and all charges. One-bedrooms start at $729 and two-bedrooms at $1,134. Each apartment is very well equipped for this price range with a washer/dryer and a dishwasher.

The James Street apartments are clustered in several buildings, one above a flower shop. Thirty-six James Street is the office of Globe Apartments, the manager and rental agency for these flats. Pubs, cafes, brasseries, and shops are on the street level, while the apartments are on the second floor and on up. There is no elevator, so climbing steps is one price to pay for these savings.

Another is that these apartments are small—well organized with an efficient use of space, but compact. The living/dining area of the studio flat, for example, is about 12 by 15 feet, and the bath has a shower but no tub. Still, the room, just right of the entrance, has tall ceilings that create an impressive space. It contains a double sofa bed against the far wall between two windows overlooking James Street. There are two end tables with lamps, a coffee table, and an easy chair that matches the sofa. A dining table with three chairs is near the entrance. On the opposite side of the room is the TV and a fireplace with a closet on either side. The small but comfortable bathroom separates the living area from the kitchen. The kitchen is completely modern and includes an under-counter refrigerator/freezer, stove, microwave, washer/ dryer, dishwasher, china for three, and good counter space.

In the one-bedroom apartment, the living/dining area (again, about 12 by 15 feet) is to the left of the entrance hallway. It has two large windows, a sofa with large matching hassock, two end tables with lamps, and a cabinet along the wall. The dining table with four matching chairs is at the end of the room nearest the entrance. The bath with tub/shower and large bath towels is opposite, and the kitchen, fully equipped, is to the right and behind the door. The bedroom is across from the kitchen and has a double bed, two tables with lamps, a closet, and coordinated drapes and bedcovers.

Management is friendly and helpful. They say to ask for what you want at the time of booking, because extras, such as cribs, beds, or VCRs, are available for an additional charge. As is, these flats are an excellent buy.

AMENITIES—Elevator (none), telephone, color TV, computer connection through telephone, fax (for hire), maid service (once a week), refrigerator/freezer (under counter), stove with oven, toaster, tea kettle, teapot, coffee maker, iron, microwave, washer/dryer, hair dryer, toiletries, welcome pack (at extra charge).

RESERVATIONS/PRICES/MISC.—Minimum stay: 1 week, with some flexibility. Reservations: Kiri Ballard. Telephone: 0207-935-9512. Fax: 0207-935-7531. E-mail: *lettings@globeapts.com*. Web site: *www.globeapt.com*. Prices per week from: studios-$648; 1 bdrm-$729; 2 bdrm-$1,134. Negotiate price? yes. Deposit? yes. Check in: 2 P.M. Check out: 12 P.M. Credit cards? yes, but at a 4.5% surcharge. Tube stop: Bond Street.

Jerome House, 14 Lisson Grove, Marylebone, London NW1 6TS

photo p. B

In a just-built, gabled building ideally located for getting around London, Jerome House's 24 apartments are spread over seven stories. While the lobby is tiny, the apartments are a good size. Since Jerome House was constructed as an apartment building, each of the three types of available flats has the same floor plan and is furnished to the same standard. Most of the flats have attractive views over the city. All have video entry phones, remote control televisions with satellite reception, VCR, radio, direct-dial telephones, and safes. Maid service is five days a week, and linens are changed midweek.

At Jerome House, the studio apartment is the biggest surprise. It is larger than most and has a bed that tucks easily into the wall when not in use. The remaining open space makes these studios especially pleasant for work or lounging. A sofa with end table and lamp offers comfortable seating. The round dining table with four chairs is in front of a window that runs the length of the room, enhancing the impression of roominess. The marbled bath is small but has a sink and tub with power shower.

All of the one-bedroom apartments have one-and-a-half baths and sofa beds that open up into a double bed. Entered via a small hallway, the living/dining area is well furnished with sofa, easy chair, coffee and end tables, and a television set. The dining table with four chairs is within a small alcove with a floor-to-ceiling window. While small, the bedroom has a queen-size bed, side tables with lamps, chair, dresser, and additional storage space. There is an additional TV on the wall. The bathroom with tub and power shower is *en suite*.

The two-bedroom apartments are similar to the one-bedrooms except for the additional bedroom with its own bathroom. The master bedroom is larger with a wider window and coordinating drapes.

All of the kitchens in Jerome House are separated by French doors from the rest of the flat. Each is equipped with stove, microwave, dishwasher, refrigerator/freezer, and washer/dryer.

Jerome House is located steps from the Marylebone train station/tube stop; the Baker Street Station is two blocks away and the Edgware Road stop a few blocks in the other direction. The Victoria and Albert, one of the few remaining station pubs, is inside the Marylebone train station. It is a pleasant and convenient place for refreshments after an evening at the theater. A famous fish and chips shop and restaurant, The Seashell, is three blocks up Lisson Grove. It's a great place for takeaway dinners.

Jerome House is represented by several agencies, and the prices can seem high. Only the resident manager, Joanne Joyce, can negotiate price, so be sure to speak to her directly.

AMENITIES—Elevator, telephone, color TV with satellite, computer connection, maid service (5 days), concierge (live-in housekeeper and manager), refrigerator, freezer (above fridge), stove, toaster, tea kettle, teapot, coffee maker, iron, microwave, dishwasher, washer/dryer, hair dryer, toiletries, welcome pack.

RESERVATIONS/PRICES/MISC.—**Minimum stay:** 1 night. **Reservations:** Joanne Joyce. **Telephone:** 0207-724-5924. **Fax:** 0207-724-2937. **E-mail:** *joanne@vienna-group. co.uk.* **Web site:** *www.vienna-group.co.uk.* **Prices per night:** studios-$175–$178; 1 bdrm-$271–$275; 2 bdrm, 2 bath-$339–$345. **Negotiate price?** yes. **Deposit?** credit card. **Check in:** 2 P.M. **Check out:** 11 A.M. **Credit cards?** yes. **Tube stops:** Marylebone, Baker Street, Edgware Road.

New Cavendish Street, London W1

photo p. B

This two-bedroom *maisonette* (two-floor apartment) right in the middle of Marylebone's most lively neighborhood is managed by Go Native, an agency that specializes in renting individual properties made available by their owners. A photographer owns this apartment. Periodically, he packs up his cameras and travels to his second home in Italy or a photo shoot elsewhere.

On the third floor (fourth for Americans) in a period building with no lift (not for those who have trouble climbing stairs), the *maisonette* is above a medical supply shop on New Cavendish Street. The climb is worth it. As soon as one steps foot into the first floor of the apartment, the open space and uncluttered look delight the eye. White walls and light provided by an abundance of windows enhance the impression of a fresh, light, and airy space. The living/dining area of the apartment actually serves as a gallery to display the owner's photographs, paintings, and sculpture. Track lighting for the paintings contributes to the brightness of the room.

In keeping with its function as a gallery, furnishings are minimal. The living room has a sofa, two tables, a fireplace, and a polished wood floor. In one corner is a dining table that will seat six. When not in use, the chairs are tucked away in a storage space.

The kitchen is at the north end of the room. Its windows provide a view of the historic Saint Mary-le-bone Church, consecrated in 1817. The kitchen is well stocked with china, cutlery, glassware, and cooking utensils, including a hand blender. There is a refrigerator with freezer, stove, microwave, dishwasher, and washer/dryer.

On the second level are the two bedrooms and one bath. At the time we visited, the bath was being refurbished. The master bedroom is above the living room so it is also south-facing and full of light. The small room has only a futon bed, dresser, desk with chair, pillows, TV, and stereo. The owner's lovely framed photographs adorn the walls.

The bathroom is down a short L-shaped hallway. It is small, tiled, and has a sink, mirror, and tub with shower.

At the north end of the L is the tiny second bedroom. Furnishings are again minimal. There is a sofa that opens up into a double bed, a wardrobe, and a window with a view of Saint Mary-le-bone.

New Cavendish Street is a convenient location. It is around the corner from Marylebone High Street with many restaurants; boutiques; a new Conran's; Patisserie Valerie (said to have the best croissants in London); and other food stores, including a just-opened Waitrose supermarket. Oxford Street, a five-minute walk, has Liberty's, Selfridges, Marks and Spencer, and much more. Ten minutes north is Regent's Park.

As is true of any flat decorated and lived in by someone else, the furnishings and style reflect the owner's needs and taste. If open space, sparkling cleanliness, and lovely works of art are your cup of tea, this flat is a find.

AMENITIES—Elevator (none), telephone, color TV with satellite, refrigerator, freezer, stove, toaster, tea kettle, teapot, coffee maker, iron, microwave, dishwasher, washer/dryer, toiletries, welcome pack (includes a light meal).

RESERVATIONS/PRICES/MISC.—**Minimum stay:** 1 week. **Reservations:** Katy Heywood-Lonsdale. **Telephone:** 0207-221-2028. **Fax:** 0207-221-2088. **E-mail:** *katy@gonative.co.uk*. **Web site:** *www.gonative.co.uk*. **Price per week:** $1,458. **Negotiate price?** no. **Deposit?** yes. **Check in:** 2 P.M. **Check out:** 10 A.M. **Credit cards?** yes. **Tube stop:** Bond Street.

Portman Square Apartments, Portman Square, London W1M 1AA

   *photo p. B*

Just off Baker Street and on the north side of the square are the Portman Square Apartments. Forty one-, two-, and three-bedroom apartments in this 1930s brick block are managed by Manors and Company, whose main office is around the corner at 1 Baker Street. The location is in the middle of the city, yet quiet, even though it is just two blocks from the bustle and crowds of Oxford Street. Across from the apartment block is a large, gated garden that tenants may use.

The 40 apartments are individually owned and decorated, most with modern furnishings and traditional fabrics. All match the high standard of the area and surroundings.

We stepped directly into the living room of the one-bedroom apartment we visited. Brightened by light-colored leather sofas, it is comfortable and cozy rather than spacious, has a working fireplace, and lovely views of the park across the way. In the inner corner is a small dining table with seating for four.

The bedroom, down a short hall, has a queen bed with dresser and bedside tables. Also off the hall is the marble-tiled bath with tub and power shower. The galley kitchen, although small, is very well supplied with cabinets, oven, stove top, microwave, freezer, refrigerator, dishwasher, washer/dryer, and coffee maker.

Each two-bedroom apartment has at least two baths. The master bath, located in the bedroom, has a tub with separate shower, sink, and bidet. The living room is spacious with two upholstered sofas, matching drapes, coffee and end tables, and oriental rugs over the lush wall-to-wall carpeting. At one end of the room is a glass dining table with seating for six.

The large kitchen is very well equipped. It has all modern appliances, including microwave, dishwasher, and washer/dryer, plus nice touches such as a breadbox with matching canister set. Plates, cups, glasses, and cutlery are ample and of good quality.

All Portman Square apartments have direct-dial telephones and color television. Maid service is provided Monday through Friday, and the reception desk in the lobby is manned 24 hours a day.

Portman Square is in a very desirable location. It is two short blocks from Selfridges and Marks and Spencer with their extensive food halls. Around the corner are all of the shops and department stores of Oxford Street. Just to the east is the Wallace Collection. A few blocks farther east is Marylebone High Street, lined with boutiques, specialty shops, and restaurants.

AMENITIES—Elevator, telephone, color TV with satellite at extra cost, fax (for a fee), maid service (5 days), concierge, refrigerator/freezer, stove, toaster, tea kettle, teapot, coffee maker, iron, microwave, dishwasher, washer/dryer, hair dryer, toiletries, welcome pack (for additional fee).

RESERVATIONS/PRICES/MISC.—**Minimum stay:** 1 night. **Reservations:** toll-free from U.S., 1-800-454-4385; in London, 0207-486-5982. **Fax:** 0207-486-6770. **E-mail:** *Sellar@manors.co.uk.* **Web site:** *www.manors.co.uk.* **Prices per night:** 1 bdrm-$227 (per week, $1,523); 2 bdrm, 2 bath-$389–$551 (per week, $2,592–$3,645); 3 bdrm, 2 bath-$503–$648 (per week, $3,240–$4,374). **Negotiate price?** yes. **Deposit?** credit card. **Check in:** 2 P.M. **Check out:** before noon. **Credit cards?** yes. **Tube stops:** Marble Arch, Bond Street.

Presidential Apartments, 102 George Street, London W1U 8NT

photo p. B

Presidential Apartments is in an unexpected but convenient location on George Street between Baker and Gloucester, and three blocks north of Oxford Street—unexpected because this is a street of boutiques and businesses, not residences. Even so, grocery shopping is not a problem with the extensive food halls of Marks and Spencer and upscale Selfridges only three blocks away.

In a modern building with elevator, Presidential Apartments occupies the second floor and up of a five-story structure. There are 23 studios and 11 one-bedroom flats. At the time of our visit, Presidential Apartments planned to begin a major rewiring and refurbishment of all its flats to be completed by 2003. In the meantime, it will rent unrefurbished flats at current rates—a real bargain. It anticipates an increase in price of about 15 percent as work on each apartment is completed.

As they are now, we were impressed with what Presidential Apartments offered for the money. The flats are spacious and comfortably furnished. Management staff is friendly, helpful, available, and welcoming.

The one-bedroom apartment opens into a small hallway with the bathroom immediately to the right, the bedroom off it, and the living/dining area to the left. The living room has a full-size sofa in a dark floral upholstered fabric with two matching easy chairs. There are end and coffee tables and lamps. A round dining table with four chairs is in a corner of the room in front of a pass-through into the kitchen alcove. The kitchen is pine paneled and very well equipped with an under-counter refrigerator/freezer, a full stove, a microwave, good-quality pots and pans, and plenty of counter space. The bedroom has twin beds with light floral bedspreads and coordinated headboards. There are two bedside tables with lamps, a dresser, and a closet.

The studios have a double bed or twin beds with one reading light and a built-in dresser along the wall. Each has either a two-person sofa and an easy chair or two easy chairs. There is a coffee table and a round dining table and chairs in a corner near the kitchen. The kitchen is the same as in the one-bedroom.

All baths have power showers and tubs, a large bath and hand towel per person, and heated towel racks.

At the time of booking, it is important to ask for the type of beds wanted. The apartments have various sleeping configurations, each with a different price. Some apartments also have balconies.

If economy with comfort rather than elegant furnishings is what you seek, the Presidential Apartments is an excellent choice. Perhaps after refurbishment, they can add glamour to their other assets.

AMENITIES—Elevator, telephone (2 lines), cable color TV with VCR, radio, computer connection in telephone, fax (through office), maid service (Monday–Friday), manager on call 24 hours, refrigerator/freezer (under-counter in studio; others, large), stove with oven, toaster, tea kettle, teapot, coffee maker, iron, microwave (not in studio), hair dryer.

RESERVATIONS/PRICES/MISC.—**Minimum stay:** 1 week, with flexibility. **Reservations:** office staff. **Telephone:** 0207-486-0097. **Fax:** 0207-487-3624. **E-mail:** *Pres ApartmentsLondon@msn.com.* **Prices from:** studios-$737 per week; 1 bdrm-$907 per week. **Negotiate price?** yes. **Deposit?** yes. **Check in:** 2 P.M. **Check out:** 12 P.M. **Credit cards?** all major except Diners, 2.5% surcharge for American Express. **Tube stops:** Marble Arch and Baker Street.

St. Christopher's Place, London W1M 5HD

At the corner of James and Barrett Streets, a block and a half behind Selfridges, is St. Christopher's Place. It is a short pedestrian street (no cars allowed) lined with boutiques, cafes, coffee shops, and restaurants. The location is convenient for all of London with the Bond Street tube a few minutes' walk and Oxford Circus four blocks away. With all the department stores on Oxford Street, the fashion hub of South Molton Street, and the Waitrose supermarket just up Marylebone High Street, even a dedicated shopper need never leave the neighborhood.

While this area is usually quite expensive (a double room at Durrants on George Street, considered moderately priced by *Frommer's* recent guide, starts at $260 a night), the three Globe apartments on St. Christopher's Place rent for $810 per week ($116 per night). While quite small, these one-bedroom apartments were recently refurbished with kitchens modernized and equipment updated for the corporate user.

Entry into each apartment is into a short hallway. A bath is off to the right, a bed-room to the left, and the living area straight ahead. The living room has a sofa and easy chair, both in the same blue and yellow striped fabric. Yellow and blue drapes and pale carpeting complement the colors of the upholstery. There are side tables, lamps, and a coffee table. A dining table with four chairs is in the corner near the entrance to the room. Table mats, china, glassware, and cutlery are supplied for four people; more are available on request. A closet is in the wall in the front of the room. For such a small apartment, the kitchen, to the right of the dining table, is very well equipped. It has an under-counter refrigerator/freezer, stove, microwave, washer/dryer, and dishwasher—the last two unusual in this price range. Kitchen walls are tiled, and there is a good supply of pots, pans, cabinets, and counter space. The bed-room has room for only a double bed, bedside tables with four drawers and lamps, and a small closet. Across the hall, the bath has a tub/shower with good pressure, large bath towels, and a hair dryer.

In spite of their diminutive size, these apartments are popular with return visi-tors: a combination of price, location, and amenities. Book as early as possible if you want to stay at St. Christopher's Place.

AMENITIES—Elevator (none), telephone, color TV, computer connection through telephone, fax (through office), maid service (once a week), refrigerator/freezer (under-counter), stove with oven, toaster, tea kettle, teapot, coffee maker, iron, microwave, washer/dryer, hair dryer.

RESERVATIONS/PRICES/MISC.—Minimum stay: 1 week, with some flexibility. Reservations: Kiri Ballard. Telephone: 0207-935-9512. Fax: 0207-935-7531. E-mail: *lettings@globeapt.com*. Web site: *www.globeapt.com*. Prices from: 1 bdrm-$810. Negotiate price? yes. Deposit? yes. Check in: 2 P.M. Check out: 12 P.M. Credit cards? yes, but at a 4.5% surcharge. Tube stop: Bond Street.

Tustin's Holiday Flats, 94 York Street, London W1H 1DP

photo p. B

Flat C, 92a York Street is truly our home-away-from-home in London. We have stayed with Tustin for 14 of our last visits to England. We consider fancier places, but the economy and comfort of Tustin's draw us back.

Tustin's 15 flats are located in a grade II–listed Georgian Terrace. They are on the second and third floors of adjoining buildings *without lifts*. From the locked exterior door, the guest enters into a hallway with the flats immediately up the stairway.

The flats vary in size, style, and convenience. The smallest one-bedroom is, indeed, quite small. The kitchenette is tiny, but contains a sink, under-counter refrigerator, convection stove, and microwave. We have managed to cook full meals in this space, but it took planning and we did bump elbows often. The living area has space for only a futon sofa, coffee table, and a dining table with two chairs. A small bathroom, with sink and bath/shower, is off the living room. The bedroom with a double bed is down the hallway. The separation of living space and sleeping space by this hallway is a big plus for the Tustin apartments, especially if one of the guests likes to read late into the night. Although there is a futon, two people are the maximum allowed in the smallest one-bedroom. If cost is a major concern, this least expensive of the Tustin's flats is a good choice. These flats overlook a school playground.

Flat C is one of the larger one-bedroom flats (maximum occupancy, four people). The living area, dining area, and kitchen are separate components of one room. There is a futon that opens up into a double bed. This section could be closed off with French doors for privacy for a couple or children. The bedroom with twin beds is down a hallway, and the bathroom is off the hallway. This second type of one-bedroom apartment does not have a dining table but a breakfast bar that separates the living area from the kitchen area. These apartments overlook York Street.

The two- and three-bedroom flats are more spacious, more elaborately decorated, and better equipped. The living area is large enough to hold two sofas, coffee table, end table, lamp, and television set. The drapes match the light floral fabric of the sofas. The dining table at one end of the room provides seating for six. The kitchen is separate. Bedrooms are again down the hall. One has a double bed and the other has a single bed. Some of these flats have an extra half bath. Flats on the first floors are preferable, if available, because of their high ceilings, moldings, and cornices.

In addition to their economy, a major attraction of Tustin's flats is their location. They are close to three tube stops (Marylebone, Edgware Road, and Baker Street) and the Marylebone train station, so that getting around London or even out of town is a breeze. The flats are a 10-minute walk to Regent's Park, the London Zoo, and the shops of Baker Street, Oxford Street, and Marylebone High Street. Supermarkets are nearby. One drawback is that check-in is only between 9:30 A.M. and 5:00 P.M., Monday through Friday.

AMENITIES—Elevator (none), telephone (with a deposit to British Telecom), color TV, refrigerator/freezer (under-counter), stove, toaster, tea kettle, teapot, iron, microwave.

RESERVATIONS/PRICES/MISC.—**Minimum stay:** 1 week. **Reservations:** Diana Voo. **Telephone:** 0207-723-9611. **Fax:** 0207-724-0224. **E-mail:** *pctustinuk@btconnect.com.* **Web site:** *www.pctustin.com.* **Prices per week:** 1 bdrm-$551–$713; 2 bdrm-$996–$1,013; 3 bdrm-$1,045–$1,061. **Deposit?** 1 week's rent. **Check in:** between 9:30 A.M. and 5:30 P.M., Monday–Friday. **Check out:** 10 A.M. **Credit cards?** 3% surcharge. **Tube stops:** Marylebone, Edgware Road, Baker Street.

Marylebone: Attractions

One of the original Georgian houses survives intact in Manchester Square. Hertford House, long the home of the Marquises of Hertford, was built in 1788 and is now the site of the Wallace Collection, one of the finest museums in London. Entrance to the house and museum is free. Inside you will find an exquisite variety of artistic treasures, ranging from Sèvres porcelain to antique clocks to Dutch masterpieces. Frans Hals' "Laughing Cavalier" occupies a central place in the great hall along with at least one Rembrandt. Eighteenth-century French furniture and paintings by Watteau and Fragonard were purchased for the house by the fourth marquis when he was British ambassador to Paris. A major renovation completed in 2000 added gallery space and the Sculpture Garden Restaurant.

Genteel residences coexisted with the most lurid part of London life in the 18th century. On the southwest corner of Marylebone stood "Tyburn Tree," the site of public executions for London until 1783. It was never a tree, but a three-sided gallows that could accommodate as many as a dozen victims at a time, from 16th-century Catholic martyrs to common thieves. Hangings in the 18th century drew large, unruly crowds of gin-drinking spectators (and pickpockets) to jeer, cheer, or just observe the spectacle. Apparently, it was this congregation of rabble rather than the executions themselves that prompted residents to pressure authorities to remove the gallows. The great Marble Arch at the corner of Hyde Park at Oxford Street and Edgware Road marks that spot today. The arch was a gateway moved from Buckingham Palace after a 19th-century renovation.

During the Regency period, the eastern and northern fringe of Marylebone became the most desirable address in London, largely because of the ego of the Prince Regent and his architect, John Nash. Nash proposed creating a grand promenade from the regent's palace in St. James's north to a rural pleasure dome set in a landscaped "Regent's Park." The plan called for replacing workers' dwellings along the route with a row of columned residences: 56 villas in the park and a ring of stuccoed terraces surrounding it. The plan won the prince's approval, but only a fraction of the residences were ever built due to the cost. Regent's Park, however, was built as planned and it is one of the glories of the Marylebone area. Between 1820 and 1830, landscapers and engineers transformed what had once been Henry VIII's hunting chase into a grand English garden. "A scene of ever-varying delight," said a visitor in 1827. A serpentine lake curves along the western side of the park, attracting all manner of water birds and children to feed them. Formal gardens with roses and hedges and a cafe anchor the center of the park, leaving large open spaces for Sunday soccer and rugby matches. In all, the park contains 400 acres of manicured, accessible green space only a couple of blocks from either the Marylebone or Baker Street tube stations. As an extra added attraction, the London Zoo occupies the north end of the park, which ends at the Regent's Canal.

Madame Tussaud's is the fifth most popular tourist attraction in all London, according to the 2000 *Frommer's* guide, and it has been a fixture in the area since 1835. The venerable founder got her start modeling death masks of French aristocrats for the revolutionary government in 1793, and took her macabre creations on the road in England in 1802. When she got tired of touring, she set up a museum in a bazaar on Baker Street. In 1884 her successors moved the exhibit, including the famous chamber of horrors, to its present location on Marylebone Road. There it survived a devastating fire in 1925 and the Blitz. Refreshed regularly with new exhibits and effigies of contemporary stars, the museum drew two-and-a-half million visitors last year. Kids love it.

The much newer Sherlock Holmes Museum around the corner at, naturally, 221 Baker Street, also attracts steady crowds, mostly foreign tourists. The narrow three-story house attempts to re-create the bedrooms and famous sitting room of Holmes and Watson as Arthur Conan Doyle described them, complete with memorabilia associated with the mysteries. Perhaps the most interesting exhibit there is the fan letters and letters from people asking for the services of the famous detective. That correspondence was once so heavy that the local bank that occupied the premises at 221 years ago kept a secretary who did nothing but answer Sherlock Holmes' mail. At least that is the story. There is also a Sherlock Holmes Collection maintained at the nearby Marylebone Public Library, open to fans and Conan Doyle scholars.

If you want more Sherlockiana, head to the Sherlock Holmes Hotel two blocks south for a snack in Mrs Hudson's Pantry or a drink in Dr Watson's Bar.

Shops, Restaurants, and Pubs

In contrast to the mercantile giants of Oxford Street, the shops on Marylebone Lane and the High Street retain the scale and character of a small town. Tiny, personalized shops specializing in buttons (The Button Queen) or sausages thrive along with pubs, newsagents, grocers, bookshops, and a smattering of new boutiques and restaurants. Biggles looks like an old, established village butcher shop, but it opened only in 1989 after the proprietor gave up a career in advertising. On the premises he makes sausages, and only sausages, of all varieties, from garlicky Toulouse to mild breakfast. Our favorites are the traditional Cumberland and Scrumpy (flavored with Scrumpy Jack cider from the West country).

Marylebone High Street also boasts what some say is the best pastry shop in London, Patisserie Valerie at Sagne, and an equally fine fishmonger, Blagden, just a few steps off the High Street on Paddington. Blagden's proudly displays its fish, as it has for decades, on a wide platform open to the street. In back it keeps an astonishing array of poultry, pheasant, grouse, quail, woodcock, and free-range eggs.

For one-stop shopping, a large Waitrose opened on Marylebone High Street in 1999. It has a full range of products, from fresh vegetables to cleaning powders to take-away meals.

East of Marylebone High Street, at 170 Great Portland Street, is Villandry. Originally it was a French grocery store with imported cheeses, bread, and vegetables. Then it began to offer sandwiches and light dinners. Eventually, demand forced it to its new, larger quarters where it opened a full-service, and expensive, restaurant. The French market remains, however, and it is the place for baguettes, a lemon tart, and a vast array of deli items.

Near the intersection of Oxford and Baker Streets, you will find two large and bustling food halls in Selfridges (on the ground floor) and Marks and Spencer (on the lower level). Selfridges is more upscale and carries products from the United States and other countries. It has extensive meat, poultry, and fish counters, as well as display cases full of cheeses, pâtés, meat pies, pastries, breads, and many various ethnic take-away dishes. Close by, inside the store proper, is a separate section with a good selection of wines, imported beers, and liquors.

Marks and Spencer carries its own St. Michaels brands only, but still has row upon row of shelves packed with high-quality items. We like their strong tea, and the fresh produce has been outstanding, especially the baby asparagus and corn. There is a large selection of frozen foods, including English savory pies, meats, main courses, and dinners to take home and reheat. It was in its dairy case that we first found Greek-style yogurt, a particularly rich variety.

On our first night in London, when we are groggy and grumpy with jet lag, we always carry out a fish or chicken dinner from The Seashell on Lisson Grove. The fish is always fresh from the boat, and everything is fried in walnut oil. The Seashell is also a sit-down restaurant, but on our first night, we prefer the privacy of eating in our own flat. Honestly, one order of chips is sufficient for two adults with leftovers.

Langan's Bistro, 26 Devonshire Street, is just off Marylebone High Street, one block north of Paddington. It is one of the restaurants owned by Michael Caine and is affordable. A three-course fixed-price dinner is about $30. We had four courses, a nice wine, and spent $50 per person. The food is quite traditional; the setting is fun; and the waiters, entertaining. Actually, we should have been content with three courses. Desserts are mammoth.

For a more varied menu in an informal setting, go to Giraffe at 6–8 Blandford at Marylebone High Street. Pan-Asian is the style here, with curries, Cantonese dishes, and several vegetarian specials. It's new, hip, and you can eat in or carry out (entrees, $11 to $16).

Bond's Brassiere serves the west side of the district (Crawford Street at Seymour Place) with French cafe food at modest prices (entrees, $13 to $20). Try the roast cod or duck breast with rosti potatoes, or anything with rosti potatoes.

The area is brimming with good pubs. We counted seven within three blocks of Tustin's and more around Marylebone High Street, too many to name but several rarities.

Barley Mow (Dorset Street) claims to be the oldest. In 1791, it served grooms and footmen from nearby estates. Part of the tavern was also a licensed pawn shop, which accounts for the private cubicles in back. Marylebone Station, built in 1902, contains its own pub. The Victoria and Albert is a rare example of the once-commonplace station pub. The spacious Edwardian interior makes a comfortable spot for travelers waiting for a train to Birmingham, or subway commuters in need of a quick "half" before home. The station houses both rail and underground lines and helps make Marylebone one of London's most accessible districts. A few blocks away, on Homer Street, a very different old-style pub survives. The Beehive is a classic "one-man bar." The small room with the counter set at an angle was designed so that a lone publican could serve the whole bar. Two are required at noontime these days because this tiny local is the best buy for lunches in this part of town. The Beehive was built as a workingman's bar in a working-class neighborhood about 1900; nevertheless, it was decorated with a molded iron fireplace and etched glass windows. In the highly competitive pub market of the time, one had to dress the bar with fittings better than the patrons would find at home to survive, and it has. The locals now tend to be neighborhood professionals in for a pint of London Pride with their shepherd's pie or omelet.

A Sunday in Marylebone

Our favorite Sunday begins with a walk through Regent's Park to the north end and either a climb up Primrose Hill for a view of the city (from its 200-foot elevation, you can see St. Paul's) or a stroll west along the canal. Regent's canal is an 1812 extension of the Grand Union Canal built a few years earlier to link the Thames to new industrial centers in the Midlands. The canal path takes you past rows of brightly painted houseboats to a basin called Little Venice where the two canals join. The ideal plan is to time your walk so that by lunchtime you reach Crocker's Folly, a pub adjacent to the canal at Aberdeen Place. On a Sunday you will find a traditional roast beef, Yorkshire pudding dinner (or lamb, pork, or chicken) with traditionally over-cooked vegetables, served in one of the grandest settings in London. Crocker's Folly—or The Crown, as it was known originally—represents the golden age of Victorian public houses. Designed in 1898 by C. H. Worley, it features marble walls and a marble-faced chimney in the saloon bar, flanked by a grand mirrored dining room and a games room. As a "free house," the bar serves a wide range of real (cask-conditioned) ales. Frank Crocker lavished money on his new pub because he had a tip that the Marylebone rail station would be located nearby. Unfortunately, it was built two miles to the east, thus the name, Folly.

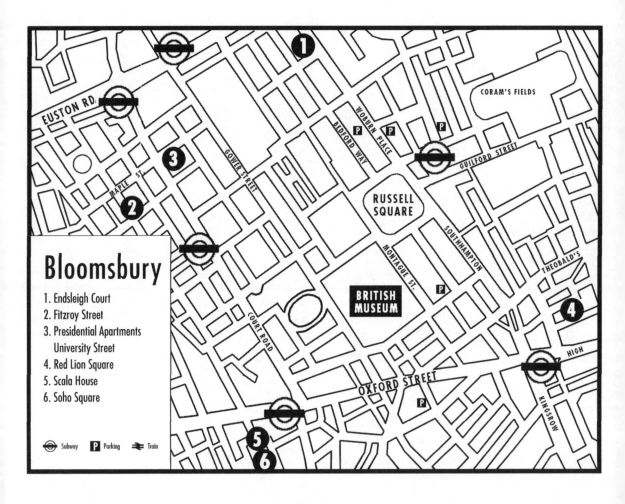

Bloomsbury

1. Endsleigh Court
2. Fitzroy Street
3. Presidential Apartments
   University Street
4. Red Lion Square
5. Scala House
6. Soho Square

Subway   P Parking   Train

Chapter 3

Bloomsbury, Fitzrovia, and Holborn

E ast of Marylebone are three neighborhoods too similar to separate. Like most London districts, the boundaries of Bloomsbury are more a matter of agreement than official definition. Consensus locates Bloomsbury between Euston Road on the north, Gray's Inn Road on the east, New Oxford Street in the south, and Tottenham Court Road to the west. For some, the name "Fitzrovia" is merely a modern affectation for the western section of Bloomsbury. Traditionally home to artists, writers, and academics, the whole district retains a modest, respectable, unpretentious air. Its chief landmarks (aside from the 600-foot British Telecom Tower), the British Museum, British Library, and University of London, make Bloomsbury a mecca for both tourists and scholars. Neighborhood shopping runs more to bookstores and specialty shops than department stores or designers, but for shops, Covent Garden is handy. Apartments here tend to be family-friendly and affordable, and the district safe, as is most of central London. Coram's Fields in the east section of the district was built especially for kids. Adults must bring a child to enjoy its seven acres of playgrounds, wading pool, and petting zoo.

Holborn, between the City and Bloomsbury, serves the legal profession, solicitors, and barristers of the inns of court, and a variety of commercial and government offices. Medieval streets and squares share the space with modern construction. Property developers recognized the value of the district's location in the 1980s and have made places like Clerkenwell, where Dickens lived, a trendy site for restaurants and flats. It is still a modest neighborhood, but ideally situated. Covent Garden shops, West End theaters, and the strand are all within an easy stroll.

Bloomsbury, Fitzrovia, and Holborn at a Glance

Apartment	Studio	1-Bedroom	2-Bedroom	3-Bedroom	Other
Endsleigh Court 1-week minimum	$85–$98 n $599–$689 w	$105–$122 n $738–$851 w	$136–$149 n $948–$1,045 w		
Fitzroy Street 1-week minimum		$139 n $972 w			
Presidential House 1-week minimum in high season		$82–$158 n $575–$1,109 w	$175–$243 n $1,223–$1,661 w (1.5 baths)	$202–$259 n $1,385–$1,844 w (1.5 baths)	
Red Lion Square 1-week minimum	$136 n $952 w		$242 n $1,694 w (2 baths)		
Scala House 3-night minimum			$211–$243 n $1,077–$1,588 w (1.5 baths)		*Penthouse* $292–$324 n $1,588–$1,988 w (1.5 baths)
Soho Square 1-week minimum	$122–$136 n $857–$952 w		$204–$218 n $1,429–$1,523 w		

NOTES: (1) All prices are in American dollars converted at $1.62 to £1 and include VAT. To convert to the current rate, divide the dollar amount by 1.62 and multiply by the rate listed in today's local paper.
(2) n=night; w=week.

Bloomsburg, Fitzrovia, and Holborn Apartments in Detail

Endsleigh Court, 24 Upper Woburn Place, WC1H 0HA

 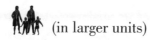 (in larger units)   *photo p. B*

Three blocks from Russell Square, four from the British Museum, and a short bus ride to Covent Garden, Endsleigh Court provides inexpensive accommodation in an area with excellent connections to all of London.

We almost missed Endsleigh Court. Our first glance at their web site (now replaced) presented a dismal picture of sparsely furnished, dreary flats. We thought they would not meet our standards for inclusion, but they were such a bargain, we had to see for ourselves.

We're glad we did. From its web site to the decor of its flats, all is changed at Endsleigh Court. The new manager, Beverly Fletcher, said she knew instantly that the web site did not present an accurate picture of what Endsleigh offered. She had it redone and made other changes. Simply by adding bedskirts to each bed she improved the look of each room exponentially.

We had to agree. From the moment we entered Endsleigh Court's highly polished and welcoming lobby with two fireplaces cheerily aglow, we were impressed and pleasantly surprised by the decor, security, and friendly assurance of the staff.

Endsleigh Court occupies a conventional multistoried 1930s building. There are 90 apartments: 79 studios, 3 one-bedroom, 7 two-bedroom, and one suite (a two-bedroom plus studio that can accommodate eight guests). All are being refurbished at the rate of one per week.

The studios enter into a small hallway. The bathroom is directly opposite the door with the living/dining area to the right. Each has a sofa or a sofa and an additional chair, a double bed with table and lamp, a dresser, and a dining table with two to four chairs, often set in front of the window. A tiny kitchen alcove is in the corner of the room. In the studios the kitchen contains only a small under-counter refrigerator (no freezer), two burners (no stove), but good-quality pots and pans. A microwave is available on request.

The one- and two-bedroom apartments are more completely furnished. All have double sofa beds. Kitchens have full stoves and microwaves. The family suite for eight has two bathrooms and a washer/dryer. Double bedrooms contain twin beds with a small chest of drawers between them. Baths are a good size, tiled, and have power showers or tub/showers and heated towel racks.

While the decor is not fancy and the flats plainly furnished, Endsleigh Court is a comfortable and secure bargain for the London traveler. Apartment rates are inclusive of VAT but not of a $47 weekly "furnishings" fee that is *not* optional. It is billed separately to pass tax savings on to the guest. Since it is not optional, we have included it in the total charge for a flat below and in our "At a Glance" table.

If you plan to stay at Endsleigh Court, book as early as possible. These inexpensive flats are much in demand. For a quieter flat, ask for an apartment at the back of the building off Upper Woburn Place.

AMENITIES—Elevator, telephone, color TV, computer connection through telephone, fax (through office), maid service (once a week), concierge/housekeeper (24 hours), refrigerator (small), stove with oven, microwave (on request), toaster, tea kettle, teapot, coffee maker (on request), iron.

RESERVATIONS/PRICES/MISC.—**Minimum stay:** 1 week. **Reservations:** Beverly Fletcher. **Telephone:** 0207-878-0050. **Fax:** 0207-380-0280. **E-mail:** *enquire@ endscourt.freeserve.co.uk* or *booking@highdorn.com.* **Web site:** *www.endsleigh court-london.com.* **Prices from:** studios-$599–$689; 1 bdrm-$738–$851; 2 bdrm-$948–$1,045. **Negotiate price?** no. **Deposit?** yes. **Check in:** 2 P.M. **Check out:** 10 A.M. **Credit cards?** Yes. **Tube stop:** Euston Station.

Fitzroy Street, 12–16 Fitzroy Street, London

photo p. C

Fitzroy Street runs only a few short blocks below Euston Road, but you can't miss it. It's in the shadow of the most prominent landmark in central London, Telecom Tower. There, in a marble-faced steel and glass building, you will find 17 modern one-bedroom flats managed by Globe Apartments.

"One size fits all" in these identical units. Each contains a 10- by 12-foot living area in front of an open-plan kitchen that is parallel to a bedroom (the same size as the living room) and a bathroom. Both living room and bedroom overlook similar modern buildings behind.

The style throughout is clean and contemporary, with pine floors accenting white walls decorated with modern prints or photographs. The living room has a comfortable small sofa, leather lounge chair, TV, cabinet, and good light. The bedroom accommodates a large double bed, dresser, closet, two bedside tables, and good reading lights—a must as far as we're concerned.

Kitchens come fully equipped with top-flight appliances, including dishwasher and washer/dryer, and a double-door, under-counter refrigerator/freezer. The only thing missing for fine dining is a dining table. Instead, the kitchen counter extends as a table for two with adjustable stools.

Like the kitchen, the bath is fully up-to-date with a power shower/tub and heated towel rack.

The building has an elevator and video entry phones for security.

All in all, Fitzroy provides stylish accommodations for two or a business traveler seeking a central location. The immediate neighborhood, recently dubbed Fitzrovia, lacks any glamorous distinction. It's a solid blend of professional offices and apartments adjacent to more celebrated districts.

Two or three blocks south, Fitzroy becomes Charlotte Street, and there you will find Elena's L'Etoile, in our opinion the best restaurant in the neighborhood. Elena has served classic French cuisine to Londoners for the past three decades (at least), first in Soho at L'Escargot and now on Charlotte Street. A few blocks beyond, across Oxford Street, you enter Soho itself with a wide range of restaurants and night life. In the daytime, the Berwick Market in Soho features fresh fruits, vegetables, and some of the best breads and pastries—and lowest prices—in town.

Chinatown and West End theaters are just beyond Soho. Two blocks east from Fitzroy on Tottenham Court Road is the nearest tube stop, Goodge Street. London University and the British Museum are two blocks beyond, and Regent's Park is a short walk north and west of the apartments.

AMENITIES—Elevator, telephone, color TV, computer connection through telephone, maid service (once a week), refrigerator, freezer, stove with oven, toaster, tea kettle, teapot, coffee maker, iron, microwave, washer/dryer, dishwasher, hair dryer, toiletries, welcome pack (for a charge).

RESERVATIONS/PRICES/MISC.—**Minimum stay:** 1 week. **Reservations:** Kiri Ballard. **Telephone:** 0207-935-9512. **Fax:** 0207-935-7531. **E-mail:** *lettings@globeapt.com.*

Web site: *www.globe.com*. **Prices from:** 1 bdrm-$972. **Negotiate price?** yes. **Deposit?** yes. **Check in:** 2 P.M. **Check out:** 12 P.M. **Credit cards?** yes, but at a 4.5% surcharge. **Tube stop:** Goodge Street.

Presidential House, University Street, London WC1E 6JQ

photo p. C

The 13 one-, two- and three-bedroom apartments of Presidential House are located in the part of Bloomsbury now called Fitzrovia. Just off Tottenham Court Road and three short blocks from the Warren Street tube station, the apartments are a 10-minute walk to Queen Mary's Garden in Regent's Park and about the same distance to the British Museum in the other direction. A supermarket is around another corner.

The entrance to Presidential House is to the left of the Abby National Bank on the corner of Tottenham Court and University. From 9 A.M. to 5 P.M. someone is on duty in the tiny entrance area to assist newcomers on their way to the flats. All of the apartments are located on the fifth floor of this modern redbrick building, and the elevator in the entry alcove is solely for the use of tenants and their guests.

Presidential House, with the same management as the Presidential Apartments on George Street in Marylebone, is similar in decor with the same friendly, upbeat, and helpful management staff, especially Mrs. B., who has overseen these apartments for the last 20 years. While the apartments are suitable for all travelers, they are a boon for families. With the exception of the one-bedroom flats, all others are split level with the sleeping rooms above and the living rooms below. The apartments are roomy, well equipped, and a bargain, too. A family of four can stay here for as little as $175 per night ($1,223 per week) in the low season. High-season rates start at $217 per night ($1,500 per week).

The split-level apartments enter into a small hallway with the stairs to the upper level immediately to the right and a half bath tucked under the stairwell. The living/dining area, through a doorway to the left, is about 25 by 18 feet, but appears more spacious because of three floor-to-ceiling windows. At the near end of the room are two easy chairs with a cabinet on the wall between them. Two matching sofas face each other across the middle of the room. At the far end is a large wooden table with six chairs. The kitchen alcove is opposite the table. Since the full-size refrigerator/

freezer would not fit in the alcove, it is just outside. All of the kitchen cabinets are pine, the floor is black and white tile, and there are a stove, microwave, basic pots, pans, and utensils, good counter space, a serving cart, and ample tableware, glasses, and cutlery. On the upper level, the full bath, with tiled floor and walls and tub/shower, is to the right of the stairway. The larger bedroom has twin beds (one flat has three), bedside tables with lamps, a wardrobe, and a large floor-to-ceiling window with curtains that match the bedspreads. The second bedroom is smaller with twin beds, a side table with lamp, wardrobe, and large window.

One-bedroom apartments are all on one level. They are similarly furnished but have smaller under-counter refrigerator/freezers, small round dining tables with two chairs, and only one sofa and easy chair. All flats have wall-to-wall pale floral carpeting.

These apartments are not glamourous, and the velvet sofas and upholstered chairs have a dated look. All are comfortable, however, and the lack of elegance may make them even more comfortable for families with small children.

AMENITIES—Elevator, telephone, color TV, computer connection through telephone, fax (through office), maid service (Monday–Friday), manager (on call 24 hours), refrigerator/freezer (large), stove with oven, toaster, tea kettle, teapot, coffee maker, iron, microwave.

RESERVATIONS/PRICES/MISC.—**Minimum stay:** 1 week, but flexible. **Reservations:** office staff. **Telephone:** 0207-486-0097. **Fax:** 0207-487-3624. **E-mail:** *PresApartmentsLondon@msn.com*. **Prices from:** 1 bdrm-$575–$1,109 (1 person), $729 (2 people); 2 bdrm-$1,223–$1,661; 3 bdrm-$1,385–$1,844. **Negotiate price?** yes. **Deposit?** yes. **Check in:** 2 P.M. **Check out:** 12 P.M. **Credit cards?** all but Diners, 2.5% surcharge for American Express. **Tube stop:** Warren Street.

Red Lion Square, London WC1

photo p. C

Holborn is an unlikely neighborhood for an elegant set of flats. Nevertheless, this busy commercial district near the Inns of Court boasts one of the nicest groups of flats in the city. Avanti Travel manages two studios and five two-bedroom flats in Halsey House, a regency building on Red Lion Square. (They are listed under the name of the square, not the name of the building.) The square, with its typical central garden, dates from 1684 and was once home to William Morris, Dante Rossetti, and Edward Burne-Jones.

But it's the apartments that count. All have been carefully decorated in the period of the building and feature high ceilings, crown moldings, fine but simple drapery, and wallpaper typical of the Arts and Crafts movement started by the above-mentioned William Morris. All of the two-bedroom flats have two baths and a central hallway but do vary in floor plan. In some, the two-bedrooms are on either side of the hall near the entrance, while in others the bedrooms are at the back with the living/ dining area and kitchen in front. Each apartment has a lovely sitting room with a fancy carved fireplace, and is large enough for a sofa, desk, easy and occasional chairs. A dining table with four chairs set in the bay window overlooks the square.

Kitchens are modern and complete with white wooden cabinets, either under-counter or large refrigerator/freezer (make preference known at booking), electric stove with gas burners, microwave, washer/dryer, and dishwasher. There are plenty of good-quality pots, pans, and cooking utensils.

The master bedrooms all have an *en suite* bath, and there is a second bath in the hall. Baths are roomy and pleasantly decorated with white walls, brass towel racks and fittings, dark wood trim, excellent counter space, and a good supply of large towels. Each flat has a hair dryer.

Master bedrooms have queen beds, and second bedrooms have either queen or twins. Second bedrooms tend to be smaller but both have bedside tables with reading lamps, dressers, and chairs.

There are additional decorative touches throughout the apartments (sculpture, prints, toy soldiers) that give them an individual and personal feel.

The studios were occupied and we could not see them. The manager described them as unusually large with either twins or a queen-size bed.

The neighborhood suffers from heavy traffic on nearby High Holborn and Southhampton Row, but the square is quiet and convenient. A 10-minute walk will take you to the British Museum or Covent Garden; a 20-minute walk, to most theaters in the West End.

These apartments are charming, elegant, and at the same time warm and welcoming. For two couples or a family, they are also an excellent buy.

AMENITIES—Elevator (none), telephone, color cable TV, VCR, computer connection through telephone, maid service (once a week), housekeeper, refrigerator/freezer, stove with oven, toaster, tea kettle, teapot, coffee maker, iron, microwave, washer/dryer, dishwasher, hair dryer.

RESERVATIONS/PRICES/MISC.—**Minimum stay:** 1 week. **Reservations:** Joan Butler. **Telephone:** 0147-470-8701. **Fax:** 0147-470-8702. **E-mail:** *avanti@avanti-london. demon.co.uk.* **Prices per week from:** studios-$952; 2 bdrm, 2 bath-$1,694. **Negotiate price?** yes. **Deposit?** yes. **Check in:** 1 P.M. **Check out:** 10 A.M. **Credit cards?** all at 3.5% surcharge. **Tube stop:** Holborn.

Scala House, 21 Tottenham Street, London W1P 9PD

photo p. C

A modern high-rise building, Scala House has been a temporary home to the business-person and tourist since 1992. Managed by the Palos since it opened, the family takes pride in providing a personal touch. They welcome each new, and many returning, visitors and are happy to assist in planning a London stay.

All of the 34 apartments in Scala House have two bedrooms and, with the exception of two penthouses on the 10th floor, all have essentially the same floor plan and same square footage. There are four flats on floors 2 through 9 and only two on the 10th.

Each of the standard flats enters into a hallway that runs the length of the apartment and has three closets. The kitchen is to the right, the sitting room opposite, and the two bedrooms beside each other at the far end of the hall. There are one and a half baths, both in the hall.

The kitchens at Scala House are outstanding. Each is a separate room that can be closed off, and each is fully fitted with a large refrigerator and separate freezer, microwave, dishwasher, and washing machine with turbo air dryer. There are ample cabinets, good counter space, and plenty of good-quality pots, pans, and cooking utensils.

Bright and airy with large windows, the living/dining room is furnished with a tufted velour sofa and two matching chairs. While comfortable and in good condition, the furniture is dark and somewhat dated, detracting from the overall look of the room. A polished wooden dining table with four chairs is at the end of the room next to the kitchen. China, glasses, and cutlery are generously supplied for eight people.

The master bedroom has a king zip-and-link bed with a cheerful floral bedspread. There are bedside tables with lamps, a dresser, mirror, and desk with chair.

Double closets provide plenty of storage space. Much smaller, the second bedroom has space only for a double bed and a dresser with lamp.

Maroon tiles cover the walls of both baths. The larger has a power shower/tub. Towels and linens are changed two times a week.

The penthouses are twice the size of the standard flat, furnished as the other flats, and have spectacular views of the London skyline.

Scala House provides comfortable but not luxurious accommodations for visitors to London. It is an especially good buy for families traveling with small or teenaged children.

Its Bloomsbury location is just minutes from the Goodge Street tube, a 5-minute walk to the British Museum, and 10 minutes from Regent's Park. If you go in the opposite direction, in the same time you will come to the department stores, boutiques, and restaurants of Oxford Street.

AMENITIES—Elevator, telephone, color TV, computer connection (modem), fax (through office), maid service (3 days a week), concierge/housekeeper, refrigerator/ freezer (large), stove with oven, toaster, tea kettle, teapot, coffee maker, iron, microwave, washer/dryer, dishwasher, hair dryer (on request).

RESERVATIONS/PRICES/MISC.—**Minimum stay:** 3 nights. **Reservations:** office staff. **Telephone:** 0207-580-6644. **Fax:** 0207-636-3406. **E-mail:** *ken@scala-house.co.uk*. **Web site:** *www.scala-house.co.uk*. **Prices from:** 2 bdrm, 1 bath plus half bath-$211 per night, $1,077 per week; penthouse, 1 bath plus half bath-$292 per night, $1,588 per week. **Negotiate price?** yes, return guests receive 10% discount. **Deposit?** yes. **Check in:** 1 P.M. **Check out:** 10 A.M. **Credit cards?** Visa and MasterCard, no surcharge, American Express and Diners at 3% surcharge. **Tube stop:** Goodge Street.

Soho Square, London WC2

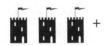 +

photo p. C

Love the theater and want to stay nearby? Try King's House on Soho Square. It's a modern apartment building with 10 flats, 6 of them short term (one studio, five two-bedrooms). The longer-term flats are often occupied by theater people. (Avanti Travel lists this property under the name of the square where it is located rather than the name of the building.)

Soho Square contains the only grass and trees in the neighborhood and is located several blocks away from the sex shops and strip clubs that gave Soho its seedy reputation several years ago. It is also only 10 minutes' walk from the playhouses of Shaftsbury Avenue, a block from Oxford Street shops, and 10 minutes from the British Museum. Berwick Street Market, just around the corner, provides wonderful baked goods, fresh fruits, vegetables, and a full range of other goodies at the best prices of any market in town.

The flats overlook the square, which at summer lunchtime fills with picnickers. The rooms are furnished comfortably and very well lighted. The two-bedroom apartment enters into a hallway that divides the living/dining area from the two bedrooms. The kitchen is opposite the door, and the bath is next to it. Matching overstuffed chairs and a sofa in the living/dining area rest upon a blue print wall-to-wall carpet. There are a wood-and-glass coffee table and side tables. On the far wall is a large bookcase/china cupboard with a desk with TV in the corner. An oval dining table for six sits off to the side in the large room. The master bedroom, also large, accommodates a queen and a single bed, with bedside tables for both. In one corner is a dresser, and a closet is along the wall. The small second bedroom has twin beds with two side tables with drawers between them. Bedcovers and curtains are in the same fabric. The room also has a dresser and closet. The galley kitchen is stylish with dark wall tiles and white wood cabinets and counters, and is very well supplied. It has a large refrigerator/freezer, full stove with double oven, microwave, washer/dryer, and dishwasher. Pots, pans, good knives, and utensils are abundant. The large modern bath has beige and white tile walls with a power shower/tub, bidet, and marble sink.

All flats have access to a roof terrace with white wrought-iron table and six chairs for summer dining.

AMENITIES—Elevator, telephone, color TV, computer connection through telephone, fax (through office), maid service (once a week), refrigerator/freezer (large), stove with double oven, toaster, tea kettle, teapot, coffee maker, iron, microwave, washer/dryer, dishwasher, hair dryer.

RESERVATIONS/PRICES/MISC.—**Minimum stay:** 1 week. **Reservations:** Joan Butler. **Telephone:** 1474-708-701. **Fax:** 1474-708-702. **E-mail:** *avanti@ avanti-london.demon.co.uk.* **Prices per week from:** studios-$857; 2 bdrm-$1,429. **Negotiate price?** yes. **Deposit?** yes. **Check in:** 1 P.M. **Check out:** 10 A.M. **Credit cards?** yes, but 3.5% surcharge. **Tube stop:** Tottenham Court Road.

Bloomsbury, Fitzrovia, and Holborn: Attractions

The name *Bloomsbury* derived from Blemondishberi, the 13th-century estate of William Blemond. In the 15th century, it became the property of Carthusian monks, who lost it soon after with the dissolution of the monasteries. Henry VIII gave it to the Earl of Southampton. Eventually, the estate fell into the hands of the Dukes of Bedford, property developers extraordinaire, and the fifth and sixth dukes shaped the neighborhood we see today. Starting in 1800, they laid out a series of squares and Georgian terraces with housing for lawyers employed at the Inns of Court. The area also attracted writers, painters, musicians, and, after the building of the British Museum, scholars. Such inhabitants established the character of the neighborhood even into the present. "A very unfashionable area, though very respectable," said a 19th-century resident. The neighborhood gained a certain avant-garde edge in the early 20th century as the home of the "Bloomsbury group" (Lytton Strachey, Virginia Woolf, Roger Fry, E. M. Forster, and other such literati).

Fitzrovia has no such historic distinction. The few blocks west of Tottenham Court Road got the name in the 1940s, and property developers apparently thought it sounded posh. Ironically, Fitzroy was a bastard son of Charles II.

Together they form a middle-class neighborhood, comfortable but not stylish, mixing residential apartments, small businesses, several colleges of the University of London, and London's most popular tourist attraction, the British Museum. The University of London—with 40,000 students, the largest in the United Kingdom—is really a consortium of colleges rather than a single campus. Senate House, which has a 200-foot tower, is the administrative center in Bloomsbury. It houses a vast library and fine collection of Elizabethan literature. The stunning new British Library, located next to St. Pancras Station, will also draw visitors. It holds many literary treasures and changing exhibitions of interest to the general public. The library displays not only books, including the Gutenberg Bible, but also historic documents such as the Magna Carta. Interactive exhibits allow visitors to turn the pages of these historic manuscripts and others, such as Shakespeare's First Folio. Many collections of private papers are generally only available to scholars, but a simple application and an ID card were sufficient to gain access to the Gladstone Papers. A reader's ticket is easily obtained to use the general collection but must be done in advance.

Fans of Dickens will enjoy a visit to his London residence on Doughty Street, now a museum with Dickens' papers, photographs, and other memorabilia.

The main attraction of the neighborhood is the British Museum. Robert Smirke's massive neoclassical structure was designed to contain the eclectic collection of royal physician Hans Sloane. It grew from its opening in 1855 to encompass a world of treasures: sculpture, painting, jewels, coins, and several libraries of books. Think of combining the Library of Congress and the Smithsonian in one building and you can understand why it attracts five million visitors a year and why each and every one of them leaves exhausted and in awe.

In 1997 the British Library moved its millions of volumes up to Euston Road next to St. Pancras Station. That freed nearly two acres of space for display galleries and the fabulous Great Court that opened in 2000. Needless to say, the museum is a must see and now more accessible than ever.

Holborn, just east of Bloomsbury, grew up around the Inns of Court, four prestigious legal fraternities established in the Middle Ages as a school and residence for barristers. Designed as self-contained communities around a series of quadrangles, the Inns include offices, dining halls, libraries, chapels, and handsome gardens inside the squares, all open to casual visitors. Temple Inn, just off Fleet Street, contains a lovely 12th-century church and a lawn along the Thames. Lincoln's Inn and Gray's Inn have extensive quiet gardens running off either side of busy High Holborn, and a block of half-timbered Elizabethan dwellings now used as shops stand on High Holborn itself.

The area is full of literary associations. The poet John Donne was a barrister of Lincoln's Inn, Charles Dickens clerked for a solicitor at Gray's Inn, and Shakespeare's *Comedy of Errors* premiered at Gray's Inn hall in 1594.

Aside from some fine old pubs like the Cittie of Yorke (22 High Holborn), the neighborhood offers little in the way of dining and nightlife. But it is only a short walk from Covent Garden, Fleet Street, and West End theaters.

Shops, Restaurants, and Pubs

Bloomsbury is not a neighborhood for a general shopping day. Leave that to Covent Garden (see p. 58). In keeping with its literary character, the neighborhood contains several good bookstores, for new books (Dillons), and used (Skoobs) on Sicilian

Avenue. But Charing Cross Road, just south of Bloomsbury/Fitzrovia, is still the mecca for books.

The area does have some outstanding specialty shops. Most unusual is John Smith and Son in Hazelwood House at 53 New Oxford Street. It is the oldest and largest umbrella and walking-stick store in Europe. Most are made in-house on the lower level from only British materials. Handles of many umbrellas and sticks come in finely crafted animal heads, from aardvark to zebra. Both can be made to order to your own specifications. Such things cost dearly, of course, but quality pays. We both bought umbrellas 15 years ago (on a half-price sale), and they are still in excellent working condition today.

Westway and Westway, 64–65, 92–93 Great Russell Street, across from the British Museum, sells a complete range of Scottish woolens. There are kilts in all tartans; Harris tweed jackets; sweaters, including cashmere; scarves; gloves; and anything else woolen you can think of. We bought our first English sweaters from Westway and Westway back in the 1970s. It's still a great place to buy high-quality British-made goods at fair prices.

Don't forget the British Museum Shop (0207-580-1788), one of the best for unusual and memorable gifts. Many items are less pricey copies of major works in the collections, including Egyptian jewelry, historic chess sets, statuary, games with history themes, and, of course, books.

One of the best reasons to stay in Bloomsbury is Charlotte Street—if you like to eat, that is. Restaurants of all prices cluster here. Starting south of Goodge Street at the corner of Charlotte and Percy is Rasa Samudra (0207-637-0222), a well-rated and expensive Indian restaurant serving dishes from Kerala (entrees, $15–$20). On the opposite corner is Bam Bou (0207-323-9130), a Vietnamese restaurant in a beautiful Georgian townhouse (entrees, $13 to $17). Moving northward, one block south of Goodge at the corner of Windmill Street is Passione (10 Charlotte Street, 0207-636-2833), an Italian restaurant known for its excellent pasta dishes (entrees, $10 to $26) and well-priced house wines. Just south of Goodge is one of our favorites, Elena's L'Etoile (30 Charlotte Street, 0207-636-7189). A few years ago, Elena moved from her former establishment, L'Escargot, in Soho to these premises in Fitzrovia. She brought with her the exceptional French cuisine that once made L'Escargot so popular. Entrees are between $30 and $48, but if you book pretheater between 6 and 7 P.M., you can take 20 percent off your total bill.

A block north of Goodge Street is Navarro's at number 67, serving authentic Spanish dishes with tapas and main courses from $4 to $20. Pied à Terre (34 Charlotte Street, 0207-636-1178), across from Navarro's, is a highly touted and very expensive restaurant featuring modern British cooking (two-course set dinner, $64; three courses, $80; eight-course tasting menu, $104). Finally, at the top of Charlotte Street at number 32 is Noho (0207-636-4445), serving Oriental fish, meat, and noodle dishes from a selection of Asian countries at the opposite end of the price spectrum (entrees from $9 to $13).

> **Hint:** Don't let the numbers confuse you. In London, address numbers can run up one side of the street and down the other—or not!

Also on Charlotte Street at number 53 is Fratelli Camisa, an Italian delicatessen. It stocks Italian cheeses, including Parmesan, along with pastas, sausages, house-made sauces, olive oils, and canned items. Assemble your own dinner here and save a bundle. Fratelli Camisa also sells delicious sandwiches at lunchtime.

Fancy fish and chips in Bloomsbury? Try the North Sea Fish Restaurant (7–8 Leigh Street, 0207-387-5892). One part is a restaurant and the other, a take-away. All main dishes are fish: fresh, well prepared, and generously proportioned. Fries are almost greaseless. Desserts—tiramisu, apple crumble, trifle—will tempt you too.

Interesting pubs abound in and around Bloomsbury. You can't miss the Museum Tavern in its location opposite the British Museum, but you may choose to, because it fills with tourists daily. When William Finch Hill designed it in 1855, he included a massive mahogany-and-glass bar and partitions to separate various classes of clientele. The present owners removed the partitions to squeeze in more customers. On the other hand, you might miss The Lamb on tiny Conduit Street (east of Russell Square), but you shouldn't. Once an inn, then a gin palace, the present decor dates from 1894 and includes a wonderful set of cut-glass "snob screens" around the bar. These short panels at head level pivot to hide the customer at the bar from his neighbor, preserving both privacy and class distinction. As a bonus, one wall is lined with antique photos of actresses of the turn of that century. Even the street is interesting. The conduit donated by Sir William Lamb in 1577 brought fresh water into the neighborhood.

The Fitzroy Tavern (16 Charlotte Street), on the western side of the district, displays interesting photographs as well. These show avant-garde writers and painters of the 1930s and 1940s who lived in this once Bohemian neighborhood. BBC staffers stop by nowadays.

A Tuesday Excursion to Covent Garden

Perhaps the best reason to stay in Bloomsbury, in addition to the British Museum, the British Library, and Charlotte Street, is its central location. It is close to Oxford Street, Soho, and Covent Garden. In fact, from all of the apartments in this chapter, you could walk to Covent Garden, a real plus because the Covent Garden tube stop is sometimes closed due to overcrowding—even in January. It's most crowded on the weekends, so go during the week. The best day is Tuesday, because this is the only weekday that the Apple Market is at Covent Garden. Apple Market is the crafts market, and most of the stalls have well-made, original items. There are handknit sweaters loomed from hand-spun yarn, quilted baby wear, jewelry, leather goods, hats, handmade puppets, batiked silks, pocketbooks, coin purses, and totes in Liberty prints, and that just scratches the surface. Apple Market is great for gifts to take home. The crafts come in all prices and all sizes.

The permanent shops have much to offer also. If there are children to buy for, the Beatrix Potter shop has dolls, clothing, socks, and all manner of items based on Peter Rabbit and the rest of Potter's animal characters. There is Paddington Bear in many forms and other traditional children's delights. Lush has a shop with natural soaps and shampoos. Enter carefully. The scent is so strong, it's hard to breathe for the first moment or two. All of us like Lush's travel shampoo. It's in cake form and fits neatly into a metal tin. No more gooey shampoo in your suitcase. Hobbs is here with its trendy gear and shoes. Thornton's has English candies in small packages that make nice gifts.

There are also many fine shops on the streets leading to the market proper,

> **Ray's Jazz Shop.** A landmark for jazz recordings, Ray's on 180 Shaftsbury Avenue at Neal Street carries everything from old 78s to the newest CDs. If it has to do with jazz, Ray or his staff know it or where to find it. New CDs cost more in Britain than in the United States, but Ray carries obscure British and European labels like Hep and Yesteryear. Check out his large bin of perfectly clean used CDs at half price. Stop in for a few minutes and spend an hour.

including the usual chain stores, Jigsaw, Monsoon, Oasis, French Connection. For teens, there's a Dr. Martens on one corner.

If someone doesn't want to shop, there's always the Theatre Museum (Tavistock Street, 0207-836-7891) or the London Transport Museum (Covent Garden Piazza, 0207-379-6344). Both are guaranteed to fascinate for hours on end. Boys especially enjoy the Transport Museum. Despite the stodgy name, the Transport Museum is great fun. Kids and adults can climb aboard 19th-century trains, learn about the amazing underground system that carries you all around town, and experience futuristic travel. The Theatre Museum lets you share in the production of *The Wind in the Willows* at the From Page To Stage Gallery, as well as view costumes and stars from Elizabethan times on.

Of course, Covent Garden is home to live theater as well: the Royal Opera House and several West End theaters. On tiny Earlham Street, the Donmar Warehouse produces the most consistently imaginative and varied theater in London. Its production of *Cabaret* went to Broadway.

> **Covent Garden Market** and the adjacent plazas and streets are alive with buskers, unicyclists, an Oriental orchestra, and myriads of street entertainers. Even if not shopping, a stroll here is a delightful diversion.

When we have finally reached our shopping limit, we gather for lunch. Perhaps at the Lamb and Flag (33 Rose Street, 0207-497-9504), a historic pub once called the Bucket of Blood, because illegal boxing matches took place there. It's been doing business since 1623 and was built during Tudor times. The first floor is crowded and rickety, but the restaurant upstairs, where basic British food is served, feels more spacious. We like the sausages on baguettes.

After our usually late lunch, we're ready to hit the food shops.

First stop is always the Tea House (15A Neal Street, 0207-240-7539). This narrow shop carries a full line of its own teas, biscuits, and jams on the first floor and a huge selection of quirky teapots on the stairway and onto the second floor. We are fond of their fruit teas, especially the peach and coconut. They are not just decaffeinated, fruit-flavored beverages, but good black tea with actual dried fruit or fruit peels in them.

Lugging half a year's supply of tea, we head off to Carluccio's (28a Neal Street, 0207-240-1487), two abutting buildings with a restaurant on the right and a delicatessen on the left. Carluccio is a world-famous chef, and we can get his restaurant sauces and prepared dishes and pastas from the deli side. Carluccio's also has Parma ham, Parmesan, ground saffron (a lovely gift in a cute container), and other individually chosen items imported from Italy. In season, as you enter the deli, you will find baskets of fresh mushrooms of all varieties on the left. On the right are equally tempting Italian breads.

Further weighed down, we set off around the corner to the best-known shop in the Neal Street enclave, Neal's Yard Dairy (17 Short's Gardens, 0207-379-7646). Here we join the line, sometimes stretching out the door, to purchase fine handmade British cheeses, aged by the proprietor to perfect ripeness. Always busy, the sales staff never hurry customers to make a choice, but ask them enthusiastically to taste this and that cheese; the staff's own favorite often became the customers'. Also on sale are yogurts, creams, olives, and outstanding breads.

After Neal's Yard Dairy, we have to head home. We can't carry anything else.

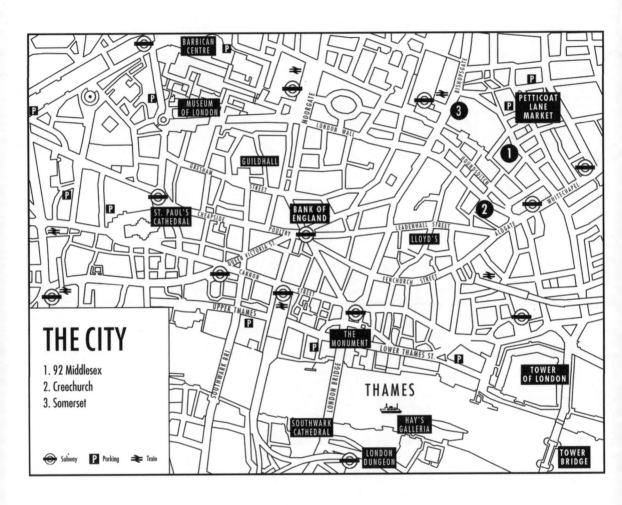

THE CITY

1. 92 Middlesex
2. Creechurch
3. Somerset

⊖ Subway 🅿 Parking 🚄 Train

BARBICAN CENTRE

MUSEUM OF LONDON

MOORGATE

LONDON WALL

PETTICOAT LANE MARKET

BISHOPSGATE

HOUNDSDITCH

WHITECHAPEL

GUILDHALL

GRESHAM STREET

ST. PAUL'S CATHEDRAL

CHEAPSIDE

BANK OF ENGLAND

POULTRY

LEADENHALL STREET

LLOYD'S

ALDGATE

QUEEN VICTORIA ST.

CANNON STREET

FENCHURCH STREET

UPPER THAMES

THE MONUMENT

LOWER THAMES ST.

TOWER OF LONDON

SOUTHWARK BRI.

LONDON BRIDGE

THAMES

SOUTHWARK CATHEDRAL

HAY'S GALLERIA

LONDON DUNGEON

TOWER BRIDGE

Chapter 4

The City

S pell "city" with a capital "C," because it was the entire city of London for hundreds of years. Romans named it and put a wall around it, but human habitation predates the Romans by a millennium. The square mile the Romans occupied stretches from the Thames at Tower Hill north to Smithfield and west to Holborn. The history of London is all inside, from Roman walls to medieval towers to church spires, but the heart of the City (if not its soul) is steel-and-glass boxes filled with bankers and market speculators. Don't be put off by that, because the City always lived by commerce. Besides, the bankers and traders leave at night. The churches, medieval fortresses, and Roman stones remain, along with fine museums, lively markets, and a giant arts center. The Tower of London and Saint Paul's Cathedral are the best-known attractions, but there are many more.

The City is just awakening to the idea of short-term apartments as an alternative to hotels. The new ones we found provide especially well for business travelers.

The City at a Glance

Apartment	Studio	1-Bedroom	2-Bedroom	3-Bedroom	Other
92 Middlesex Street 1-week minimum 🏰🏰🏰🏰	$162 n $1,133 w	$228–$238 n $1,609–$1,666 w	$295–$324 n $2,065–$2,665 w (2 baths)	$419 n $2,931 w (2 baths)	
The Creechurch 1-week minimum 🏰🏰🏰🏰		$246–$270 n $1,721–$1,888 w	$254–$293 n $1,777–$2,054 w (2 baths)		*Penthouse* $317–$397 n $2,221–$2,776 w
Somerset Bishopsgate No minimum stay 🏰🏰🏰🏰	$187–$200 n $1,237–$1,329 w	$248–$276 n $1,647–$1,837 w	$305–$352 n $2,025–$2,341 w (some, 2 baths)		*Penthouse* $476 n $3,166 w (2 baths)

NOTES: (1) All prices are in American dollars converted at $1.62 to £1 and include VAT. To convert to the current rate, divide the dollar amount by 1.62 and multiply by the rate listed in today's local paper. (2) n=night; w=week.

The City Apartments in Detail

92 Middlesex Street, London, E1 7EZ

photo p. D

Middlesex Street is one of the defining boundaries of the City, London's oldest neighborhood and its financial heart. Relegated exclusively to the businessperson for some time, the whole area is now enjoying redevelopment and eager to welcome other visitors.

As 92 Middlesex Street demonstrates, much is new in this oldest part of London. There are 5 studios, 12 one-bedroom, 9 two-bedroom, and 3 two-bedroom penthouse apartments in this reconstructed building. All furnishings are new and bright. Each flat has a sofa bed for an extra person.

The studios at 92 Middlesex are a pleasant surprise. Instead of the usual one room, there are two, although the bedroom lacks a door to close it off from the living area. The living/dining room is supplied with a sofa bed in bright blue, an end and a coffee table, a small dining table and two chairs, and a kitchen along one wall. The kitchen is complete with all appliances except a dishwasher. Both the living room and bedroom have a bath. For two travelers on a budget, it can be used as a small two-bedroom apartment (two smart businessmen were doing just that at the time of our visit).

Although it is a modern conversion, not all flats of the same type are the same size at Middlesex. One particular one-bedroom apartment with a bath and a half seemed larger to us than a two-bedroom, two-bath flat. Ask for size details when you book.

In the two-bedroom apartment, one enters into a central hallway. Two side-by-side bathrooms are off to the right, and two bedrooms are off to the left. The hall ends in the living/dining area with the kitchen off to the right. In all of the flats, the furnishings are contemporary. The living room has two sofas, one yellow and one blue. There is a glass-and-wrought-iron coffee table and a matching dining table with four chairs. Chair seats are in the same fabric as the curtains. The carpeting throughout is beige. The decor is pleasant and light.

The kitchen is separate and complete. It has blond wood cabinets on three white tiled walls. There are a full-size refrigerator/freezer, electric stove with four gas burners, microwave, washer/dryer, and dishwasher. Pans, tableware, glasses, and utensils are plentiful.

In the master bedroom is a king bed with wrought-iron-and-glass bedside table along with a dressing table, a chair, and a second TV. Bedcovers and curtains are in a yellow and blue floral pattern. The second bedroom is slightly smaller and has a double bed, two bedside tables, and no TV.

Baths are opposite each bedroom and are tiled in white. One has a tub/shower while the other has only a shower.

These apartments are comfortably furnished and light and airy rather than lavish. Dishwashers and washer/dryers are a plus in this price range, as are a friendly and helpful on-site management staff.

Amenities—Elevator, telephone with answering machine, color satellite TV, VCR, CD/stereo player, radio, computer connection ("Inntouch" Internet access system), fax (through office), maid service (Monday–Friday), concierge/housekeeper, refrigerator/freezer (large), stove with oven, toaster, tea kettle, teapot, coffee maker, iron, microwave, washer/dryer, dishwasher, toiletries.

Reservations/Prices/Misc.—**Minimum stay:** 1 week. **Reservations:** office staff. **Telephone:** 0207-377-1763. **Fax:** 0207-247-1266. **E-mail:** *parklane@cpd.co.uk.* **Web site:** *www.parklane.co.uk.* **Prices per week from:** studios-$1,133; 1 bdrm-$1,609; 2 bdrm, 2 bath-$2,065; penthouse-$2,931. **Negotiate price?** yes. **Deposit?** yes. **Check in:** 2 P.M. **Check out:** 12 P.M. **Credit cards?** yes. **Tube stop:** Liverpool Station.

The Creechurch, 2–20 Creechurch Lane, London EC3

photo p. D

Creechurch perfectly illustrates the practice of transforming old properties for new uses in the City. The Tea Consumers' Company occupied the premises as a warehouse until 1920. Large iron cranes with pulleys bolted on the exterior walls hauled the tea bales from the street below and swung them into the building through broad doors on each of the warehouse floors. Those doors are now floor-to-ceiling windows for the 33 ultramodern one- and two-bedroom apartments. The only reminders of its warehouse history are iron cranes still mounted on the wall.

The narrow lane, named for the medieval Christi Church that stood nearby, can be a bit hard to find, especially if you approach it in a pelting rain as we did. But it is in the heart of the City, located between Aldgate tube station and Liverpool Street tube and rail terminus.

Once inside, contemporary comforts take the place of warehouse history. Although each flat has a different floor plan and slightly different dimensions, the style of decor is uniform throughout. Pristine white walls surround Scandinavian furniture on pine floors. The decorators have gone for clean lines and functional efficiency. Wood-stained venetian blinds or Roman shades cover the windows instead of curtains and drapes in the living rooms. They use glass and simple wood veneers for coffee and dining tables, yet the apartments feel luxurious rather than plain or cold.

The kitchens come with the very best in quality appliances (Neff and Bosch), including full-size refrigerator/freezer, dishwasher, washer/dryer, electric oven, gas

66

burners, and microwave. Blond wood cabinet fronts conceal the larger appliances. Most baths contain tubs and power showers decorated in marble tile. All the rooms, except the baths, have large windows, and living rooms have more than one. Good light is hard to come by in the City with its narrow streets.

The living room in one-bedroom apartments has a sofa and lounge chair, while in the two-bedroom flats there are two sofas. Sofas are either blue or beige and coordinate with the upholstery on the dining chairs. All have coffee and occasional tables and design details, such as Scandinavian area rugs, plants, and sculptures, that give these flats their opulent feel. Bedrooms all have double beds with curtains, bedcovers, and wallpapers in beige tones. There are bedside tables and dressers in each bedroom. In the standard two-bedroom, the master bath is *en suite* with another bath with tub off the hallway.

Seven luxury penthouses (four two-bedroom and three one-bedroom) crown the buildings. They share the same general decor and quality of appliances but in more spacious rooms. The living/dining room in one measures 28 by 14 feet, an impressive setting for an executive cocktail party. Arched ceilings or skylights make them seem even larger. Private balconies, fireplaces, and somewhat better views distinguish them.

These apartments are a fine choice for the executive who needs to be in the City and perhaps entertain clients. Creechurch has a catering arrangement with Poets Restaurant. Certainly, to stay here, an expense account helps. Not only are prices high, but Creechurch has a bizarre rate structure: it considers a week to be six nights and seven days! If you pay its weekly rate and expect to stay a week, you will be disappointed. When we questioned the manager about this, she could only say that it was the way they did it and everyone understood. The only benefit we could see is that it allows a guest to arrive and check in at any time of the day or night. In the rates below, we have also included prices for a *true* week, seven nights, and the VAT for both (the VAT is not included in Creechurch's posted prices, perhaps because visitors often stay more than 28 days, when the VAT is substantially reduced).

AMENITIES—Elevator, telephone, satellite color TV, radio, computer connection through telephone, fax (line in each flat), maid service (Monday–Friday in penthouse, once a week otherwise), concierge/housekeeper (8 A.M.–8 P.M., Monday–Friday), refrigerator/freezer (large), stove with oven, toaster, tea kettle, teapot, coffee maker, iron, microwave, washer/dryer, hair dryer, toiletries, welcome pack.

RESERVATIONS/PRICES/MISC.—**Minimum stay:** 6 nights, 7 days (one "week," see text above). **Reservations:** office staff. **Telephone:** 0207-623-5019. **Fax:** 0207-623-5021. **E-mail:** *reservations@thecreechurch.fsnet.co.uk.* **Web site:** *www.johndwood.co.uk.* **Prices from:** 1 bdrm-$1,475 for 6 nights, $1,721 for 7; 2 bdrm, 2 bath-$1,529 for 6 nights, $1,777 for 7; penthouse-$1,904 (1 bdrm) for 6 nights, $2,221 for 7. **Negotiate price?** no. **Deposit?** yes. **Check in:** anytime. **Check out:** anytime. **Credit cards?** yes. **Tube stop:** Aldgate.

Somerset Bishopsgate, 190 Bishopsgate, London EC2M 4NR

photo p. D

Located in a former printing house in the heart of the City, Somerset was under construction for two years, opening as serviced apartments in April 2000. In contrast to this most ancient part of London, it is completely 21st century, from its streamlined Neff kitchens to its digital telephone system and analog Internet lines. Part of a chain of executive residences from the Asian Pacific, Somerset Bishopsgate provides all-modern amenities in the middle of London's financial district.

There are 21 studio, 12 one-bedroom, and 12 two-bedroom apartments, including two penthouses. Studios come in two types, deluxe and executive. The executives are larger with more separation between the sleeping and living area. Both enter into a foyer with a full bath off to one side. A glass door opens into the rest of the flat. At one end of the room is a double bed with bedside table, lamps, and dresser. A sofa, matching easy chair, and coffee table are in the middle, and a glass dining table with four chairs is at the other end. Each flat has a desk with stereo and CD player. Floors are polished pine with scatter rugs and, in keeping with the modern style, the windows have blinds rather than drapes. The ultramodern kitchen alcove is behind the dining table. The kitchens are striking with gray tiled floors, gray cabinets, black marble counters, and black exhaust hoods. They have recessed lighting, full-size refrigerator/freezers, stove with four burners, microwaves, and washer/dryers. There are no dishwashers, but maids do the washing up in the mornings.

One-bedroom apartments open into a foyer off which are three doorways. The one to the right leads to the bath; the one to the left, to the living room; and the center one, to the bedroom. The bedroom has a king bed, bedside tables with lamp, and closets.

Two glass doors lead into the living/dining room. There are a blue sofa, matching easy chairs, tables, a Scandinavian rug, and a desk with stereo and CD player. A dining table with four chairs is in front of the kitchen, similar to the one in the studios.

There are two types of two-bedroom apartments. Both have only one bath, but one type is a dramatic split-level. The single-level type has a long hallway off which the bath and two bedrooms open on the right side, while the living/dining/kitchen section opens off the far left end of the hall. While similarly furnished, the split-level apartments are distinguished by white wooden stairways and beamed room dividers in the bedrooms on the second level. Balconies with outdoor furniture open off both of the bedrooms on the upper level.

These bright and airy apartments provide many amenities in a part of London that is just becoming familiar to tourists. There is an enticing combination of old with new in the neighborhood. The modern Liverpool tube and train station is directly across from Somerset, while the revived, traditional Spitalfields Market with crafts, organic foods, and baked goods is just a few blocks away. The City now welcomes all visitors—businessperson and tourist alike.

AMENITIES—Elevator, telephone (ISDN digital telephones), satellite color TV, radio, computer connection, maid service (Monday–Friday), concierge/housekeeper (24 hours), refrigerator/freezer (large), stove with oven, toaster, tea kettle, teapot, coffee maker, iron, microwave, washer/dryer, dishwasher, hair dryer, toiletries.

RESERVATIONS/PRICES/MISC.—**Minimum stay:** 1 night. **Reservations:** office staff. **Telephone:** 0207-621-8788. **Fax:** 0207-621-8700. **E-mail:** *juliacook@somerset.com.* **Web site:** *www.somerset.com.* **Prices from:** studios-$1,237 per week, $187 per night; 1 bdrm-$1,647 per week, $248 per night; 2 bdrm, 1 bath-$2,025 per week, $305 per night; penthouse, 2 baths-$3,166 per week, $476 per night. **Negotiate price?** no, but discounts to frequent guests, and corporate discounts. **Deposit?** yes. **Check in:** 3 P.M. **Check out:** 11 A.M. **Credit cards?** all major. **Tube stop:** Liverpool Station.

The City: Attractions

The city is both the oldest and newest London neighborhood. Its winding streets date from Saxon times, but the towering steel-and-glass structures looming overhead are as new as today, part of the continual rebuilding process since World War II. Originally Londinium, when Romans laid out the square mile, the City *was* London until the 17th-century expansion beyond its walls. Age and a long reputation as a banking center (500 of them now) suggest stability and order, but a glance at a street map or a walk between Aldgate and Threadneedle Streets proves otherwise. The City is still a work in progress, new buildings set swiftly on old foundations to make every inch of the expensive real estate profitable. Half a million people work in the city, but only a few thousand live here, so by day it's a beehive; at night and on weekends, quiet compared with Chelsea or the West End.

Nevertheless, there is plenty to do and see. The Tower of London, the premier tourist attraction, anchors the southeast corner of the City and Saint Paul's Cathedral, the southwest. In between, dozens of gemlike small churches also designed by Sir Christopher Wren lend elegant contrast to the gray office blocks nearby.

The Barbican Center for Art and Conferences occupies 20 acres of the City combining concert halls, theaters, and an art gallery with its own tube station. It is home to the Royal Shakespeare Company and the London Symphony Orchestra. Given its size, you can't miss the Barbican, but you might not notice the Museum of London nearby. That would be a shame because this "gem" of a museum (as Kettler and Trimble [2001] call it in their *Amateur Historian's Guide to Medieval and Tudor London*) is unique to the city. It illustrates the history of London from prehistoric times, with special attention to the changing conditions of life in London. The address is London Wall for the Roman wall just outside. If you enter after 4 P.M., admission is free.

Shops, Restaurants, and Pubs

For a more worldly experience in this mercantile center, try one of the giant street markets. Petticoat Lane on Middlesex Street has drawn crowds hunting bargain clothing every Sunday for decades (open between 9 A.M. and 2 P.M.). Among the junk, you will find good-quality clothes, bags, and shoes. Petticoat Lane's designer section is worth a look off Goulston Street. Brick Lane Market, too, has plenty of junk but it also has High Street "seconds" at great discount and several shops selling high-quality leather at good prices (Xen, Mordex, and Unique Leatherwear). If hunger strikes as you shop, stop at the Brick Lane Bakery at 159 for inexpensive bagels (or *beigels,* as they spell it). There is only one flavor, except on the weekends, when a salty bagel is added.

But the best market these days is Spitalfields, a covered city block on Commercial Street near the Liverpool Street tube. Here the range of goods attracts more than just bargain hunters. Organic producers offer fruit, vegetables, and baked goods on Friday, and Sunday craftsmen and women join them with jewelry, hand knits, leather goods, handmade dresses, and French soaps, as well as new and used clothing and toys. We found lambswool scarves at two for $16 and a homemade bird whistle for $1.60. On the outer edge of the market, the Victorian Kitchen provides a traditional Sunday lunch that's good and reasonably priced. (Be careful going up the steep steps.)

In addition to the Victorian Kitchen, there are good restaurants in and around Spitalfields Market. Inside is the Arkansas Cafe. It serves barbecue, coleslaw, and potato salad to eat in or take away for later. Arkansas Cafe gets a gold star for both quality and price (entrees, $6 to $20), but it's only open at lunch. Some say it's the best barbecue in London. Just outside at 16–18 Brushfield Street (0207-377-9877; entrees, $16 to $30) is City Limits, a wine bar that also serves well-prepared, traditional food. The wine list is extensive and heavily French. Downstairs is a bistro. On the other side of the market at 8a Lamb Street is a Spanish restaurant, Mesón Los Barriles (0207-375-3136) with tapas, but the fresh fish and seafood specials ($10 to $18) are the best bets.

At 1 Poultry Street in the center of the City near Bank Tube Station is Le Coq d'Argent (0207-395-5000; entrees, $15 to $34), a Conran restaurant. It's named for its address, and not what it serves, because seafood is the specialty here. Preparation is mainly French. If you feel adventuresome, try the plateau de fruits de mer, a tower of crab, oyster, clams, cockles, winkles, and every sort of shellfish ($30). On a pleasant evening, enjoy sitting outside on the roof terrace. For modern British cooking in a modern setting, go to City Rhodes (1 New Street Square, 0207-583-1313; entrees, $25 to $39). The prices reflect the fame of the chef, Gary Rhodes.

Banking has brought many Japanese businesspeople into the city and with them a number of Japanese restaurants. If you have a taste for *kaiten zushi* (sushi revolving on a conveyor belt), there is K-10 at 10 Copthall Avenue (0207-562-8510, $2 to $6). Quality and preparation are outstanding and the setting is breathtaking. Those tasty little mouthfuls can add up, though, so you may pay more than expected. Less expensive is the noodle bar Noto Ramen House in Bow Bells House at 7 Bread Street (0207-329-8056; entrees, $10 to $12), which sells authentic Japanese noodles at a bargain price.

Old pubs abound, such as Samuel Johnson's favorite, Ye Olde Cheshire Cheese, on Fleet Street. It's just around the corner from his house on Gough Square (worth a visit). The Blackfriars at the entrance of Blackfriars Bridge may be the most distinctive pub in London. The wedge-shaped art nouveau building commemorates a Dominican monastery that once stood nearby. Henry Poole, a leader in the Arts and Crafts movement, decorated the interior with wonderful bronze and terra-cotta carvings depicting jolly friars making and drinking wine. A rotund Friar Tuck–type figure stands smiling above the entrance, inviting you to share the fun inside.

For something completely different, how about sipping your pint in a grand ballroom? Hamilton Hall was the ballroom of the Great Eastern Hotel at the Liverpool Street tube and rail station. The hotel was refurbished in the 1980s, but the ballroom remains as it looked in 1901—30-foot ceilings and gilt-edged paintings of Greek gods and goddesses in the style of Louis XIV over a rich carpet. To that was added a bar, and real ale, and it's just across the street from Somerset Bishopsgate. By contrast, Dirty Dick's pub and wine bar is all brick and bare wood, with a macabre history.

If you are stopping at Creechurch apartments, you might look in at the Hoop and Grapes at 47 Aldgate High Street. It occupies the only timber-frame building in the City that survived the Great Fire of 1666. The owners claim it as the oldest pub in London.

Westward in Holborn, you'll find a gem of decorative craftsmanship in Princess Louise, 208 High Holborn (a few blocks from Red Lion Square). Named for one of Queen Victoria's daughters, it represents the peak of public house design in the 1890s. The magnificent etched-glass mirrors, elegant wood panels, and tiled floor came from the best craftsmen of the time. The builders of the Cittie of Yorke at 22 High Holborn reacted against the elaborate 1890s style. Built just a decade later than the Princess Louise, the owner opted for a medieval-inn look with a black, timbered ceiling and leaded glass, and applied an old name from a "deceased" bar in the neighborhood. Samuel Smith of Yorkshire owns both pubs.

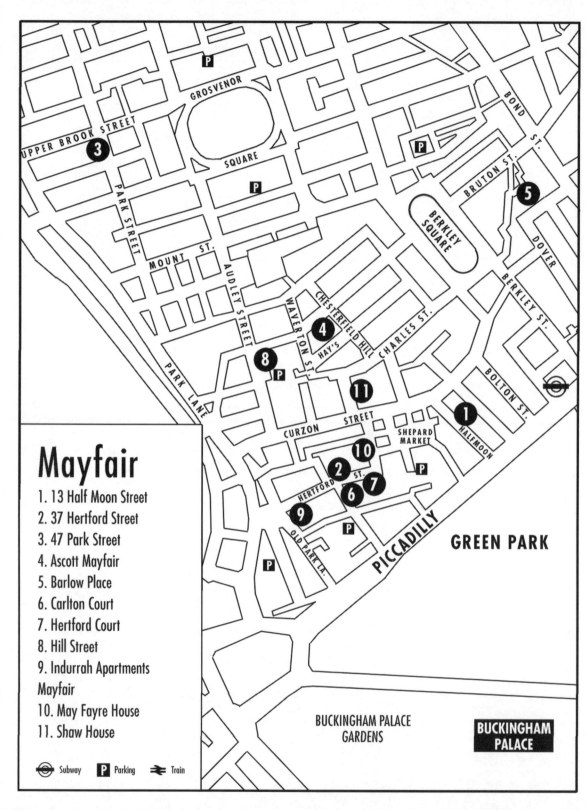

Mayfair

1. 13 Half Moon Street
2. 37 Hertford Street
3. 47 Park Street
4. Ascott Mayfair
5. Barlow Place
6. Carlton Court
7. Hertford Court
8. Hill Street
9. Indurrah Apartments
Mayfair
10. May Fayre House
11. Shaw House

⊖ Subway   P Parking   ⇌ Train

Chapter 5

❦

Mayfair

U nlike many neighborhoods that went in and out of fashion with the times, Mayfair has always been a stylish address. Its central location between Piccadilly and Oxford Streets, proximity to the royal palaces, and the fine Georgian homes that line its streets made it home to Britain's social elite then and now. The neighborhood blends old residential dwellings with newer, post–World War II commercial properties and office blocks. Nevertheless it is a quiet area, especially the western half where most of the luxury apartments are situated.

The posh hotels and embassies in Mayfair tend to make it a bit more stuffy than Chelsea or nearby Marylebone, but there is plenty to do here. Fine museums are at hand. You are only a few blocks from West End theaters, and adjacent to a great park (Hyde Park) for the kids to play and adults to walk in. And Mayfair is the center for elegant shopping. Liberty's, Austin Reed, and the world-famous Hamley's, a five-floor toy store, attract every shopper to Regent Street. Bond Street has antiques, galleries, and Sothebys' auction house. Mayfair's famous hotels, Claridge's, the Connaught, and the Dorchester are expensive, but to experience equal luxury at a more reasonable (but still expensive) price, the area contains many superb apartments with all the amenities of a five-star hotel.

Mayfair at a Glance

Apartment	Studio	1-Bedroom	2-Bedroom	3-Bedroom	Other
13 Half Moon Street No minimum stay		$619 n $4,333 w	$752–$942 n $5,264–$6,596 w	$847 n $5,929 w	
37 Hertford Street No minimum stay	$116–$162 n $810–$1,134 w	$203–$266 n $1,418–$1,863 w	$284–$405 n $1,985–$2,835 w (2 baths)		
47 Park Street No minimum stay	$400–$547 n $2,800–$3,829 w	$523–$1,095 n $3,661–$7,665 w	$971–$1,190 n $6,797–$8,328 w (2 baths)		
Ascott Mayfair No minimum stay	$370 n $2,475 w	$545 n $3,607 w	$798 n $5,178 w (2 baths)	$1,095 n $7,376 w (2 baths)	
Barlow Mews 1-week minimum		$302–$354 n $2,113–$2,475 w			
Carlton Court 1-week minimum		$286 n $1,999 w	$394–$489 n $2,760–$3,140 w (1.5–2 baths)	$579 n $4,050 w (2.5 baths)	Townhouse $1,020 n $7,138 w (4 baths)
Hertford Court Apts. No minimum stay		$209–$238 n $1,428–$1,942 w	$324–$400 n $2,056–$2,513 w (1 or 2 baths)		
Hill Street 1-week minimum		$220 n $1,542 w			

76

Apartment	Studio	1-Bedroom	2-Bedroom	3-Bedroom	Other
Indurrah Apts. Mayfair No minimum stay	$130–$190 n $891–$1,134 w	$146–$243 n $972–$1,701 w	$243–$405 n $1,701–$2,754 w (2 baths)	$332–$567 n $2,268–$3,402 w (2 baths)	*Penthouse* $356–$599 n $2,430–$3,726 w
May Fayre House 1-week minimum		$281–$298 n $1,971–$2,080 w	$408–$436 n $2,856–$3,046 w (2 baths)	$470 n $3,284 w (3 baths)	
Shaw House 1-week minimum		$337–$503 n $2,360–$3,521 w (2 baths)	$504–$690 n $3,521–$4,827 w (2 baths)	$653–$1,074 n $4,568–$7,519 w (2 baths)	*4-bedroom* $824–$1,494 n $5,768–$10,460 w (2.5 baths)

NOTES: (1) All prices are in American dollars converted at $1.62 to £1 and include VAT. To convert to the current rate, divide the dollar amount by 1.62 and multiply by the rate listed in today's local paper. (2) n=night; w=week.

Mayfair Apartments in Detail

13 Half Moon Street, Flemings of Mayfair, 13 Half Moon Street, London W1Y 7RA

photo p. D

Thirteen Half Moon Street's 10 apartments are in two buildings that are on either side of the delightful small hotel, Flemings of Mayfair. The listed buildings date from 1730, and the middle section opened as a hotel in 1851. Both apartment buildings have their own entrances, but guests register through the hotel. There they may enjoy the Georgian parlor with its intricate moldings, elaborate fireplace, and fine chandelier. Guests are invited to use all the amenities of the hotel, including its restaurant, bar, and 24-hour concierge service.

Each of the apartments is individually designed and decorated in styles ranging from regency to Louis XIV pastoral, and each is named for an English literary figure. We visited the Jane Austen and George Eliot apartments, both two-bedroom flats, and a three-bedroom flat very popular with families.

The living/dining area of the Austen apartment is decorated with pale-yellow striped wallpaper. The yellow is matched in the upholstered sofas and side chair and in the floral fabric of the floor-to-ceiling drapes. A marble fireplace with finely carved wooden mantle and brass fittings dominates the room where there is a desk in its own alcove and a polished, round dining table and four chairs. Double-crown moldings decorate the ceiling. The master bedroom with *en suite* bath and dressing room is wallpapered in red and white; a matching floral bed canopy is hung from the wall. The smaller second bedroom, also with *en suite* bath and in red and white, has a striped red canopy and matching bedcovers. Both baths are marble tiled with a power shower/tub, telephones, ample towels, guest robes, and toiletries. The galley kitchen is a separate room with door and is fully fitted with modern appliances, including large refrigerator/freezer, dishwasher, and washer/dryer.

The much larger living area of the Eliot apartment is in blue and white with two sofas on either side of the marble fireplace. The dining room is separate with table, chairs, and server. Elaborately traditional, the master bedroom has a king-size bed, blue and white floral wallpaper that matches the bedcovers, drapes, canopy, and privacy screen. The kitchen has all appliances and is large enough to hold a small table and two chairs.

With its own entrance and door preserved from 1730, the three-bedroom apartment feels like a separate townhouse because of its very large rooms and two levels. All bedrooms are upstairs. The living room is richly decorated in crimson and gold with a crystal chandelier, sofas, chairs, and a desk. The master bedroom has an English double bed, while the second has twin beds, and the third, a single bed. Each bedroom has an *en suite* bath with an additional bath off the hall on the lower level. In addition to the above appliances, the large kitchen has a built-in counter grill.

Although all of the apartments are elaborately decorated, children are very welcome. When we were visiting over the holidays, management even gave a Christmas tree to each family that wanted one.

All flats have marble-and-wood fireplaces, desks, real plants, and (by January 2001) new carpets and drapes.

AMENITIES—Elevator, telephone, color cable TV, radio, computer connection and computer, maid service (twice a day, 7 days), concierge/housekeeper, refrigerator/freezer, stove with oven, toaster, tea kettle, teapot, coffee maker, iron, microwave, dishwasher, washer/dryer, hair dryer, toiletries, welcome pack.

RESERVATIONS/PRICES/MISC.—Minimum stay: 1 night. **Reservations:** Sylvie Cartiser. **Telephone:** 0207-493-2088. **Fax:** 0207-7499-1817. **E-mail:** *sylvie@no13halfmoon street.co.uk*. **Web site:** *www.flemings-mayfair.co.uk*. **Prices from:** 1 bdrm-$619 per night, $4,333 per week; 2 bdrm, 2 bath-$752 per night, $5,264 per week; 3 bdrm, 2 bath-$847 per night, $5,929 per week. **Negotiate price?** yes, discount through American Express Travel. **Deposit?** yes. **Check in:** 2 P.M. **Check out:** 12 P.M. **Credit cards?** yes. **Tube stop:** Green Park.

37 Hertford Street, Mayfair, London W1J 7SF

photo p. D

A red and white brick building with four stories, 37 Hertford is one of the smaller townhouses on this residential street. It offers studios, one-, and two-bedroom apartments, and shares the closeness of Hyde, Green, and St. James's Parks with the other short-term rental units on this block. On the edge of Mayfair, access to the rest of London is easy by subway, and the shopping pleasures of Harrods and Knightsbridge's designer boutiques are an agreeable walk along Knightsbridge Road (about three-quarters of a mile away). On the other hand, Mayfair has many delights itself, including restaurants, pubs, and grand old buildings.

At present, 37 Hertford is in the midst of refurbishment, with hopes of eventually securing permission for the installation of an elevator in this listed building. Although it has no lift, in other ways Hertford Street is very up-to-date. For example, there is a laundry room, soap powder provided, for guest use on the third floor.

Each of the apartments opens into a foyer. In the two-bedroom flat, both bedrooms are off to the right, a bathroom is straight ahead, the living/dining room is to the left, and the kitchen is beyond. The decor is modern. The living/dining area has pale-yellow walls, two sofas in a pale-yellow stripe, a matching easy chair with large hassock, a fireplace (unfortunately blocked off with an unsightly wood slab), a mirror, end tables, and a coffee table. An alcove contains an étagère with vases and other decorative objects. In front of a wide window stands a glass dining table with four yellow and white upholstered dining chairs. A large kitchen with rose-colored walls and white cabinets runs off the alcove. There are a full-size refrigerator/freezer, full stove with four gas burners, microwave, large stainless steel sink, pots, pans, dishes, and more counter space than usual—a kitchen to really cook in. Both bedrooms feature the same yellow and white as the living room. The master bedroom with *en suite* bath has a queen bed, bedside tables, recessed lights, a chair, and a built-in dressing table between a cabinet and closet. The master bath is small but still has a tub with shower. A larger bath is off the hall.

In the one-bedroom apartment on the ground floor, the living/dining area is smaller with room for only one sofa and two easy chairs, all in a soft red fabric, and white wood-and-glass end and coffee tables. Across from the sofa is a breakfast bar and pass-through to the kitchen alcove, and a round glass dining table as well. Both bar and table have four chairs or stools in fabric that matches the sofa. The kitchen, while not a separate room, is well set off and as fully equipped as the one in the two-bedroom apartment. The bedroom has a double bed, side tables with reading lamps, and a mirrored dressing table set into the wall between two closets. The bath is tiled in pale yellow and has a tub/shower.

These are pleasant, spacious apartments with great kitchens. In some of the flats, the yellows were of different hues—clashing more than complementing, a small point. Management made it clear that they will negotiate price based on length of stay and vacancy rate.

AMENITIES—Elevator (none), telephone, color cable TV, radio, computer connection through telephone, fax (through office), maid service (Monday–Friday), housekeeper (9 A.M.–5 P.M., on call otherwise), refrigerator/freezer (large), stove with oven, toaster, tea kettle, teapot, coffee maker, iron, microwave, laundry room for guest use, hair dryer, toiletries.

RESERVATIONS/PRICES/MISC.—**Minimum stay:** 1 night. **Reservations:** Nabeel Safadi. **Telephone:** 0207-499-3623. **Fax:** 0207-499-2808. **E-mail:** *nabeelsafadi@ hotmail.com.* **Prices per week from:** studios-$810; 1 bdrm-$1,418; 2 bdrm, 2 bath-$1,985. **Negotiate price?** yes. **Deposit?** yes. **Check in:** 1 P.M. **Check out:** 12 noon. **Credit cards?** yes, but 4% surcharge. **Tube stops:** Green Park, Hyde Park.

47 Park Street, Mayfair, London W1K 7EB

photo E

Forty-seven Park Street was built by the first Baron Milford in 1926, and it *looks* baronial. It is a seven-story building with Corinthian columns constructed in the style of a grand Edwardian townhome. In 1981 Michelin star–winning chef Albert Roux moved his restaurant, La Gavroche, into 47 Park Street and subsequently became its manager. His wife, Monique, decorated the 52 one- and two-bedroom apartments in an Edwardian manner tweaked with French *art de vivre* style.

Now, guests at 47 Park Street get priority reservations at La Gavroche, which also provides the 24-hour room service menu. For the last three years, Conde Nast's *Traveler Magazine* has recognized the excellence of 47 Park Street by listing it as one of the top 500 hotels of the world.

The apartments themselves are luxurious. Each has two telephone lines, including private direct-dial phone/modem line, air conditioning, bathrobes and slippers for each occupant, fine toiletries, bone china tableware, and crystal wine glasses. A gym two minutes away provides sauna, jacuzzi, and swimming pool. A house florist cares for the living plants in each apartment. Original artworks decorate the walls of common areas and individual flats as well.

Each apartment conveys the feeling of an individual residence, perhaps because of the inside hallways with chair-rail and ceiling moldings, period prints, and occasional tables. In the one-bedroom apartment, the hall is L-shaped with the bedroom and living room on the far side and the kitchen near the entrance. A sofa and two easy chairs in a soft blue and beige print line adjacent walls in the living/dining room, with a bar and desk opposite. Ornate window treatments are in the same fabric as the sofa and chairs. The bedroom has a king bed, bedside table with lamps, dresser, easy chair, and wooden wardrobe.

The two-bedroom is similar in layout with an additional bath. The carpeting is blue throughout complemented by paler blue walls. The master bedroom has a king bed, chaise, and TV, while the second bedroom has a double bed and TV.

Marble bathrooms with a built-in sink and power shower/tub add to the luxury of these flats. Kitchens are fully equipped, as expected, with under-counter refrigerator/freezer, full stove, ample china, glassware, pots, and pans; a microwave is available on request.

All of the apartments at 47 Park Street are decorated lavishly, with attention to fine period details. Flats on levels 1 through 4 have the highest ceilings. A stay here is very expensive, even for Mayfair, but you do have access to one of the finest restaurants in Europe. Also it is just two blocks away from a favorite pub, the Audley, at 4143 Mount Street. If it is within your budget or your business expense account, 47 Park Street is a convenient, luxurious, and friendly place to stay.

AMENITIES—Elevator, telephone (2 lines), color satellite TV, radio, computer connection through telephone, fax, maid service (7 days), concierge/housekeeper, refrigerator/freezer, stove with oven, toaster, tea kettle, teapot, coffee maker, iron (on request), microwave (on request), hair dryer, toiletries, welcome pack.

RESERVATIONS/PRICES/MISC.—**Minimum stay:** 1 night. **Reservations:** office staff. **Telephone:** 0207-491-7282. **Fax:** 0207-491-7281. **E-mail:** *reservations@47park street.com*. **Web site:** *www.47parkstreet.com*. **Prices per night from:** studios-$400; 1 bdrm-$523; 2 bdrm, 2 bath-$971. **Negotiate price?** yes. **Deposit?** credit card information. **Check in:** 2 P.M. **Check out:** noon. **Credit cards?** all major. **Tube stop:** Marble Arch.

The Ascott Mayfair, 49 Hill Street, London W1J 5NB

photo p. E

At the Ascott Mayfair, luxury is in the details—bone china tableware, fine cotton linens, your own personal maid seven days a week, health club with gym, sauna and solarium, terrycloth robes, air conditioning, and complimentary breakfast in The Terrace overlooking the garden. Built in 1920, the sophisticated art deco style is maintained throughout the public areas and in quality-design details (paintings, lamps, clocks) in the individual apartments.

There are 56 studio, one-, two-, and three-bedroom apartments at the Ascott Mayfair, all of which have desks equipped with fax and computer connection. Each also has its own music system with CD player, and a golf umbrella! Some have fireplaces. Complimentary tea and coffee are always available in front of the fire in The Terrace, and an "honesty" bar is open at all times.

The flats themselves are smallish but lavishly furnished. Entry into the one-bedroom is through a foyer. The open-plan kitchen nook is straight ahead with the living area to the right and the bedroom with *en suite* bath to the left. Striking with its gray marble counters, glass burners, pale wooden cabinets, and chrome sink, it has an under-counter refrigerator and a microwave, but no stove. There is a convenient pass-through into the living/dining room near a round dining table that seats four. Across from the table against the wall is a brown velvet sofa, matching easy chair, side table, and coffee table. The desk is in the corner near the door. The bedroom has a king bed or zip-and-link (specify your preference at booking), side tables, chest of drawers, easy chair, closet, and TV. The bath is tiled with marble counters, mahogany details, and a power shower/tub. The washer/dryer is in the hallway.

In the two-bedroom, two-bath, the furnishings are similar but there is a marble fireplace and a large oriental rug over the blue wall-to-wall carpet. The kitchen has a dishwasher, even though the maid washes up each day. The master bedroom includes a king bed, easy chair with hassock, tables with reading lamps, dresser, and TV in a cabinet. The second bedroom has a queen bed with tables, lamps, chair, and closet. Both baths are *en suite.*

All of this luxury comes at a price, of course: studios start at $370 per night. Mayfair is an expensive area and the Ascott does provide a prestigious address to impress business clients. Full secretarial services are available through the office. Children are welcome, and the Ascott Mayfair is close to both Hyde Park and Green Park with plenty of space for kids to romp. The Duke of Wellington Museum, a grand Regency townhome, is nearby, as is Berkeley Square, where you will search in vain for nightingales.

AMENITIES—Elevator, telephone (3 lines in each flat), color satellite TV, radio, computer connection (modem), fax (in flat), maid service (7 days a week), concierge/housekeeper, refrigerator/freezer, toaster, tea kettle, teapot, coffee maker, iron, microwave, hair dryer, toiletries.

RESERVATIONS/PRICES/MISC.—**Minimum stay:** 1 night. **Reservations:** office staff. **Telephone:** 0207-499-6868. **Fax:** 0207-499-0705. **E-mail:** *ascott@the-ascott.com.* **Web site:** *www.the-ascott.com.* **Prices from:** studios-$370 per night, $2,475 per week; 1 bdrm-$545 per night, $3,607 per week; 2 bdrm, 2 bath-$798 per night, $5,178 per week; 3 bdrm, 2 bath-$1,095 per night, $7,376 per week. **Negotiate**

price? yes, discount through American Express Travel. **Deposit?** yes. **Check in:** 2 P.M. **Check out:** noon. **Credit cards?** all major. **Tube stops:** Green Park, Bond Street, Hyde Park Corner.

Barlow Mews, 3 Barlow Place, Mayfair, London

photo p. E

Barlow Mews is an almost hidden asset for Park Lane Apartments. This modern building is tucked away in a lane south of Bruton Street very near New Bond Street. The location could not be better, but it is tricky to find.

The five one-bedroom flats in Barlow are all the same. Each one opens into a short hallway with a closet. The hallway opens into the living/dining area which is L-shaped; the dining alcove with table and four chairs is in the short leg of the L. The long leg is the sitting room, brightly furnished with an overstuffed chair and sofa bed in a red and gold fabric. The dining chairs are covered in the same material as the sofa, and the wall-to-wall carpet is dark red. There are coffee and end tables, CD/stereo system, and VCR. There is a free video library for guest use. Two good-sized windows are in the wall opposite the dining alcove.

To the right of the hall is the bedroom with *en suite* bath. It has a double bed and bedside tables with reading lamps. There are a dresser with mirror along one wall and a closet along another wall. Drapes and bedcovers are in coordinating colors. The bath has a power shower/tub.

The kitchen is to the left off the hallway. It has all the appliances that a modern cook needs—full electric stove with gas burners, microwave, under-counter refrigerator/freezer, washer/dryer, and dishwasher.

Each apartment has a video entry phone for security and an Inntouch Internet access system. Towels and linens are changed twice a week.

Park Lane Apartments offers guests use of a local gym without charge, one pass per flat to a local attraction, a complimentary bus pass, and full office services for business travelers. While cribs and high chairs are available at an extra charge, children receive a complimentary gift pack.

These apartments are small but comfortable. The location is most convenient.

AMENITIES—Elevator, telephone, color satellite TV, radio, computer connection (Inntouch Internet access system), fax (machines available), maid service (Monday–Friday), refrigerator/freezer, stove, toaster, tea kettle, teapot, coffee maker, iron, microwave, dishwasher, washer/dryer, hair dryer.

RESERVATIONS/PRICES/MISC.—**Minimum stay:** 1 week. **Reservations:** office staff. **Telephone:** 0207-629-0763. **Fax:** 0207-493-1308. **E-mail:** *parklane@cpd.co.uk.* **Web site:** *www.parklane.co.uk.* **Prices from:** 1 bdrm–$2,113. **Negotiate price?** yes. **Deposit?** $810. **Check in:** 2 P.M. **Check out:** noon. **Credit cards?** all major. **Tube stops:** Green Park, New Bond Street.

Carlton Court, 10 Down Street, Mayfair, London W1Y 7DS

photo p. E

A brick Dutch Colonial built as apartments in 1996, Carlton Court provides modern amenities in a fine old neighborhood. Very centrally located near Hyde Park Corner and just off Piccadilly in the heart of Mayfair, Carlton Court is within easy walking distance of Buckingham Palace, Hyde and Green Parks, Fortnum and Mason, and the exclusive boutiques of Jermyn Street. Ten one-, two-, and three-bedroom apartments occupy 10 Down Street, and around the corner on Brick Street there is an additional five-bedroom, four-bath townhouse, excellent for large families or business groups.

Decorated by the owner/manager, each apartment has its own style. There is only one flat per floor, allowing maximum privacy. Each flat enters into a long hallway. The living/dining areas are at one end of the hall, while bedrooms open off the opposite end. The apartments all have crown molding throughout and deep-blue wall-to-wall carpeting. White marble fireplaces enhance each living room, which has two upholstered sofas, matching easy chair, lamps, coffee table, and dining table. Several of the dining tables expand to provide more seating. The china, serving eight, is Chodziez; the glassware, crystal; and there are two sets of silverware, one for every day and one for special occasions. The three-bedroom has sufficient china for 12. The kitchens are all separate rooms with mahogany cabinets, marble countertops, glass burners, and double wall ovens. There is a full-size refrigerator/freezer, microwave, and washer/dryer. Each kitchen also has a small table with chairs. Pots and pans are high quality and in generous supply. There is even a full set of fine, sharp Chamberlain knives.

The two-bedroom apartments come with two baths (some have one and a half baths), the master bath *en suite,* the other in the hall. The master bedroom accommodates a king bed with matching red and blue bedcovers and drapes, bedside tables with reading lamps, dresser, two closets, and a TV. The second bedroom has a double bed, bedside tables, lamps, and closet. Both baths are large and elegant with gray tiled floors, mahogany cabinets, and power showers/tubs. Robes and toiletries are supplied. In the three-bedroom, you get an additional half bath.

The apartments at Carlton Court are large, luxurious, and convenient. The townhouse, which has two reception rooms, is excellent for a traveling business group that needs space for meetings or entertaining clients.

AMENITIES—Elevator, telephone, color satellite TV, radio, computer connection (through telephone), fax (through office), maid service (Monday–Friday), concierge/ housekeeper (9 A.M.–11 P.M.), refrigerator/freezer, stove with oven, toaster, tea kettle, teapot, coffee maker, iron, microwave, dishwasher, washer/dryer, hair dryer, toiletries.

RESERVATIONS/PRICES/MISC.—**Minimum stay:** 1 week. **Reservations:** office staff. **Telephone:** 0207-483-0597. **Fax:** 0207-629-3225. **E-mail:** *ccourt@dial.pipex.com.* **Web site:** *www.carltoncourt.com.* **Prices per week from:** 1 bdrm-$1,999; 2 bdrm, 1.5 baths-$2,760; 2 bdrm, 2 bath-$3,140; 3 bdrm, 2.5 bath-$4,050; townhouse-$7,138. **Negotiate price?** yes. **Deposit?** credit card information. **Check in:** anytime. **Check out:** 11 A.M. **Credit cards?** all major. **Tube stop:** Green Park.

Hertford Court Apartments, 14–15 Hertford Street, Mayfair, London W1Y 7DX

 +

photo p. E

A series of brick-and-stone art deco townhouses line Hertford Street in Mayfair. Hertford Court is one of several that have been converted to apartments for short-term visitors. While Mayfair is known for its high prices, this side street of elegant residences provides some relative bargains. A block east of Hyde Park and one block north of Green Park, the location combines the convenience of city living with access to the rural pleasures of these great parks.

At Hertford Court there are 12 one- and two-bedroom apartments, and one three-bedroom penthouse on the sixth floor. The penthouse is less expensive than the two-bedroom, perhaps because the elevator runs only to the fifth floor.

Each of the apartments opens into a small foyer. The living/dining area is straight ahead, with the bathroom to the right and the bedroom at the far end of the flat. Furnishings are modern. In the one-bedroom, the living room has two striped uphol-stered sofas, a table between them with lamp, and a glass coffee table. At the end of the room in front of two wide French doors is a square glass dining table with four chairs. The blue wall-to-wall carpeting picks up one of the stripes in the sofa cov-ers. The large white-tiled bathroom has a tub/power shower with etched-glass show-er guard, bidet, and heated towel racks. Next to the bath is the kitchen with white wooden cabinets, marblelized countertops, a stove with four gas burners, a microwave, and better-quality pots and pans. The more casually decorated bedroom has a king bed with red and yellow checked spread, two bedside tables with lamps, dressing table with mirror, small wicker chair, and a closet that runs the length of one wall.

Similar in general layout, the second bedroom of the two-bedroom apartments is across from the master bedroom and the kitchen is beside it. In this case, the sofa is blue with white dots, and the carpet is red. A bath is *en suite* in the master bedroom, which is more formal with floral bedspread and velvet curtains. Headboard, dress-ing table, and wardrobe are in blond wood. The smaller bedroom has twin beds, side tables with lamps, dressing table, and large closet. An additional bath in the hallway has a shower but no tub, and, as in all two-bedrooms flats, there is a washer/ dryer.

These are roomy, comfortable, and pleasantly furnished apartments in a great location. They are a good buy in a pricey neighborhood.

AMENITIES—Elevator, telephone, color cable TV, computer connection (through telephone), fax (through office), maid service (Monday–Friday), concierge/housekeeper (9 A.M.–6 P.M., Monday–Friday), refrigerator/freezer, stove, toaster, tea kettle, teapot, coffee maker, iron, microwave, washer/dryer (in 2-bdrm flats), hair dryer (at extra charge).

RESERVATIONS/PRICES/MISC.—**Minimum stay:** 1 night. **Reservations:** Baba Zakari. **Telephone:** 0207-403-2372. **Fax:** 0207-493-0637. **E-mail:** *cavendish@ukonline.co.uk*. **Prices from:** 1 bdrm-$209 per night, $1,428 per week; 2 bdrm, 1 bath-$324 per night, $2,056 per week; 2 bdrm, 2 bath-$362 per night, $2,284 per week. **Negotiate price?** no. **Deposit?** credit card information. **Check in:** 2 P.M. **Check out:** 1 P.M. **Credit cards?** all major. **Tube stops:** Green Park, Hyde Park Corner.

Hill Street, Mayfair, London

photo p. F

The London Connection manages a lovely flat in the residential west section of Mayfair. It is in a modern building on Hill Street in a quiet block minutes from Hyde Park. The apartment complex desk provides 24-hour security coverage and each flat has a security entry phone.

A lift took us to a corner flat on an upper story. The door (with three locks) opens into a green and white tiled foyer with a mirror, dresser, lamp, and coat closet. Across from the door is the bath, tiled in green, with sink and marble counter, tub with power shower, and bidet. The double window offers a pleasant view over Mayfair.

The bedroom holds a king-size bed, and it, too, has a fine view from a large window framed by coordinated drapes. A dresser, wardrobe, and closet along one wall offer ample storage space.

The living/dining area is elegant and comfortable. A sofa, in a light floral print that matches the drapes, and two side chairs provide seating. A side table with lamp and several floor lamps give plenty of light. Oriental rugs accent the rose-colored wall-to-wall living area carpeting. At the far end of the room is a dining table for four in front of a window overlooking the street below. Shelves with knickknacks, vases for flowers, and bowls for fruit line the wall. Tucked into another corner in front of another shelf is a TV with satellite reception. In both the living room and bedroom, ceiling moldings add to the impression of Georgian elegance.

In contrast, the large kitchen is very modern with light wood cabinets and new appliances. A convection oven, microwave, dishwasher, disposal, and washer/dryer are included. With its white-tile walls and light wood cabinets, the kitchen is a bright and airy place to work.

AMENITIES—Elevator, telephone, color TV with satellite, maid service (5 days), concierge, refrigerator, freezer, stove, toaster, tea kettle, teapot, coffee maker, iron, microwave, dishwasher, washer/dryer, hair dryer.

RESERVATIONS/PRICES/MISC.—**Minimum stay:** 1 week. **Reservations:** London Connection. **Telephone:** toll-free, 888-393-4530, ext. 10. **Fax:** 801-621-4933. **E-mail:** *Sales@LondonConnection.com.* **Web site:** *www.londonconn.com.* **Price per week:** $1,542 all year. **Negotiate price?** no. **Deposit?** credit card. **Check in:** 2 P.M. or by arrangement. **Check out:** 10 A.M. **Credit cards?** yes. **Tube stops:** Hyde Park Corner, Bond Street.

Indurrah Apartments Mayfair, 20 Hertford Street, Mayfair, London W1J 7RX

photo p. F

The building at 20 Hertford Street is one of a series of fine period townhouses that line this quiet street in Mayfair. The location is excellent. A short street, Hertford ends in Park Lane with Hyde Park just across. A block south is Green Park, and Buckingham Palace and Gardens, which merge into lovely St. James's Park, a happy habitat for many of the Queen's swans. Midway between Hyde and Green Park tube stops, the rest of London is easily accessible. Apsley House, the Duke of Wellington Museum, is a short walk away. The immediate neighborhood is primarily residential but Shepherd's Market, a shopping square with pubs, restaurants, and grocers, is down the block and around the corner.

Twenty Hertford Street is an elegant stone and redbrick house. Wrought-iron balconies grace the exterior and the entrance hallway appeals with high ceilings, arched doorways, and classical moldings and wainscoting on white walls.

There are four studio, three one-bedroom, and three two-bedroom apartments. Decor becomes simpler in each as the stories get higher. The studio at the back of the ground (first) floor retains the original features of this fine house. There are cornices and friezes with a molded rose motif, chair rail moldings, an ornate chandelier, and a fireplace. The wallpaper is a red-and-blue stripe, and the blue is picked up in the bedcovers and elaborate drapes in the same pattern on the tall window. A dining table with two chairs is in front of the window. The bed is queen size; tables with drawers and lamps are on either side. A sofa and closet are along the wall. Tucked into a recessed corner next to the fireplace is a kitchenette in a waist-high wooden cabinet. While it has no oven, it does have two burners, a microwave, a small refrigerator, and more than enough pots, pans, china (stoneware by Samsonite), and cutlery for two people. The bath is small but has a tub/shower and pedestal sink.

The two-bedroom apartment on the first floor (second, for Americans) is even more ornately decorated. The rooms are large, and there are the same high ceilings, cornices, friezes, and a marble fireplace. In the living room the wallpaper is gold and white with very fancy gold and black drapery on the two floor-to-ceiling windows. The two sofas, rug, and fabric on the dining chairs are all in a blue and white dotted pattern. Tables, cabinets, mantel mirror, server, and oval dining table with six chairs also fit into this large room without crowding. The kitchen is between the living room and master bedroom. It is complete with beige wooden cabinets, full stove, under-counter refrigerator, and microwave. The master bedroom with *en suite* bath is dominated by a king bed with oriental canopy in a rose floral pattern matched on bed-covers and drapes. In front of the window are a small table and two chairs. The second bedroom, off the other end of the living room, is similarly furnished but with less elaborate canopy. The master bath has a tub with shower. A second bath in the hall has only a shower.

These two apartments are "superior" and cost more than flats on the upper levels. If this sounds like too much decoration for you, the flats on the higher floors are plainer.

If, on the other hand, you want a taste of traditional English high style, then the Indurrah Apartments have it in abundance and at a reasonable price for Mayfair.

AMENITIES—Elevator, telephone, color cable TV, radio, computer connection, fax (through office), maid service (Monday–Friday), concierge/housekeeper, refrigerator/freezer, stove (except studio), toaster, tea kettle, teapot, coffee maker, iron, microwave, hair dryer (on request), toiletries.

RESERVATIONS/PRICES/MISC.—**Minimum stay:** 1 night. **Reservations:** Nik Ibrahim. **Telephone:** 0207-629-3946. **Fax:** 0207-629-3690. **E-mail:** *admin@ indurrahapartment.freeserve.co.uk*. **Web site:** *www.indurrahapartment.freeserve.co.uk*. **Prices from:** studios-$130 per night, $891 per week; 1 bdrm-$146 per night, $972 per week; 2 bdrm, 2 bath-$243 per night, $1,701 per week; 3 bdrm, 2 bath-$332 per night, $2,268 per week; penthouse-$356 per night, $2,430 per week. **Negotiate price?** yes. **Deposit?** 1 night's rent. **Check in:** 2 P.M. **Check out:** noon. **Credit cards?** all major. **Tube stops:** Green Park, Hyde Park Corner.

May Fayre House, 22–28 Shepherd Street, Mayfair, London W1Y 7LJ

May Fayre House sits in the village center of Mayfair, on the very street where Edward Shepherd built the market house that put an end to the "riotous" annual May Fairs that wealthy residents would no longer tolerate. A modern building on a historic site, May Fayre House has 20 one- and two-bedroom apartments and one three-bedroom penthouse. While the flats contain all modern amenities, their decor and furnishings are traditional and elaborate.

One- and two-bedroom apartments come in small and large. All open into a foyer, but in the smaller flats the living/dining areas are more compact, with only one sofa, chair, end tables, very intricately carved coffee table, and ornate mirror. A round wooden dining table is in the corner with four matching chairs.

Large one- and two-bedroom flats hold an additional sofa, an upholstered chair, an extra cabinet, and perhaps an oriental rug over the wall-to-wall carpeting. Each apartment is individually decorated with its own color scheme and design details. Window treatments throughout are lush with rich fabrics, drapes, valences, and sconces. Walls, in contrast, are plain, usually white with only ceiling moldings for decoration. Bedrooms, while not large, all have their own bathrooms and canopied beds. Headboards, bedcovers, and drapes are all in matching or coordinating fabrics. Master bedrooms have king or queen beds, while second bedrooms have queen or double beds. Each has mahogany bedside tables with drawers and lamps, dressing table, upholstered chair with foot stool, and wardrobe.

Large white tiled baths come with pedestaled sinks, heated towel racks, bidets, tubs with power showers, and wall-mounted hair dryers. Towels are changed daily.

Ample kitchens with light wood cabinets, marble counters and back splashes, and marble-tiled floors complete the picture. The wood paneling conceals full-size refrigerator/freezers. There are wall-mounted ovens and microwaves, and washer/dryers.

May Fayre House seems to come with everything. It is one of the few London properties to provide air conditioning in every apartment and also offers garage parking. Even the elevator has a TV with continual CNN coverage.

The only drawback at May Fayre House is the price. The small one-bedroom in low season starts at $2,093 per week. Prices climb skyward from there. The location is some compensation. Shepherd's Market is thick with antique stores, shops, pubs, and restaurants. The nearby Green Park tube provides access to the rest of London, if you should want to leave such elegant lodgings.

AMENITIES—Elevator, telephone, color satellite TV with more than 90 channels (multi-language), radio, computer connection through telephone, fax (through office), maid service, concierge/housekeeper, refrigerator/freezer, stove, toaster, tea kettle, teapot, coffee maker, iron, microwave, washer/dryer, hair dryer, toiletries.

RESERVATIONS/PRICES/MISC.—**Minimum stay:** 1 week. **Reservations:** office staff. **Telephone:** 0207-491-0000. **Fax:** 0207-491-4444. E-mail: *mayfayrehouse@ btinternet.com.* **Web site:** *www.mayfayrehouse.co.uk.* **Prices per week from:** 1 bdrm-$1,971; 2 bdrm, 2 bath-$2,856; 3 bdrm, 3 bath-$3,284. **Negotiate price?** yes. **Deposit?** credit card information. **Check in:** 2 P.M. **Check out:** noon. **Credit cards?** all major. **Tube stops:** Green Park, Hyde Park Corner.

Shaw House, 6 Chesterfield Street, Mayfair, London

photo p. F

Three redbrick Edwardian townhouses, one of which was the home of Somerset Maugham, make up the 10 apartments in Shaw House. The one-, two-, three-, and four-bedroom flats are all completely refurbished and modernized. Still, they retain some of the pleasing characteristics of a 1900s-style building. The wide entrance hall and grand central staircase are graceful remnants of that opulent era. All apartments have tall windows and high ceilings, not just those on the lower levels, and all furnishings are traditional and tasteful (never overdone).

In the two-bedroom, a hallway runs the length of the flat and separates the bedrooms. As one enters, the master bedroom is on the left and the second bedroom is to the right. The living/dining room is beside the second bedroom. It is a large room full of light from two windows. The wallpaper is in a white and soft pink stripe that complements the carpeting. A china cupboard holds crystal wine and other glassware. In a corner of the room, a wooden cabinet hides the TV, VCR, stereo, and CD player. Management stocks a free video library for guest use. A dining table with six chairs is in the corner closest to the door. On the wall opposite, there are a sofa in a white-on-white fabric with another sofa to its right, and the appropriate lamps and tables. The kitchen is a small but efficient space with large refrigerator/freezer, four-burner stove, microwave, washer/dryer, and dishwasher.

The master bedroom, about 12 by 14 feet, has a queen-size bed, bedside tables with lamps, dresser, and closet. The bath is *en suite.*

In the second bedroom, the beds are twin and a second bath is down the hall.

These pleasant apartments are on a residential street in the middle of Mayfair. They are well taken care of by two managers who live on site and have overseen the property for many years. Park Lane, the rental agency, provides guests with extra services, such as free use of a local gym, complimentary bus service, and complimentary entry to local attractions (one per apartment).

The neighborhood has many amenities. Shaw House is a five-minute walk to the Green Park tube, and Hyde Park is just a few blocks to the west. Shepherd's Market, with its pubs, cafes, greengrocers, and boutiques, is right around the corner.

AMENITIES—Elevator, telephone, color satellite TV, radio, computer connection (Antic Internet access system), fax (machines available), maid service (Monday–Friday), concierge/housekeeper, refrigerator/freezer, stove, toaster, tea kettle, teapot, coffee maker, iron, microwave, dishwasher, washer/dryer, hair dryer, toiletries.

RESERVATIONS/PRICES/MISC.—**Minimum stay:** 1 week. **Reservations:** office staff. **Telephone:** 0207-629-0763. **Fax:** 0207-493-1308. **E-mail:** *parklane@cpd.co.uk.* **Web site:** *www.parklane.co.uk.* **Prices from:** 1 bdrm, 2 bath-$2,360; 2 bdrm, 2 bath-$3,521; 3 bdrm, 2 bath-$4,568; 4 bdrm, 2.5 bath-$5,768. **Negotiate price?** yes. **Deposit?** yes. **Check in:** 2 P.M. **Check out:** 11 A.M. **Credit cards?** all major. **Tube stop:** Green Park.

Mayfair: Attractions

The May Fair lasted less than a century before complaints by wealthy residents suppressed it, but the name stuck. A bawdy folk celebration of the planting season seems the least likely name to give London's most aristocratic neighborhood. The area lacks space for more than a patch of grass, never mind a field or garden, although it borders two of London's finest parks.

Hyde Park and Green Park mark the western and southern boundaries of Mayfair, with Oxford and Regent Streets defining the north and east. From the outset, Mayfair has been the home of wealth. Half a dozen noblemen built palaces on the north side of Piccadilly near St. James's Palace and the royal parks in the 1660s, and one survives magnificently. Burlington House, enlarged in the 18th century in the Palladian style with its grand forecourt and painted ceilings, became the Royal Academy in 1854. Its spacious galleries offer year-round exhibitions of both classical and modern art. The Summer Exhibition shows and sells work by living British artists, some at affordable prices.

Many Georgian mansions survive from the first century of settlement in the more residential western section, as do the original squares—Hanover, Berkeley, and Grosvenor. But modern hotels, office blocks, and embassies now surround those squares. Grosvenor Square, the largest of London's town squares, struggles to accommodate the massive American embassy on its west end. Its modern gray stone hulk seems at war with the redbrick Georgian or neo-Georgian neighborhood.

Five-star hotels, luxury apartments, and aristocratic residences dominate the western half of Mayfair, while commerce rules the east, from Berkeley Square to Regent Street. There you will find the tailors of Savile Row; Sotheby's auction house on New Bond Street; antique stores, especially Grays Antique Market; boutiques on South Molton; and grand department stores on Regent Street.

The two most popular tourist attractions in Mayfair are the Royal Academy of Arts and Apsley House.

The Royal Academy of Arts (Burlington House, 0207-300-5959) is the oldest art society in the country and the most prestigious. George III was its patron and Joshua Reynolds, the first president. Selection for one of its juried exhibitions guaranteed lucrative commissions, if not an entire career, for an artist. Pictures by all the great names of British painting and most of Europe's classical artists line the walls of its 17 galleries. Far more eclectic and often interesting are the modern pictures chosen for the annual Summer Exhibition. It is the event of the art calendar.

Apsley House, once called "No. One London," at 149 Piccadilly (0207-499-5676) is now the Wellington Museum. The Duke of Wellington lived in this great city house, built by Robert Adam in the 1770s, from 1817 until his death 35 years later. Ten of the rooms are restored to their original condition and are crammed with gifts from grateful monarchs to Wellington. There are many treasures—silver, porcelain, paintings, statuary—and the house itself is grand to see.

Shops, Restaurants, and Pubs

Most of Mayfair's shops have names known to all. Liberty (214–220 Regent Street, 0207-734-1234), with its Tudoresque facade and interior, is perhaps the most famous. Liberty print fabrics and lesser copies of them decorate homes around the globe. It not only sells material but is a full-service department store with cosmetics, ladies and menswear, and household goods. The scarves, gloves, slippers, address books, and assorted small items on the first floor make excellent gifts, especially if you buy them at the January sale.

Just across the street from Liberty is Dickens and Jones, a shop on Regent Street since 1835. It too was known originally for its fine fabrics. Today it is a large and fashionable department store. There is a branch of Laura Ashley on Regent Street also, with additional shops on Oxford Street. And don't forget Hamley at 188–196 Regent Street: five stories of everything a child could wish for. Enter, do, but hang on to your pursestrings.

Nearby Bond Streets (both New and Old) hold an abundance of houses of the "haut-est" of fashion: Bally, Chanel, Donna Karan, Ferragamo, Gucci, Jaegar, and Versace, just to name a few.

Savile Row, between Regent and New Bond, is the street for the gentleman shopper. "Bespoke" (made to order) three-piece suits and shirts are the specialties here at Gieves and Hawkes, Anderson and Sheppard, Henry Poole, and others. Bespoke suits range in price from $800 to four figures and upward. But they last for 20 years.

South Molton Street is the place for trendy British designers. Check out Browns, which stocks most of them. Luckily, it has a 50-percent-off rack with last year's now-cooled hot items. You might even be able to buy something here.

Food shops in Mayfair are just as high quality and high price as you might expect. Allen and Company (117 Mount Street, 0207-494-2000), butcher to the Ritz and other exclusive restaurants, has finely aged British beef, lamb, pork, and a full array of game. James Knight of Mayfair (8 Shepherd's Market, 0207-499-2664), fishmonger to the Prince of Wales, in addition to the freshest of fish, carries an interesting assortment of fish products (soups, butters, terrines) as well as fine cognacs and other goodies on its lower level. For sweet gifts for chocoholic friends, yourself included, stop at Charbonnel et Walker (Royal Arcade, 28 Old Bond Street, 0207-491-0939).

Some say it makes the best chocolates in the world. They come already boxed in beautiful presentations, or you can pick your own assortment.

Some of the best restaurants in the world are in Mayfair. The Dorchester Grill Room, cheznico, The Connaught, and Le Gavroche are hallowed names to devout gourmets.

For those of us who want some money in our pockets after we dine, there are also excellent moderately priced restaurants. For fine Chinese dining, try Kai (65 South Audley Street, 0207-493-8988; entrees, $13 on up). The duck with glass noodles cooked in a clay pot is especially succulent. Or try Mulligans of Mayfair (13–14 Cork Street, 0207-409-1370; entrees, from $16 to $26) for high-quality Irish (yes, Irish!) country cooking in a relaxed, comfortable setting. Guinness is on draft and there is also a selection of outstanding Irish whiskies. Chez Gerard (31 Dover Street, 0207-499-8171), the reliable steak and fries restaurant chain, also has a branch in Mayfair (entrees, $8 to $36).

Our very favorite pub in Mayfair is the Audley (see below), but others worth a visit are Ye Grapes, Shepherd's Tavern, the Guinea, and the Windmill. Ye Grapes (16 Shepherd Market) and Shepherd's Tavern (50 Hertford Street) are both historic pubs in Shepherd's Market. Both are reputed to have been places of assignations for gentlemen and "working girls" in Victorian times. The Guinea (30 Bruton Place) and Windmill (6–8 Mill Street) are also historic pubs, owned by the same couple. They are Young's pubs serving fine ales and the Smith's prize-winning beef-and-kidney pies, sandwiches, and other pub standards.

A Monday in Mayfair

A great way to start the week is with a visit to the Royal Academy of Arts. We might enjoy one of the temporary exhibits—Turner watercolors in 2001, for example—or wander among the permanent collection's works by Reynolds, Constable, or Turner. It's a pleasure just to spend time in this fine Palladian building with its grand staircase and painted ceiling.

Enlightened and uplifted, we can then goof off for the rest of the day with a clear conscience. First stop is the Burlington Arcade, just down the street from the Royal Academy. This Regency-style covered archway is full of small, exclusive specialty stores. Here you will pay top price for the best-quality Irish linens, cashmeres, silks, jewelry, perfumes, men's shirts, dressing gowns, ties, and pajamas. Usually we window-shop, but sometimes we find a small item we can't resist.

Then we proceed up and down Bond, Regent, and Oxford Streets until we can shop no more. It's past time for lunch anyway, so we drag ourselves and our packages to the Audley (41–43 Mount Street). The lunch crowd, most intense in London between 1 and 2 P.M., has thinned and we can spread out in comfort for a peaceful lunch. The setting is elegant. Designed by Thomas Verity and built by Watney's in 1889, the Audley's brick Edwardian exterior opens into a spacious pub with red ceilings, golden plasterwork, chandeliers, red leather banquettes, and richly paneled walls. Fine meat pies, fish and chips, salads, and sandwiches are served until 9:30 P.M.—a lovely spot to while away an hour or so. Then we're off to rest and ready ourselves for a night at the theater.

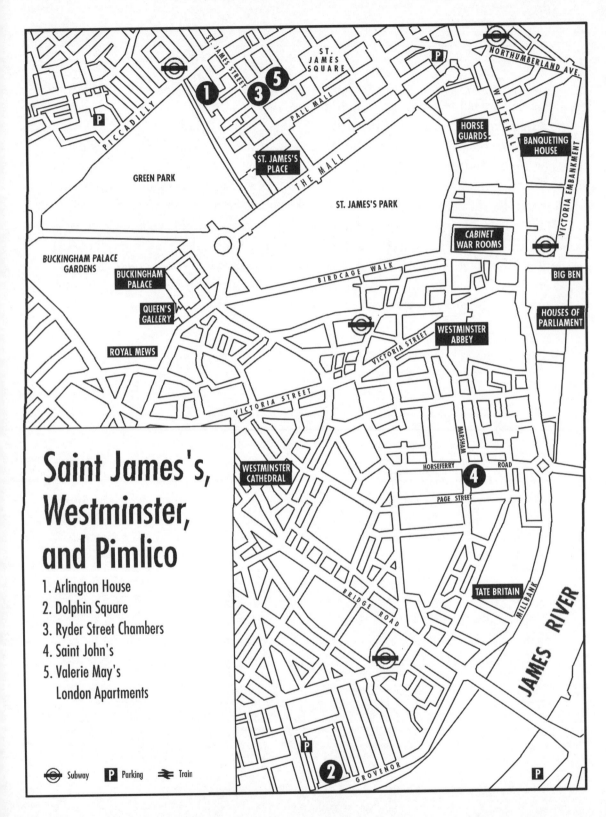

Saint James's, Westminster, and Pimlico

1. Arlington House
2. Dolphin Square
3. Ryder Street Chambers
4. Saint John's
5. Valerie May's
   London Apartments

⊖ Subway 🅿 Parking 🚆 Train

Chapter 6

✤

St. James's, Westminster, and Pimlico

These three districts run north to south from Piccadilly to the Thames. They include Victoria Station, the rail hub that serves south England and Gatwick Airport. You will find three excellent apartment buildings just off Piccadilly and Jermyn Streets in the heart of St. James's. Buckingham Palace, Westminster Abbey, and the Houses of Parliament are the best-known attractions. Westminster is the seat of government, while the Queen lives on the opposite side of St. James's Park.

Pimlico, an altogether more modest neighborhood, draws crowds only for the Tate Gallery at Millbank. It also contains the oldest and largest full-service apartment complex in the city, Dolphin Square.

This is a sophisticated and busy area with wealthy city dwellers, government officials, and diplomats filling its small streets. It is the center of power for Great Britain with easy access to the whole of London.

St. James's, Westminster, and Pimlico at a Glance

Apartment	Studio	1-Bedroom	2-Bedroom	3-Bedroom	Other
Arlington House 3-week minimum, summer; 1 week otherwise 🏠 🏠 🏠 🏠 +	$122–$163 n $857–$1,142 w	$188–$265 n $1,313–$1,856 w (1.5 baths)	$266–$503 n $1,860–$3,521 w (1.5 and 2.5 baths)	$521–$870 n $3,645–$6,091 w (2.5 baths)	*4-bedroom* $579–$680 n $4,051–$4,759 w (2.5 baths)
Dolphin Square No minimum 🏠 🏠 🏠 🏠 🏠 refurbished 🏠 🏠 🏠 🏠 unrefurbished	$211–$267 n $1,474–$1,871 w	$267–$316 n $1,871–$2,211 w	$397–$486 n $2,665–$3,402 w (1 or 2 baths)	$585 n $4,082 w (3 baths)	
Ryder Street Chambers No minimum 🏠 🏠 🏠		$171–$210 n $1,199–$1,466 w			
St. John's House 1-week minimum 🏠 🏠 🏠 🏠			$284 n $1,620 w (2 baths)		
Valerie May London Apts. 1-week minimum 🏠 🏠 🏠 🏠		$139 n $972 w			

NOTES: (1) All prices are in American dollars converted at $1.62 to £1 and include VAT. To convert to the current rate, divide the dollar amount by 1.62 and multiply by the rate listed in today's local paper. (2) n=night; w=week.

St. James's, Westminster, and Pimlico Apartments in Detail

Arlington House, 25 Arlington Street, London SW1A 1RL

 +

photo p. F

With sweeping views over Green Park that suggest the countryside, Arlington House is nevertheless in St. James's in the heart of the West End. Although it overlooks the park, two blocks behind it on Piccadilly are Fortnum and Mason; Burlington Arcade; the Wedgewood/Waterford store; and, one block closer, the exclusive shops of Jermyn Street. Buckingham Palace is a short stroll through the park, the Green Park tube stop is a block away, and a new Waitrose supermarket is just across Piccadilly in Mayfair.

Arlington House was built in 1934 as an apartment block of 107 studio, one-, two-, three-, and four-bedroom flats. The lobby, hallways, and other public spaces reflect its art deco origins. The apartments themselves are well equipped and elegantly furnished. All have fireplaces, most have washer/dryers, and all flats with two or more bedrooms have two and a half baths. The china is Wedgewood and the wine glasses are crystal.

A central hallway runs the length of the one-bedroom. To the left is the living/dining area with floral wallpaper, ceiling moldings with floral border, and a fireplace with intricate plasterwork. The blue of the wall-to-wall carpeting coordinates with the blue-green stripes of the drapes and the matching fabric of the sofa and two easy chairs. A table with four chairs in front of the window gives diners a view of Green Park. A corner chest holds china, glassware, and table mats. In the bedroom are twin beds with brass headboards, side tables, reading lamps, wardrobe, and easy chair. French doors open to a balcony, again overlooking the park. The bath is *en suite*. The kitchen with blond wooden cabinets has full-size refrigerator/freezer, stove with glass burners, and quality pots and pans.

In the two-bedroom, the central hallway separates the living area from the bedrooms and kitchen. The living room has three wide windows, ceiling molding, ornate chandelier, wooden/marble Georgian fireplace, and built-in cabinets with arched display shelves. There are two easy chairs, matching sofa, and a dining table with six chairs. Colors are all coordinated shades of blue, including the wall-to-wall carpeting. The master bedroom has twin beds, reading lamps, dresser, and closet. The second bedroom has a single bed, dresser, and closet. Both have *en suite* baths with a half bath at the end of the hall. The kitchen is similar to that in the one-bedroom but larger, with table and chairs and a washer/dryer.

These luxury apartments are a relative bargain in an exclusive location. They are especially handy for theater lovers. Half a dozen West End shows are an easy walk away.

Amenities—Elevator, telephone, color satellite TV, computer connection through telephone, fax (in some), maid service (Monday–Friday), concierge/housekeeper, refrigerator/freezer, stove, toaster, tea kettle, teapot, coffee maker, iron, microwave, washer/dryer (in most larger flats), hair dryer (on request), toiletries.

Reservations/Prices/Misc.—**Minimum stay:** 1 week; 3 weeks May–September 3, with discretion. **Reservations:** office staff. **Telephone:** 0207-629-0021. **Fax:** 0207-823-9244. **E-mail:** *LupusPrty@aol.com.* **Prices per week from:** studios-$857; 1 bdrm, 1.5 bath-$1,313; 2 bdrm, 2 bath-$1,860 (3 people), $2,450 (4 people); 3 bdrm, 2.5 bath-$3,645; 4 bdrm, 2.5 baths-$4,051. **Negotiate price?** yes. **Deposit?** $486. **Check in:** anytime. **Check out:** midday. **Credit cards?** all major. **Tube stop:** Green Park.

Dolphin Square, Chichester Street, London SW1V 3LX

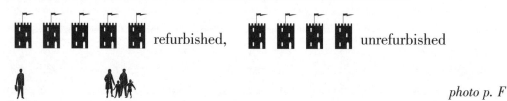

refurbished,   unrefurbished

photo p. F

Dolphin Square is a world unto itself. Created in 1935 by Sirs Richard and Albert Costain, it is a full city block backed by three and a half acres of gardens. The River Thames is immediately south of the square.

Instead of a mansion block of flats, Dolphin Square describes itself as one of Europe's first all-suite hotels. The average length of stay has changed from a week to two and a half days, reflecting the needs of modern business travelers. It offers all the amenities of a five-star hotel. It has conference facilities, a 60-foot swimming pool, gym, aerobics/dance classes, drugstore, florist, bar, brasserie, and a world-class restaurant, Rhodes in the Square (Gary Rhodes's latest). Maid service is seven days a week. Room and concierge services are available around the clock. But Dolphin Square is also all suites or flats. For those who wish to cook for themselves there are a greengrocer and food shop.

All of the apartments are in the process of refurbishment. The ones not yet redone are called "standard" and are the less expensive. The standard studio we saw did look a bit old-fashioned but not worn. From the corridor we entered into a small hall-way. The kitchen is across from the door, the bath next to it, and the living/dining room at the end of the hall. A double bed is against the near wall. Opposite the bed is a white table and two black bentwood chairs. A blue, upholstered easy chair is in the corner with a reading lamp behind it. In the other corner is a TV with a trouser press behind it. Since the apartments are all in a square, each has an expansive view over the large central gardens. The drapes are of the same fabric as the bedcovers. Even in this older studio, the kitchen is complete with small refrigerator/freezer; stove; good-quality pots, pans, and utensils; plenty of cabinets and counter space; and a pantry for storage tucked into the corner. The bath has a tub/shower, large hand and bath towels, and a facecloth—all on a heated towel rack.

As expected, the deluxe studio in the same amount of space is more luxuriously decorated. All furnishings were color-coordinated with print wallpaper, a TV cabinet, and a small round dining table with matching chairs.

The deluxe two-bedroom, two-bath would be an excellent choice for two couples or two businessmen. The living/dining space and kitchen are between the two bedrooms and bathrooms (one *en suite* and one off the entry hall) for maximum privacy. The *en suite* bedroom has twin beds while the other has a king. Both have a dresser and bed-side tables with reading lamps. A sofa and matching easy chair provide seating in the living room and there is a dining table for four. Carpeting, wall covering, drapes, and bedcovers are color-coordinated. Kitchen and baths are standard and fully stocked. All rooms have several windows. There are additional closets in the hall.

Families are welcome at Dolphin Square, but it is especially well equipped for the business traveler. In spite of its large size and business orientation, we found the staff uniformly friendly and informal.

AMENITIES—Elevator, telephone, color satellite TV, radio, computer connection in telephone, fax (request at time of booking), maid service (7 days a week), concierge/housekeeper, refrigerator/freezer, stove, toaster, tea kettle, teapot, coffee maker, iron, microwave, washer/dryer (in some), hair dryer, toiletries, welcome pack.

RESERVATIONS/PRICES/MISC.—**Minimum stay:** 1 night. **Reservations:** office staff. **Telephone:** 0207-798-8890. **Fax:** 0207-798-8896. **E-mail:** *reservations@dolphin squarehotel.co.uk*. **Web site:** *www.dolphinsquarehotel.co.uk*. **Prices from:** studios-$211 per night (1 person), $251 per night (2 people); 1 bdrm-$267 per night; 2 bdrm-$397 per night; 2 bdrm, 2 bath-$437 per night; 3 bdrm, 3 bath-$585 per night. **Negotiate price?** yes. **Deposit?** credit card information. **Check in:** 2:30 P.M. **Check out:** 11 A.M. **Credit cards?** all major. **Tube stop:** Pimlico.

Ryder Street Chambers, 3 Ryder Street, St. James's, London SW1Y 6PY

photo p. G

At the corner of Ryder and Duke Streets in a brick and white stone Edwardian building are the Ryder Street Chambers, 11 one-bedroom apartments that sleep from one to four people. The Chambers sits among the art galleries and traditional shops that mark this historic neighborhood, a block from Jermyn Street and Fortnam and Mason, and an easy walk to West End theaters. Two blocks to the west is Green Park, and St. James's Park is nearby to the south. What a location for a city lover!

Ryder Street Chambers are the only apartments in this book that do not have cooking facilities. Fire regulations forbid it. We include them because of their charm, economy, and location in an area with few such choices.

All of the flats are on the upper stories, accessed through an old-fashioned open-grill elevator that said "1920s Paris" to our imaginations. There are three types of apartments, priced according to space and number of persons accommodated. The least expensive ($171 per night) is a corner apartment with double bed and single sofa bed. The most expensive ($210 per night) has twin beds and a double sofa bed. Furnishings are all in a traditional style.

While small, the corner apartment is pleasantly decorated, and the "corner" in question is a cozy nook with small round dining table and two chairs in front of its three casement windows. The ceiling above it is recessed and has three moldings. The rest of the room has dropped molding with a floral border that matches the fabric of the drapes, sofa, and easy chair. The carpet is a deeper blue. There are additional tables, lamps, and a breakfast bar that holds china, glassware, cutlery, and a small refrigerator. The bath with tub and shower attachment is between the living room and bedroom. In the bedroom are a double bed, end tables with drawers and reading lamps, and closet.

In the largest one-bedroom, the apartment opens into a hallway. To the left is the bath with a door separating the sink from the tub/shower and toilet. To the right through a doorway is the sitting room with a commanding bay window. In front of the window is a large dining table. There are ceiling moldings, a dropped molding, and a floral border. A sofa is against the wall and a matching chair is to the left. A breakfast bar and small refrigerator are in the corner. The bedroom has twin beds.

All baths have large bath and hand towels, and facecloths.

We were delighted to discover these relatively inexpensive apartments in tony St. James's. Their only drawback is their lack of cooking facilities. The manager, Valerie May, explained that these are traditionally "gentlemen's chambers," and that no gentleman could be expected to cook. While you cannot cook, the flats are fully equipped for eating with china and wine glasses. You can carry out from Fortnum's extensive food hall or have meals delivered by local restaurants that provide these services to guests at Ryder Street. For wine, there is Berry Bros. and Rudd around the corner, the oldest wine shop in London.

AMENITIES—Elevator, telephone, color TV, radio, computer connection through phone (with adapters available), fax (through office), maid service (Monday–Friday), live-in housekeeper, refrigerator, tea kettle, teapot, coffee maker, dryer, hair dryer, toiletries, welcome pack.

RESERVATIONS/PRICES/MISC.—**Minimum stay:** 1 night; **Reservations:** Valerie May. **Telephone:** 0207-930-2241. **Fax:** 0207-839-2108. **Prices per night from:** corner 1 bdrm (sleeps 3)-$171; standard 1 bdrm (sleeps 3)-$190; large 1 bdrm (sleeps 4)-$209. Prices are for single or double occupancy, extra person at $29 per night. **Negotiate price?** yes. **Deposit?** yes. **Check in:** on arrangement. **Check out:** on arrangement. **Credit cards?** all major. **Tube stop:** Green Park.

St. John's House, 79 Marsham Street, London SW1

photo p. G

In a modern glass-and-steel high-rise at the corner of Masham Street and Horseferry Road, Go Native manages 20 two-bedroom apartments available for short-term rental. This luxury block supplies all the latest in amenities, including gym with weight equipment, tidal pool, sauna, and massage therapist.

While these apartments are designed with the corporate traveler in mind, the location in Westminster is an excellent spot for tourists as well. Nearby are the Tate Gallery, the Houses of Parliament, Westminster Abby and Cathedral, Buckingham Palace, the Cabinet War Rooms, and the Royal Banqueting House, Inigo Jones' masterpiece in Whitehall Palace. If you are coming from or going to other parts of the United Kingdom, Victoria Station is a five-minute cab ride away.

Although in the busy heart of London, many of these apartments overlook a pleasant park at the side of the building. Decor ranges from traditional to modern, and several floor plans are available, one of them on two levels. Except in the bedrooms, which have wall-to-wall carpeting, all floors are wood.

In the split-level, the lower floor contains the second bedroom with queen-size bed and *en suite* bath. Up the stairs is the master bedroom with king-size bed, bathroom, living/dining room, and kitchen.

In the more typical apartment, the master bedroom has a king-size bed, lovely view of the garden, and an *en suite* bath with a tub/shower. In front of the entrance and next to the master bedroom is the second bedroom. It has a double bed and the same view.

The living/dining area is to the left off the hall and is nicely furnished with sofa and easy chair in matching blue fabric and pale carpeting. The dining table occupies a corner alcove with a server with mirror above. A balcony opens off the main part of the room.

To the left of the entrance is the thoroughly modern kitchen. Its dark-wood cabinets and black countertops are dramatic against the white tile walls. The designers fit two eye-level, stainless steel ovens in one corner, and glass burners are built into the counter. A full-size refrigerator/freezer, washer/dryer, and dishwasher are behind cabinet fronts.

As is typical of new buildings in the center of London, individual rooms are small and public areas are large. Although each flat appears to be professionally decorated, the amenities and styles vary, because these apartments are owned by different individuals with their own tastes. Request what you like at time of booking, especially if bed size is important. We found a range of king, queen, double, and twin beds.

Amenities—Elevator, telephone, color satellite TV, radio, computer connection through telephone, fax (through office), maid service (Monday–Friday), concierge/housekeeper, refrigerator/freezer, stove, toaster, tea kettle, teapot, coffee maker, iron, microwave (in some), welcome pack (at extra charge).

Reservations/Prices/Misc.—**Minimum stay:** 1 week. **Reservations:** Go Native. **Telephone:** 0207-221-2028. **Fax:** 0207-221-2088. **E-mail:** *enquiries@gonative.co.uk*. **Web site:** *www.gonative.co.uk*. **Prices per week from:** 2 bdrm, 2 bath-$1,620. **Negotiate price?** yes. **Deposit?** yes. **Check in:** 2 P.M. **Check out:** 10:30 A.M. **Credit cards?** all major. **Tube stop:** St. James's.

Valerie May London Apartments, St. James's, London SW1Y 6PY

photo p. G

Valerie May London Apartments, 13 one-bedroom flats in a period building on a side street in St. James's, are delightful pieds-à-terre for a week's stay in London. Their location could not be better—close to Hyde, Green, and St. James's parks, half a block from Fortnum's, and walking distance to the half-price ticket booth at Leicester Square and many West End theaters. High-quality shops abound, from shirtmakers and bespoke tailors on Jermyn Street to the Wedgewood/Waterford shop around the corner. Private art galleries line the street, and now, at last, a full-service Sainsbury grocery is just a few blocks away. And the icing on the cake is that these apartments, each with a sofa bed in the living room, starting at $972 per week, are quite a bargain for St. James's, or anywhere in central London for that matter.

The apartments are slightly different in layout and specific furnishings, but all are decorated in a traditional style with features that make each individual. Access to the apartment is through a lobby complete with doorman and a grilled open-work elevator to the upper stories.

A typical apartment opens into a small foyer. On the right is the kitchen, ahead the bedroom with the bath, and the sitting room is to the left. The sitting room of one flat we visited has wall-to-wall blue carpeting and a coordinating sofa along one wall. An ornately carved fireplace and built-in china cupboard give the room elegance, and a desk makes it functional as well. A TV cabinet, easy chair, and dining table complete the setting. The bedroom is papered in pale-blue polka dots and contains a queen-size bed, lamp tables, closet, and wardrobe. In the kitchen are a full-size stove, an under-counter refrigerator, and a microwave. Some flats have a washer/dryer. There is a full bath with a tub/shower.

A second apartment is essentially the same except for the location of the rooms. It, too, has a fireplace and a sofa bed in the sitting room.

Other apartments have slight variations—some have only two burner stoves, some have a double bed, some have fireplaces, so it is important to specify your preferences at time of booking.

We think these small but comfortable apartments are a find. They are traditional and have individual touches that make them feel like a home. An additional plus for us is that one of our favorite galleries (Chris Beetles at 8–10 Ryder Street) is just across the road. If you book a stay here between November and January, you can enjoy Beetles' annual show, a selection of British cartoons and illustrators' art from the 1850s to the present. It's free, but you must ring for admittance.

AMENITIES—Elevator, telephone, color TV, radio, computer connection through telephone, fax (through office), maid service (once a week), refrigerator/freezer, stove, toaster, tea kettle, teapot, coffee maker, iron, microwave, washer/dryer (in some), hair dryer.

RESERVATIONS/PRICES/MISC.—**Minimum stay:** 1 week. **Reservations:** Valerie May. **Telephone:** 0207-930-2241. **Fax:** 0207-839-2108. **Prices per week from:** 1 bdrm-$972. **Negotiate price?** yes. **Deposit?** yes. **Check in:** on arrangement. **Check out:** on arrangement. **Credit cards?** all major. **Tube stop:** Green Park.

St. James's, Westminster, and Pimlico: Attractions

Technically, Westminster encompasses all three districts as part of the City of Westminster, but in character and attractions, they are distinct.

St. James's takes its name from a medieval hospital for leper women that Henry VIII rebuilt as St. James's Palace. The adjacent neighborhood and park evolved in the 17th century initially to serve the palace and its courtiers. The streets between Piccadilly and Pall Mall, St. James's Street, and Haymarket still cater to an affluent, if not aristocratic, clientele. Two properties from the 18th century occupy their original premises on St. James's: the hatter, Locks, and Berry Brothers and Rudd, a most unusual wine merchant.

Merchandise has not squeezed out the main architectural treasure, St. James's Church Piccadilly by Christopher Wren, though even this church has a market in its courtyard on Thursdays.

St. James's Park is the oldest royal park in London and the prettiest. Its man-made lake, set between Buckingham Palace and Horseguards Parade, attracts more than 30 species of birds, including pelicans and Australian black swans. James I established an aviary there and his grandson expanded it, adding Birdcage Walk as a private street through the park. The Ornithological Society built a lodge on an island in the park in 1849. At lunch hour, the benches fill with clerks and bureaucrats from the public offices surrounding the park.

Government ministries, Parliament, and Westminster Abbey dominate Westminster proper from Trafalgar Square to Millbank. The forbidding gray facades that line Whitehall offer both obvious and hidden treasures. Of the latter, the Banqueting House ranks number one. Inigo Jones built it in 1622 as a ceremonial room for Whitehall Palace. Peter Paul Rubens painted the ceiling for Charles I who lost his head on a scaffold just outside. The entrance can be hard to find on Horseguards Avenue just off the east side of Whitehall.

You can't miss the Houses of Parliament, however, farther down Whitehall. The neogothic seat of both Lords and Commons is open to the public most mornings and, on a limited basis, during evening debates. We recommend the guided tours of both houses, which can now be arranged for the summer recess (August–September) by calling Ticketmaster at 0207-344-9966 (or *www.ticketmaster.co.uk*). Overseas visitors can apply for permits to visit at other times through the Parliamentary Education Unit. See the extensive web site *(www.parliament.uk)* for details.

Westminster Abbey is a must for first-time visitors or anyone who hasn't seen it since the exterior was cleaned. Turns out it is white, not black, and full of interest (and tour groups in all languages).

The Cabinet War Rooms, Churchill's underground headquarters, is another popular attraction off Whitehall at King Charles Street (admission, $7.50).

A bus from Trafalgar is probably the best way to visit Westminster and Pimlico, because most of the sites are on the main route—Whitehall to Millbank—and along the Thames. Westminster is the seat of government, while the Queen lives on the opposite side of St. James's Park.

The Tate Museum (now Tate Britain, since there are two) faces the Thames on Millbank and is Pimlico's chief attraction. As the new name implies, Tate Britain devotes its space to British art from the 16th century, including the incomparable Turner collection.

For the most part, Pimlico is a modest residential neighborhood. Located between Westminster and Chelsea, the Thames and Belgravia building dates only from the 1830s when Thomas Cubitt bought leases in the area. Cubitt, who built fashionable Belgravia, saw a profit in small homes for the less affluent. Despite its prized location, Pimlico has never enjoyed the status of its neighbors Chelsea and Belgravia, but it contains one of the largest fully serviced apartment blocks in Europe, Dolphin Square, and the best brew pub in London, the Orange.

Shops, Restaurants, and Pubs

Fashionable men's shops, often a century old, run the length of Jermyn Street in St. James's. Shirtmakers Turnbull and Asser, and Herbie Frogg; Russell and Bromley or Fostor and Son shoemakers; Paxton and Whitfield, selling cheese since 1740; George Trumper, barber and perfumer; Pink tie emporium; and Alfred Dunhill—all make for wonderful window shopping, whether you can afford to buy or not. Prince's Arcade, between Jermyn and Piccadilly, is another old-fashioned shopping experience. Along the south side of Piccadilly, Fortnum and Mason still makes up picnic hampers, and near Piccadilly Circus, Waterstone's just opened the largest bookstore in Europe.

Step into the past when you enter Berry Bros. and Rudd at 3 St. James's Street. Wine and spirits merchants for more than 200 years, the building they have occupied for all that time has changed very little. It could be in a Dickens novel. You will notice immediately that there are no wine bottles on the wall nor any clerks, although one appeared very quickly in response to our footsteps across the uneven floor. The wines are kept cool in the basements below, and you will make your selection from a wine ledger that the clerk presents to you from the high Victorian desk. Prices in this historic shop are no higher than elsewhere, and their own label wines are good value. Sit in an original Windsor chair as you choose. They also carry a full line of sherries and ports.

There are fewer restaurants than you might expect in this area, mainly because the many civil servants who work here leave the central city at night. Good choices still remain. Le Caprice (0207-629-2239; entrees, $15 to $35) in Arlington House on Arlington Street is one of them. It's been a top restaurant for many years, so book as far in advance as possible if you plan to dine there in the evening. The food is excellent but not fussy, and the atmosphere sophisticated but not pretentious.

Four fine options are on St. James's Street. L'Oranger is at 5 St. James's (0207-839-3774; two courses, $56; three courses at $64), elegant dining considered to be good value even at these prices. Petrus at 33 serves classic cuisine (0207-930-4272; three courses at $64), and The Avenue at 7–9 (0207-321-2111; entrees, $20 to $27) prepares modern food in a minimalist setting and offers bargain dinners pre- and post-theater (two courses, $23; three, $27). Call for exact times.

For less-pricey dining, try Al Duca at 4–5 Duke of York Street (0207-839-3090; two courses, $29; three, $34). Modern Italian dishes are served in relaxed and stylish surroundings at good prices for the outstanding quality of the food.

In Pimlico the choice for fine dining seems to be one—Rhodes in the Square at Dolphin Square, Chichester Street (0207-798-6767; one course set dinner, $20; two courses, $40; three, $50). In steel and deep blue, this 1930s-style dining room is comfortable and welcoming at the same time. Add to this the inventive cooking of Gary Rhodes and you have the ingredients for a memorable night out.

There are three pubs named "Red Lion" in St. James's, and each is worth a visit. The Red Lion at 23 Crown Passage, a lane of old-fashioned shops off Pall Mall, claims to be the oldest village pub in London. Although it may be more than 350 years old, this pub is still a cozy spot to spend an hour sipping an Adnams beer. A restaurant serving traditional food is upstairs. The Red Lion, at 2 Duke of York Street since the 1820s, is famous for the etched-glass mirrors added in 1890. These mirrors make the pub a festive place, and the wooden benching along the wall offers a comfortable seat for your Adnams beer (again). The Red Lion at 48 Parliament Street has been on that site since 1733 when it was owned by the crown. Now it is patronized more by political types than royalty and has a division bell to call MPs back to vote when needed. The pub food is good, and real ales are on tap.

After your stroll through St. James's Park, stop in at The Two Chairmen (39 Dartmouth Street). It's not named after two CEOs, but after the men who transported the well-off by sedan chair throughout the city. It's been in business since the 17th century and has a mural of the chairmen on its wall.

23 Greengardens, Marylebone

Barrett Street, Marylebone

Cavendish Apartments, Marylebone

Chiltern Street, Marylebone

A

Jerome House, Marylebone

New Cavendish, Marylebone

Portman Square, Marylebone

Presidential Apartments, George Street, Marylebone

P. C. Tustin's, Marylebone

Endsleigh Court, Bloomsbury

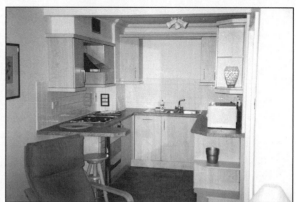

Fitzroy, Fitzrovia

Presidential House, University Street, Bloomsbury

Soho Square, Bloomsbury

Scala House, Bloomsbury

Red Lion Square, Holborn

C

92 Middlesex, The City

Creechurch, The City

Somerset Bishopgate, The City

13 Half Moon Street, Mayfair

37 Hertford Street, Mayfair

47 Park Street, Mayfair

Ascott Mayfair, Mayfair

Barlow Mews, Mayfair

Carlton Court, Mayfair

Hertford Court, Mayfair

Hill Street, Mayfair

Indurrah Apartments, Mayfair

Arlington House, St. James's

Shaw House, Mayfair

Dolphin Square, Pimlico

Ryder Street Chambers, St. James's

St. John's, Westminster

Valerie May London Apartments, St. James's

Basils, Knightsbridge

Beaufort House, Knightsbridge

Cheshams, Belgravia

G

Cheval Apartments, Knightsbridge

Clifton Lodge, Knightsbridge

Knightsbridge Service Flats, Knightsbridge

Snow White Properties, Knightsbridge

Club Suites, Chelsea

Draycott House, Chelsea

Nell Gwynn House, Chelsea

Sloane Apartments, Chelsea

130 Queensgate, Kensington

Allen House, Kensington

Ashburn Gardens, Kensington

Astons, Kensington

Chequers of Kensington, Kensington

Collingham Gardens, Kensington

Eight Knaresborough, Kensington

Five Emperor's Gate, Kensington

Huntingdon House, Kensington

John Howard Hotel, Kensington

Kensington Court, Kensington

Kensington Park, Kensington

The Lexham, Kensington

Queensgate, Kensington

K

Belgard, Paddington

Europa House, Maida Vale

One Hyde Park Street, Bayswater

Porchester Place, Bayswater

Princes Square, Bayswater

Two Hyde Park Square, Bayswater

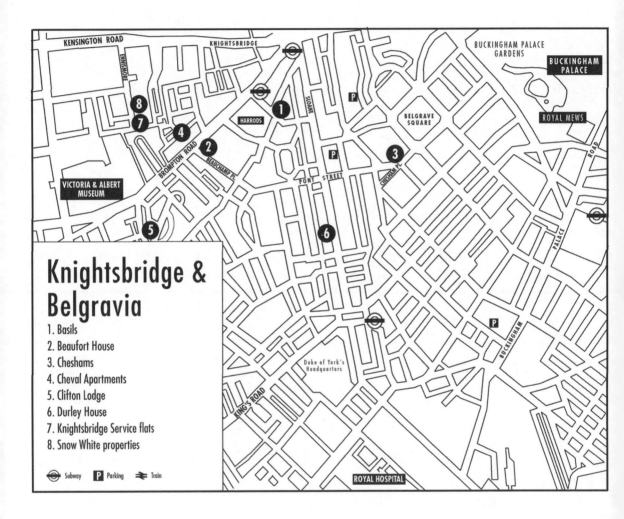

Knightsbridge & Belgravia

1. Basils
2. Beaufort House
3. Cheshams
4. Cheval Apartments
5. Clifton Lodge
6. Durley House
7. Knightsbridge Service flats
8. Snow White properties

Subway   P Parking   Train

Chapter 7

~~~~~~~~~

Knightsbridge and Belgravia

F amous for Harrods, Harvey Nichols, and other such shopping icons, Knights-
bridge also offers the free, bucolic pleasures of Hyde Park and Kensington
Gardens. It is a narrow, wedge-shaped neighborhood stretching westward from
Hyde Park Corner between Sloane Street and along Knightsbridge and Brompton
Roads to South Kensington. Belgravia joins it on the east side of Sloane Street. At
Hyde Park Corner stands the treasure-filled home of the Duke of Wellington, and the
subway line running through the area whisks travelers to West End theaters in 10
minutes.

Knightsbridge has a selection of tasteful apartments in seven mansion blocks;
tiny, tony Belgravia, one. They are handy not only for the shops and fine restaurants,
but also for the museums and concert hall in South Kensington.

Knightsbridge and Belgravia at a Glance

Apartment	Studio	1-Bedroom	2-Bedroom	3-Bedroom	Other
Basils No minimum stay	$227 n $1,532 w	$227 n $1,532 w	$437–$510 n $2,916–$3,402 w (2 baths)	$607–$632 n $3,564–$4,212 w (2 baths)	*Penthouse* $608–$729 n $4,050–$4,860 w
Beaufort House No minimum stay		$343–$476 n $2,332–$3,265 w	$552–$666 n $3,797–$4,597 w (1.5 or 2 baths)	$733–$942 n $5,063–$6,529 w (2.5 or 3 baths)	*4-bedroom* $933–$1,047 n $6,462–$7,262 w (3.5 baths)
Cheshams No minimum stay		$227 n $1,523 w	$389–$446 n $2,592–$2,297 w (2 baths)		
Cheval Apts. 1-week minimum			$286–$360 n $1,999–$2,522 w (2 or 2.5 baths)	$453–$469 n $3,169–$3,284 w (2 baths)	*Townhouse* *2–3-bedroom* $317–$488 n $2,218–$3,417 w
Clifton Lodge 5-night minimum	$130–$146 n $907–$1,022 w	$178–$211 n $1,247–$1,477 w			
Durley House 3-night minimum		$476–$562 n $3,332–$3,934 w	$714–$904 n $4,998–$6,328 w		*Piano Suite* $914 n $6,398 w
Knightsbridge Service Flats 1-week minimum	$130–$146 n $907–$1,021 w				
Snow White Properties 1-week minimum	$154–$181 n $1,079–$1,264 w	$174–$227 n $1,215–$1,588 w			

NOTES: (1) All prices are in American dollars converted at $1.62 to £1 and include VAT. To convert to the current rate, divide the dollar amount by 1.62 and multiply by the rate listed in today's local paper. (2) n=night; w=week.

Knightsbridge and Belgravia Apartments in Detail

Basils, 15 Basil Street, London

photo p. G

Located facing the back of Harrods, Basils is in a shopper's paradise. Not only is it a few steps from the world's most famous department store, it is also only a block from the boutiques of Beauchamp Place. Around the corner is Harvey Nichols, another up-market, world-class department store. A block to the east is Sloane Street with representatives of many of London's major fashion emporiums. If that isn't enough, the subway is just three minutes away.

While in traditional surroundings, Basils itself is a modern brick building with elevator. Many of the eight apartments have balconies. All contain reproduction antique furniture in the opulent style typical of apartments managed by Manors and Company. The flats range from studios to three-bedrooms with two baths plus a penthouse, and all are comfortably sized. (All of the studios were occupied at the time of our visit, so we were unable to see them.)

Each apartment opens into a small hallway with the living/dining area to the right. The one- and two-bedroom apartments have an overstuffed sofa and two easy chairs, while the three-bedroom living room has two sofas. Windows are either full length or in small alcoves that also hold a large color TV. The dining area is at the far end of the room with a round table, the appropriate number of chairs, and a good supply of fine china and cutlery. Floor and table lamps provide ample light.

In the two- and three-bedroom flats, the master bedroom contains an *en suite* bath. There is an additional large bath across the hall. King or queen beds occupy all of the master and second bedrooms; twin beds are in the third. Bed linens are color-coordinated with window coverings and both are of high quality. As in most flats, second and third bedrooms are smaller than the master bedroom. The second bedrooms at Basils have an additional TV.

Baths have power showers and tubs. There are plenty of towels and toiletries, and hair dryers are available on request.

The kitchens are well supplied with full ovens, microwaves, washers/dryers, and pots and pans. Refrigerators are under-counter size.

While Basils is in a modern building, it provides neither satellite television nor air-conditioning. Fans are available during unusually hot spells. There are two phones in larger flats and one phone line. Computer connection is through the phone line. A fax machine is available at the visitor's request.

Basils has fewer amenities than other Manors and Company properties and is showing its age. Still, in this very expensive neighborhood, it represents good value for comfort and some luxury, especially since price is negotiable.

AMENITIES—Elevator, telephone, color TV, radio, computer connection through telephone, fax (on request), maid service (Monday–Friday), concierge/housekeeper (9:30–5:30, Monday–Friday), under-counter refrigerator, small freezer compartment, stove with oven, toaster, tea kettle, teapot, coffee maker, iron, microwave, washer/dryer, hair dryer (on request), toiletries, welcome pack (at extra cost).

RESERVATIONS/PRICES/MISC.—**Minimum stay:** 1 night. **Reservations:** Mr. Seller. **Telephone:** 0207-486-5982; toll-free U.S.: 1-800-454-4385. **Fax:** 0207-486-6770. **E-mail:** *enquiry@manors.co.uk.* **Web site:** *www.manorsco.co.uk.* **Prices from:** studio and 1 bdrm-$227 per night, $1,532 per week; 2 bdrm, 2 bath-$437 per night, $2,916 per week; 3 bdrm, 2 bath-$607 per night, $3,564 per week; penthouse-$608 per night, $4,050 per week. **Negotiate price?** yes. **Deposit?** yes. **Check in:** 2 P.M. or earlier, if available. **Check out:** 12 P.M. **Credit cards?** yes. **Tube stop:** Knightsbridge.

Beaufort House, 45 Beaufort Gardens, Knightsbridge, London SW3 1PN

   *photo p. G*

Beaufort House won the 1999 London Tourist Award for Self-Catering Holiday of the year, and the reasons are evident from the moment one walks through the flower garden entrance into the reception area. The room is large with high ceilings and fireplace, as befits a grand Regency townhouse, and is furnished with comfortable sofas and stuffed chairs. The setting is formal but the staff is warm, friendly, and quick to meet the requests of guests.

The location of Beaufort House is superb. It is one of a series of Regency buildings on a quiet cul-de-sac in Knightsbridge. Around the corner to the right on Brompton Road is Harrods. Around the corner to the left is Beauchamp Place with its exclusive boutiques and esoteric restaurants (Borshtch 'n' Tears has been there since our first visit to London many, many years ago).

The 21 one-, two-, three-, and four-bedroom apartments at Beaufort House are classified as standard, superior, and executive, the higher rankings reflective of larger flats and more amenities. Whatever the classification of the flat, all are furnished in a rich traditional style with sofas, easy chairs, desk, fireplace (some flats have more than one), and coordinated drapery and slipcovers. Dining areas are well set off or are separate rooms with formal dining tables and sufficient seating for the number of occupants and guests. All have video entry phone, individual safes, satellite TV, stereo and CD players, VCRs, radios, direct-dial telephones, voice mail, ISDN, and dataports. Each kitchen has stove, microwave, refrigerator, washer/dryer, and iron and can be closed off. Three- and four-bedroom flats also have dishwashers and larger refrigerator/freezer units. Bedrooms are elegantly decorated with lots of closet space, a bureau, bedside tables with lamps, and an additional chair. Bathrooms are sizable with marble walls, power showers/baths, and ample towels. Maid service is seven days a week.

The standard one-bedroom is the only flat with just one bathroom, but on the ground-floor level it does have an outside terrace with seating for a morning cup of coffee in a private, tranquil setting. Standard and superior one-bedrooms have one and a half baths, one *en suite*. The standard two-bedroom has one and a half baths, and the other two-bedrooms, two and a half baths, two *en suite*. All three- and four-bedroom flats have at least two and a half baths and are split-level, with the bedrooms on the upper level. Some flats have balconies or gardens.

All of the flats have been recently refurbished and all open into a foyer with fresh wallpaper and carpeting. These flats are very well maintained at an address that is excellent for the businessperson, and all provide an appropriate setting for meeting with or entertaining business clients.

AMENITIES—Elevator, air conditioning, telephone, color satellite TV, radio, computer connection, fax (in flat), maid service (Monday–Friday), refrigerator/freezer, stove, toaster, tea kettle, teapot, coffee maker, iron, microwave, dishwasher (in 3- and 4-bdrm), washer/dryer, hair dryer, toiletries, welcome pack.

RESERVATIONS/PRICES/MISC.—Minimum stay: 1 night. **Reservations:** office staff. **Telephone:** 0207-584-2600. **Fax:** 0207-584-6532. **E-mail:** *info@beauforthouse.co.uk.* **Web site:** *www.beauforthouse.co.uk.* **Prices from:** 1 bdrm-$343–$476 per night; $2,332–$3,265 per week; 2 bdrm, 1.5 or 2 bath-$552–$666 per night; $3,797–$4,597 per week; 3 bdrm, 2.5 or 3 bath-$733–$942 per night, $5,063–$6,529 per week; 4 bdrm, 3.5 bath-$933–$1,047 per night, $6,462–$7,262 per week. **Negotiate price?** yes. **Deposit?** 1 week's rent. **Check in:** 2 P.M. **Check out:** 10 A.M. **Credit cards?** all major. **Tube stop:** Knightsbridge.

Cheshams, 11–12 Chesham Place, London SW1

 +

photo p. G

Cheshams is situated in one of the most exclusive neighborhoods of London, Belgravia. It is two short blocks from Sloane Street with its designer boutiques, and within easy walking distance of Harrods, Harvey Nichols, and Beauchamp Place.

An elegant white stone mansion, Cheshams is on a quiet street of similar houses. Inside its Georgian exterior are 13 completely refurbished one- and two-bedroom apartments. The rooms are large with only two flats per story. Apartments on the first floor have high ceilings, crown moldings, and iron balconies with small topiary trees.

All of the flats open into a small hallway with a bathroom off to the right. In the one-bedrooms, there is an overstuffed sofa in a blue fleur-de-lis design with two matching easy chairs. The TV is tucked into a corner opposite the sofa. The dining table with four chairs is in front of a window. Along one wall a cabinet holds china, wine glasses, and other supplies. The kitchen opens to the right of the table into a different room. The bedroom is to the left of the hallway. It has a queen bed with bedside tables for storage, a desk with chair, and a large closet along the wall opposite from the bed.

The two-bedroom flat is very bright with two large windows; their decorative treatments coordinate with the light-colored furnishings, an upholstered sofa, and two easy chairs. There is a large glass-fronted cabinet with china and glasses, and the dining area, again with round table and sufficient chairs, is at the interior end of the room. A bathroom is off the hallway, while another is in the master bedroom. The

120

master bedroom has a second telephone. Both bedrooms and the kitchen are down the hallway. Generally, the bedrooms are good-sized and similarly furnished, but in some two-bedroom apartments, the second is quite small, while in others, it is large. It's important to make your preference known at time of booking.

All of the kitchens at Cheshams have large refrigerator/freezers, gas stoves, washer/dryers, and plenty of cabinet space. Management provides washing-up liquid. The two-bedroom apartments have a dishwasher.

Baths have power showers with tub and have large bath and hand towels. Toiletries are supplied.

All in all, these are large, airy apartments beautifully decorated in a lovely neighborhood.

AMENITIES—Elevator, telephone, color cable TV, radio, computer connection through telephone, fax (through office), maid service (Monday–Friday), housekeeper (9:30–5:30), refrigerator/freezer, stove, toaster, tea kettle, teapot, coffee maker, iron, microwave, washer/dryer, hair dryer (on request), welcome pack (on request at extra charge).

RESERVATIONS/PRICES/MISC.—**Minimum stay:** 1 night. **Reservations:** office staff. **Telephone:** toll-free from U.S., 1-800-454-4385; in UK, 0207-486-5982. **Fax:** 0207-486-6770. **E-mail:** *enquiry@manors.co.uk.* **Web site:** *www.manors.co.uk.* **Prices from:** 1 bdrm-$227 per night, $1,523 per week; 2 bdrm, 2 bath-$389 per night, $2,592 per week. **Negotiate price?** yes. **Deposit?** yes. **Check in:** 2 P.M. **Check out:** noon. **Credit cards?** all major. **Tube stop:** Sloane Street.

The Cheval Apartments: 140 Brompton Road, Knightsbridge, London SW3 1HY

 +

photo p. H

In addition to several properties for longer-term stays, the Cheval Group manages three sets of apartments and townhouses in the center of Knightsbridge. Collectively, they are called The Cheval Apartments and are located on Brompton Road, Cheval Place, and Montpelier Mews.

The first group, in a modern building right on Brompton Road, is made up of five identical apartments, each with two double bedrooms, one single bedroom, and two full baths, one *en suite.* For maximum privacy, there is only one flat on each floor with an elevator to bring visitors directly to each apartment. Although Brompton Road is a busy, bustling street with Harrods just one block to the east, the apartments themselves are quiet with double-glazed windows throughout, and all of the bedrooms at the back of the flats. As is typical of all properties managed by the Cheval Group, the apartments are a good size with traditional, comfortable furnishing. The living rooms have attractive ceiling moldings, two upholstered sofas, end tables with lamps, and coffee tables. Each has a balcony overlooking Brompton Road. The dining area is at the far end of the living room and contains a large table with six chairs and a window onto the balcony. The large walk-in kitchen is behind the dining area, can be closed off to conceal clutter from guests, and is spacious enough to hold a breakfast table and chairs. The kitchen's built-in appliances are concealed neatly behind cabinet fronts. Down the hallway is the master bedroom, bath *en suite,* with a double bed, tables, lamps, dresser, mirror, and extra chair. The second bedroom is twin-bedded, while the third has just a single. Windows, closets, and storage space are plentiful.

The second group, at 11–25a Cheval Place, is one street behind Brompton Road. There are eight apartments and four townhouses. The apartments all have one double and one single bedroom, and two bathrooms. The apartments on Cheval Place are the smallest in square footage and least expensive accommodations in the Cheval Group. While smaller, the living/dining area still holds, without crowding, two sofas, coffee and side tables, and a circular dining table. Several of these flats have balconies with outside seating. The two bedrooms are nicely furnished with coordinated comforters and wallpaper, side tables, dresser, mirror, and extra chair. All of the townhouses are more spacious. Three have three double bedrooms and three and a half baths, while the fourth is smaller: two double bedrooms and two and a half baths. The three larger townhouses have a separate dining room with a large table, seating for six, and a server. All have walk-in kitchens with breakfast tables.

The third group, within Montpelier Mews, one block north of Brompton Road, includes eight apartments, and one large and four smaller townhouses. One apartment has three bedrooms, the rest two. The building is modern with circular balconies off the living area of each flat or townhouse. There are only two flats per floor. The living/dining areas are comfortably furnished with a sofa, two easy chairs, side tables, and circular dining table with chairs. A large, completely furnished kitchen is behind the dining area with a pass-through to the dining room for convenience. The master bedroom with bath *en suite* has a queen bed, dressing table and mirror, and a walk-in closet large enough to hold a year's worth of Harrods purchases and Imelda Marcos' shoes. The small townhouses, called courtyard houses by the Cheval Group, seem spacious with two sofas, mirrors, tables and lamps in the living area, and a formal dining table and chairs at one end. The bedrooms are cheerful with bright, color-coordinated bedspreads and drapes, bedside table with lamps, dressing table, mirror, bureau, and closets.

All of these apartments and townhouses are continually refurbished and scrupulously clean. All kitchens have a refrigerator/freezer (in larger accommodations, these are separate units), stove, microwave, washer/dryer, dishwasher (except at the smallest apartments in Cheval Place), a large supply of good-quality pots and pans, utensils, dish towels, and washing-up liquid. All have two sets of dishes—one for everyday use and one of Portmerion china. Baths are well stocked with towels and face cloths that are changed twice each week, and they have power showers and tubs. Many also have bidets. Membership in a nearby health club is included in the rental fee. Parking is available at an additional cost of $154 per week.

AMENITIES—Elevator, air conditioning (none, but has fans and will assist tenant in rental of mobile unit), telephone (direct-dial line with two phones), color TV with satellite, radio (2), computer connection through telephone, fax (will provide on request), maid service (Monday–Friday), refrigerator, freezer, stove, toaster, tea kettle, teapot, coffee maker, iron, microwave, dishwasher (in all but the four smallest flats at Cheval Place), washer/dryer, hair dryer, toiletries, welcome pack (generous, with supplies for a full breakfast).

RESERVATIONS/PRICES/MISC.—**Minimum stay:** 1 week. **Reservations:** office staff. **Telephone:** 0207-225-3325. **Fax:** 0207-581-2869. **E-mail:** *cheval@chevalgroup.com.* **Web site:** *www.chevalgroup.com.* **Prices from:** Brompton Road Apartments, 3 bdrm, 2 bath-$3,169 per week. Cheval Place Apartments, 2 bdrm, 2 or 2.5 bath-$1,999 per week; large townhouse-$3,417 per week; small townhouse-$2,808 per week. Montpelier Mews Apartments, 2 or 3 bdrm, 2 or 3 bath-$2,189–$3,284 per week, townhouse, 2 bdrm, 2.5 bath-$2,846 per week. **Negotiate price?** for long-term stays. **Deposit?** required. **Check in:** 12 noon. **Check out:** 10 A.M. **Credit cards?** yes. **Tube stop:** Knightsbridge.

Clifton Lodge, 45 Egerton Gardens, London SW3 2DD

photo p. H

Clifton Lodge began life as a townhouse designed by T. H. Smith in 1886. Knightsbridge, then and now, is a very smart neighborhood, and Egerton Gardens is a quiet, residential street just off Brompton Road. Ten minutes' walk east takes you to Harrods, five minutes' west to Victoria and Albert Museum.

Inside and out, the building retains its Victorian style but the atmosphere is one of homey informality, thanks to the caring presence of the long-time resident manager, Mrs. Scovil. Its six studios and four one-bedroom flats vary modestly in size, but all are intended for only two people; the smallest studio is probably best for one. Living space is maximized in most of the studios with well-designed wall cabinets for the twin beds when not in use (the American term "Murphy bed" doesn't do them justice). Kitchen facilities are located in a corner of the living rooms in both the studios and one-bedrooms. Despite limited space, all living rooms are bright with two or three large windows. Three of the front apartments feature big bay windows. The furniture mixes modern and traditional styles, comfortable and undistinguished, but walls and window treatments are stylish and carefully chosen. Appliances are modern, ample for the needs of short-term visitors. The studios have two stove-top burners and the one-bedrooms all have ovens as well. All have private baths with tub and power showers, clean and well maintained.

The rates are very reasonable for this neighborhood, and the small staff is exceptionally helpful, especially for guests new to the city or apartment holidays.

Amenities—Elevator, telephone, color satellite TV, maid service (Monday–Friday), concierge/housekeeper (live-in), refrigerator/freezer, stove (some), toaster, tea kettle, teapot, coffee maker, iron, microwave, washer/dryer (laundry room in basement), hair dryer (on request).

Reservations, Prices, Misc.—Minimum stay: 5 nights. **Reservations:** Mrs. Scovil. **Telephone:** 0207-584-0099. **Fax:** 0207-823-9194. **E-mail:** (coming soon). **Web site:** (coming soon). **Prices from:** studios-$130 per night, $907 per week; 1 bdrm-$178 per night, $1,247 per week. **Negotiate price?** yes. **Deposit?** $405. **Check in:** noon. **Check out:** 10:30 A.M. **Credit cards?** Visa and MasterCard. **Tube stop:** Knightsbridge, South Kensington.

Durley House, 115 Sloane Street, London SW1X 9PJ

   *photo cover*

Our visit to Durley House was a return one. We stayed in a two-bedroom apartment there many years ago and thought it elegant then. Now it has undergone a complete metamorphosis and assumed the shape of a posh apartment house with all the services of a luxury hotel, including an on-site chef.

Durley House is located on Sloane Street, one of the most exclusive addresses in London. It is also a convenient location just north of Sloane Square and all the boutiques and restaurants of King's Road, and a 10-minute walk from Harrods and Beauchamp Place with its rows of shops.

The entrance to Durley House is through modern wood-framed doors into a paneled anteroom, then through a doorway to the right into reception. In front of the reception desk is a large stairway to the 11 one- and two-bedroom apartments. There is also an elevator tucked behind the stairway.

All of the apartments at Durley House are spacious with high ceilings, and decorative moldings and cornices. Three large windows cross the living area and fill the room with natural light. Furnishings are elaborate, many in a traditional country manor style with genuine antiques. Others are quite flamboyant with bright red color schemes and faux-fur animal prints. The living rooms all have fireplaces with a sofa and two overstuffed easy chairs grouped in front. A desk is at one end of the room, and a small dining table is placed in front of a window for meals prepared in the flat. For meals prepared by the chef, however, food arrives directly from the kitchen via an old-fashioned dumbwaiter and is served by a live waiter on an antique table supplied for the occasion.

The elaborate decor continues into the bedrooms with bold colors, striking window treatments, and coordinated fabrics on comforters, drapes, wall coverings, and furniture. All the beds are oversized (seven feet by seven feet) zip-and-link with linens made especially to fit them. There is good storage space with a closet and bureau, and a dressing table with mirror and chair.

The two-bedroom apartment, similar in style to the one-bedroom, is larger and opens into a hallway that runs the width of the flat. The one-bedroom opens into a foyer. The kitchen in the two-bedroom is also larger with more counter space. Kitchens are supplied with necessities. Since many guests cook very little and rely on Durley House's 24-hour room service, most utensils, baking equipment, microwaves, teapots, and so forth are supplied by staff at the guests' request. It is surprising, given the level of luxury here, that the two-bedroom apartment has only one bath.

One of the loveliest and most expensive apartments at Durley House is the Piano Suite. The living room is grand with three full-length windows, a floral-patterned upholstered sofa and chairs, dramatic yellow draperies, an antique fireplace mantel, and its own baby grand piano at the far end of the room.

As a luxury apartment hotel, Durley House emphasizes the services and facilities it places at the disposal of its guests. Staff will prepare cocktail and dinner parties in the guests' apartments. Maid service is twice daily, seven days a week. Room service for full meals and snacks is available 24 hours a day. Full secretarial and office services are available on request. Each guest has keyed access to Cadogan Garden and its tennis courts just across the way.

Each flat has a fax machine, dataport, two telephone lines, telephones in living room and bedroom, VCR, two radios, individual safes, toiletries, and a hair dryer. Although Durley House is elegant and somewhat formal, children are welcome and management will arrange for babysitters.

The prices at Durley House may take your breath away, but they do have specials. They offer packages at Christmas, Easter, and other holidays, and August is one of their quietest months.

AMENITIES—Elevator, air conditioning (currently being installed for all flats), telephone (two lines and two phones for each flat), color satellite TV, radio (2), computer connection, fax (machine in flat), maid service (twice daily, 7 days a week), concierge, valet, refrigerator, freezer, stove, toaster, tea kettle, teapot, coffee maker, iron, microwave (on request), washer/dryer (available in basement, but laundry service available), hair dryer, toiletries.

RESERVATIONS, PRICES, MISC.—**Minimum stay:** 3 nights, usually. **Reservations:** office staff. **Telephone:** toll-free from U.S., 1-800-553-6674; in UK, 0207-235-5537. **Fax:** 0207-259-6977. **E-mail:** *durley@firmdale.com.* **Web site:** *www.firmdale.com.* **Prices per night:** 1 bdrm-$476, luxury 1 bdrm-$562; 2 bdrm-$714, deluxe 2 bdrm-$904; Park Suite-$714; Piano Suite-$914. **Negotiate price?** seasonal. **Deposit?** credit card number. **Check in:** 1 P.M. **Check out:** 12 noon; **Credit cards?** all but Diners Club. **Tube stop:** Sloane Square.

Knightsbridge Service Flats, 45 Ennismore Gardens, London SW7 1AQ

photo p. H

Martin Raphael's apartment townhouse stands across from lovely Ennismore Gardens. The best view is from the French doors of the first-floor front studio. The high ceilings and windows give this flat a great sense of space, but the dozen studios into which the building is divided all have good light, even the singles.

The size of the flats varies considerably, and the first- and second-floor flats contain more decorative features, such as crown moldings and chandeliers. Most flats consist of a sitting room with twin beds, a kitchen, and a bathroom with a tub/shower. The largest flat is suitable for three, containing two single beds and a sofa bed in its own alcove, a dresser, and easy chairs. It also has a large kitchen with under-counter refrigerator/freezer, a stove with four burners, and a microwave; it is adjacent to the small back garden. The two smallest flats are best for just one person since they are small rooms with just a twin bed, desk, kitchenette, easy chairs, dining table with chairs, TV, and bath. Some flats have balconies and/or fireplaces.

A typical flat has twin beds off one wall with the living area in front of the beds. There are two easy chairs, coffee table, and TV. Against the opposite wall are a wooden chest of drawers and a matching wardrobe. The kitchens are set off in separate rooms or alcoves. Some have breakfast bars. All, except in the two smallest flats, have four-burner stoves. The dining table may be in the kitchen or at one end of the living area. In each flat, there is a good supply of pots, pans, china, and cutlery.

Window treatments are simple: coordinated drapes and curtains. Quiet print or floral-patterned wallpaper runs throughout the house, and small framed prints decorate the walls. Furnishings are modern, serviceable, but of no particular style. The kitchen, bath fixtures, and appliances are up-to-date and well maintained. The whole building is scrupulously clean and fresh.

These are homey, comfortable flats in a fine building situated in a prime location. Harrods and busy Brompton Road are only two blocks away through the churchyard of Holy Trinity Brompton, but the church grounds and Ennismore Garden insulate the square from noise and traffic. The actress Ava Gardner kept a flat in another house on this square for many years for that very reason.

AMENITIES—Elevator, telephone, color satellite TV, fax (through office), maid service (Monday–Friday), concierge/housekeeper, refrigerator/freezer, stove, toaster, tea kettle, teapot, coffee maker, iron, microwave, welcome pack.

RESERVATIONS/PRICES/MISC.—**Minimum stay:** usually 1 week. **Reservations:** office staff. **Telephone:** 0207-584-4123. **Fax:** 0207-584-9058. **E-mail:** *info@ksflats.demon. co.uk.* **Web site:** *www.ksflats.demon.co.uk.* **Prices from:** studios-$907–$1,021 per week. **Negotiate price?** occasionally. **Deposit?** $486. **Check in:** 1 P.M. **Check out:** 11 A.M. **Credit cards?** Visa and MasterCard. **Tube stop:** Knightsbridge.

Snow White Properties, 55 Ennismore Gardens, London SW7 1AJ

photo p. H

Custard the cat was away on holiday when we called at Snow White Properties, but otherwise, everything was just as usual, that is, shipshape and lovely.

These elegant apartments are located in a grand, white-stone Regency-style townhouse in a row of similar buildings on a square built by Viscount Ennismore in 1843. The townhouse faces Ennismore Gardens, a leafy oasis in the heart of Knightsbridge. The garden is private, but guests at Snow White Properties have keyed access and can enjoy its quiet charms even though it is just two blocks north of the hurry and hustle of Brompton Road.

There are 11 apartments: 2 studios and 9 one-bedroom, all slightly different in floor plan and size. The larger flats are more expensive. Small or large, each apartment is carefully decorated in a traditional style with wallpaper, drapes, upholstery, rugs, and even towels and face cloths color-coordinated. A cat theme is repeated throughout in small touches, such as feline-shaped doorstops.

The large studio on the ground floor has a small patio off the kitchen. Two sofa beds provide comfort and can be closed up in the daytime for uncluttered living space. The view of the garden is a big plus in this studio that has the feel of a larger flat. Decor is in a striking black-and-white motif. The fully equipped galley kitchen overlooks the living area from a raised gallery that also contains the bath and door to the patio.

Also on the ground floor is a one-bedroom apartment that opens onto a garden with table and chairs for morning coffee or afternoon tea. The French doors off this terrace fill the living room with light and offer a restful and refreshing view. It is furnished with sofa, stuffed chair, coffee and lamp tables, breakfront, and circular dining table at the end of the room. The kitchen, which can be closed off, is behind the dining area. The bedroom has twin beds, a bureau, ample closet space, an additional chair, and a view of the garden. A second one-bedroom on the first floor has floor-to-ceiling windows in both living room and bedroom. Rich blue comforters, headboards, and pillows decorate the bedroom, but the *pièce de résistance* is the view of the garden beyond the beds.

Interior design for all of the flats at Snow White Properties is by the owner. Each one has been done with care. In fact, our notes for Snow White Properties are full of words like "beautiful," "well coordinated," "lovely colors," and "very, very pretty." While the apartments are not large, furnishings are chosen and arranged to make maximum use of available space. All flats have direct-dial, metered telephones compatible for computer use plus satellite TV and radios. Kitchens contain ample china and utensils as well as under-counter refrigerator with small freezer, stove, and microwave. Baths have power showers/tubs and heated towel racks.

Children are welcome at Snow White Properties, and management can supply cribs.

Snow White Properties was a favorite of all three of our reviewers. For the quality of these flats and their location in tony Knightsbridge, they are a good buy.

AMENITIES—Elevator (some flats require walk up half flight of stairs), air conditioning (mobile units supplied when necessary), direct-dial telephone, color TV with satellite, radio, computer connection through telephone, fax (available through office), maid service (Monday–Friday), housekeeper (9:30–5:30, Monday–Friday, with emergency number provided), refrigerator, freezer, stove, toaster, tea kettle, teapot, coffee maker, iron, microwave, washer/dryer (in basement for guest use), hair dryer, toiletries, welcome pack.

RESERVATIONS/PRICES/MISC.—**Minimum stay:** 1 week. **Reservations:** Ann. **Telephone:** 0207-584-3307. **Fax:** 0207-581-4686. **E-mail:** *snow.white@virgin.net.* **Web site:** *freespace.virgin.net/snow.white.* **Prices from:** studios-$1,079–$1,264; 1 bdrm-$1,215–$1,588. **Negotiate price?** for longer stays. **Deposit?** $1/2$-week's rent. **Check in:** 2 P.M. **Check out:** 12 noon. **Credit cards?** all major. **Tube stops:** Knightsbridge, South Kensington.

Knightsbridge and Belgravia: Attractions

You will look in vain for the bridge that named the village in the 11th century, but legend has it that two knights fought it out on the site. The stream has also disappeared after being dammed to form Serpentine Lake in Hyde Park in 1730. The lake enhanced a park that had become fashionable after Charles II adopted it for royal promenades. The royal presence attracted anyone who wished to be noticed to Hyde Park for a stroll or a canter along *route du roi,* the road between Kensington Palace and St. James. Now called Rotten Row, the road still accommodates horseback riders, especially on Sundays. Horse lovers can also watch a column of the Household Cavalry trot through the park on their parade to the changing of the guards.

Among the free attractions in this expensive neighborhood is the Serpentine Gallery, a former tea house given over to contemporary art exhibits sponsored by the Arts Council.

Harrods began as a village grocery 150 years ago and now employs a staff of 4,000. The main attraction for many is still groceries in the seven elaborate food halls that anchor the ground floor. But the store's enduring popularity depended upon a reputation of service, established when the original building was destroyed by fire in December 1883. Charles Digby Harrod wrote his customers that their orders would be delayed "a day or two." And so they were, but he fulfilled all his Christmas orders despite the fire and won a loyal following for his new store. The present store dates from 1906, a full block of neogothic grandeur, and it sells everything. The reputation for service survives but the controversial antics of the present owner, Mohamed Al Fayed, has undermined customer loyalty substantially. If you have friends to whom the name Harrods is magic, check out the lower level. Walk past the Egyptian gallery and you will enter a hall full of Harrods souvenir items: from teddy bears to fountain pens to totes, everything has a Harrods logo.

Harvey Nichols, nearby, is now reckoned the more fashionable of London's department stores. Designer shops and boutiques occupy almost every inch of the neighborhood surrounding these two giants, especially along Upper Sloane Street, Brompton Road, and Beauchamp Place.

For aesthetic or spiritual relief, you are welcome to stop off Brompton Road at Thurloe Place for a look at Brompton Oratory. It's a Catholic church built in the

1880s to imitate an Italian baroque church of the 16th century, complete with an Italian altarpiece and statuary.

Shops, Restaurants, and Pubs

The largest food halls in London are at Harrods. More than 34,000 feet on the first floor make up seven separate rooms devoted to every food imaginable. The fish and meats departments are outstanding. There are many prepared dishes from around the world to take home and heat, and savory pies available whole or by the slice. The confectionery room has excellent candy gifts, and the produce room has an extensive selection of fruits and vegetables from all over the globe. Everything, of course, is expensive.

Harvey Nichols also has an excellent and expensive food hall. If you're shopping only for food, take the express elevator to the top floor. There you will find an impressive display of fish, meats, charcuterie, fruits, vegetables, fresh mushrooms, breads, and pastries. There are also kits for some dishes, such as risotto, containing all the necessary ingredients for the complete dish—just the thing for the traveling cook.

Behind Harrods at 5 Walton Street is La Picena, an Italian delicatessen. From the front window you might think it just a butcher shop, but inside it holds a full range of Italian delicacies, including house-made sauces, fruits and vegetables imported from Italy, and many dishes ready to go (cannelloni, gnocchi, lasagna, cooked chicken).

Both Harrods and Harvey Nichols have a variety of restaurant choices. Harvey Nichols is the current "in" place, the Fifth Floor Cafe. The food is excellent, not as expensive as you might expect (entrees, $14 to $24; two-course set menu, $28; three-course set menu, $32). If you want to be seen, however, be sure to be there at lunchtime.

There are inexpensive options at Harvey Nichols also. Yo! Sushi is off the food hall on the fifth floor. You take your sushi from a conveyer belt as dishes pass in front of you. Wagamama, the burgeoning noodle chain, has a branch on the lower ground level. The food, Japanese noodles and other selections, is organic and healthful. At the opposite end of the price spectrum is La Tante Clair (The Berkeley, Wilton Place, 0207-823-2003). The chef is world famous, the food French and exquisite, and the prices amazing. The minimum at dinner is $80 per person.

For great food in a posh modern setting and at slightly lower prices, try Isola (145 Knightsbridge, 0207-838-1044; entrees, $27 to $36). At lunch the set menu at $16 seems a real bargain.

The Bunch of Grapes (207 Brompton Road), down the street from Harrods, is a comfortable and historic stop for a pint after a day of shopping. A working pub since before the 1780s, the Bunch of Grapes is known for its lobby mirror and etched-glass snob-screens. East of Harrods at 53 Kinnerton Street is the Nag's Head, an old pub reopened in 1979. It's stuffed with interesting antique odds and ends, including two 1930s game machines that require old pennies. You get them from the bartender.

Belgravia boasts two fine pubs, the Grenadier (18 Wilson Row) and the Star Tavern (6 Belgrave Mews). Both are in flower-bedecked mews settings without loud music and irritating game machines. Off the beaten path, they have more locals than tourists. An authentic sentry box marks the doorway of the Grenadier, and it is said that the Duke of Wellington was a regular visitor. In its earlier days, the Star Tavern was a gathering place for servants of the uppermost class. Rigidly segregated by status, only the butlers of the very grandest houses, some of the grandest in Europe, in fact, were accepted in the coveted back room. Now it is an open and airy pub, welcoming to all. House-made meat pies, stews, and vegetarian dishes are served from the counter at the far end of the bar.

The Australian (29 Milner Street), between Brompton Road and Kings Road, also does without piped music. It serves a fine range of beers (Marston and Adnams, when we were in) across a unique copper-topped bar. It's a friendly, unpretentious place where folks play darts or chess and enjoy food above the average pub grub.

The Swag and Tails (10–11 Fairhold Street, 0207-584-6926) is a "gastropub" in a charming floral-covered mews cottage not far from Harrods, west of Montpelier Street above Brompton Road. It is hard to find on the short mews streets but well worth the search. Our party enjoyed squash soup, pear-and-blue-cheese salad, and spring rolls for appetizers, and pasta with a walnut Gorgonzola sauce, duck with leeks, and a steak for our main courses. Appetizers run from $3 to $9; sandwiches, from $10 to $14; and entrees, from $14 to $19.

A few blocks southwest of Harrods is Beauchamp Place, with pricey boutiques and restaurants, but also some reasonable ethnic choices. Borshtch 'n' Tears (45–46 Beauchamp Place, 0207-589-5003) has been there for years. We ate there the first time we stayed in a London apartment. The Russian food is tasty, the setting is relaxed and fun, and a set meal of three courses is only $30, and that includes a glass of vodka. At 9 Beauchamp Place is Patara (0207-581-8820; entrees, $13 to $24), a sophisticated restaurant with white tablecloths and Thai textiles on the wall; spiciness can be turned up or down. At 39 and 49–50 Beauchamp Place are Caravela and O Fado, respectively, two Portuguese restaurants. Caravela (0207-581-2366) has a nautical theme and a menu that emphasizes fish and seafood (entrees, $13 to $20). O Fado (0207-589-3002), the oldest Portuguese restaurant in London, serves a full traditional menu (entrees, $11 to $23) and well-priced wines.

In nearby Belgravia, for a fine French meal in a modern country setting, try Roussillion (16 Saint Barabas Street, 0207-730-5550; set dinner, two courses, $40; three courses, $47). Vegetarian dishes and meals are outstanding.

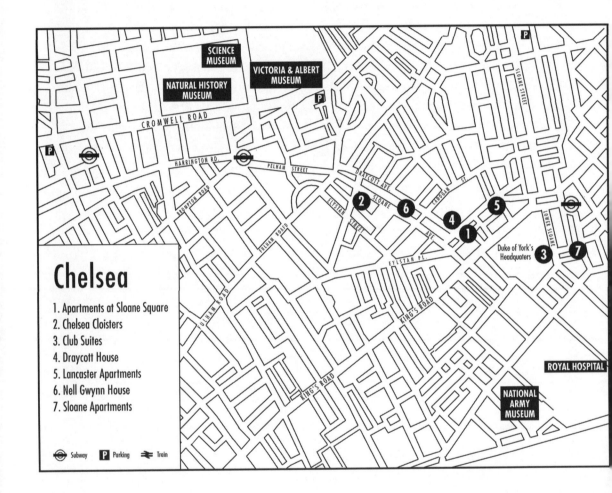

Chelsea

1. Apartments at Sloane Square
2. Chelsea Cloisters
3. Club Suites
4. Draycott House
5. Lancaster Apartments
6. Nell Gwynn House
7. Sloane Apartments

Subway   P Parking   Train

SCIENCE MUSEUM

NATURAL HISTORY MUSEUM

VICTORIA & ALBERT MUSEUM

CROMWELL ROAD

HARRINGTON RD.

PELHAM STREET

BROMPTON ROAD

FULHAM ROAD

DRAYCOTT AVE.

SLOANE

ELYSTAN STREET

CADOGAN ST

SLOANE STREET

LOWER SLOANE

EYLSTAN PL.

AVE.

KING'S ROAD

KING'S ROAD

Duke of York's Headquaters

ROYAL HOSPITAL

NATIONAL ARMY MUSEUM

Chapter 8

Chelsea

The street signs designate it grandly as part of the Royal Borough of Kensington and Chelsea, but Chelsea is quite distinct on its own. It's a wedge-shaped district running along the Thames from Sloane Square to the point where Fulham Road brushes King's Road. King's Road bisects the district for the whole of its length and has defined it in the minds of many people since the 1960s as a trendy shopping center for the young or would-be young.

To the clothes conscious, Chelsea means the King's Road, lined with boutiques and Saturday shoppers. To gardeners, it is Mecca, the site of a world-class flower show each May and one of the oldest gardens in England, the Physic Garden. For residents it is a chic neighborhood of well-kept townhouses and good restaurants. Visitors will also find a 17th-century village here, including the Royal Hospital, the National Army Museum, and a major London theater, the Royal Court.

Chelsea is an expensive and exclusive residential district, but many flats, especially the studios, are a relative bargain. Don't worry, though, there are plenty of expensive apartments in Chelsea also. The choice is yours.

Chelsea at a Glance

Apartment	Studio	1-Bedroom	2-Bedroom	3-Bedroom	Other
The Apts. Sloane Square No minimum stay (studios) 1-week minimum (1-bdrm)	$171–$231 n $999–$1,618 w	$204 n $1,428 w			
Chelsea Cloisters 1-week minimum (Unrated)	$111–$126 n[a] $778–$883 w	$171 n[a] $1,199 w	$226–$237 n[a] $1,580–$1,661 w (1 bath)		
The Club Suites No minimum stay	$238 n $1,668 w	$289–$305 n $2,025–$2,132 w	$289–$371 n $2,025–$2,598 w (1 or 2 baths)		*Maisonette* $510 n $3,571 w (2 baths)
Draycott House No minimum stay		$327–$398 n $2,073–$2,572 w	$607–$792 n $3,858–$5,040 w (1 or 2 baths)		
Lancaster Apts. 2-night minimum		(Only long term)	$334 n $1,666 w (2 baths)		*Penthouse* $371 n $1,999 w
Nell Gwynn House 1-week minimum	$114–$156 n[b] $795–$1,090 w	$175–$238 n[b] $1,222–$1,669 w	$217–$338 n[b] $1,516–$2,364 w (1 or 2 baths)		
Sloane Apts. No minimum stay	$219–$247 n $1,533–$1,732 w	$266–$371 n $1,865–$2,598 w	$371–$400 n $2,598–$2,800 w		

NOTES: (1) All prices are in American dollars converted at $1.62 to £1 and include VAT. To convert to the current rate, divide the dollar amount by 1.62 and multiply by the rate listed in today's local paper.

    a. Excludes electricity ($8–16 p.w.), lease ($114), linens ($97–$130), and onetime cleaning ($113–$146) and laundry charges ($113–$163).

    b. Includes cleaning charge.

(2) n=night; w=week.

Chelsea Apartments in Detail

The Apartments Sloane Square, Chelsea, London SW3 2SH

The Apartments at Sloane Square have four locations. Only one, 41 Draycott Place, is licensed for short-term stays. The others, at 1 Sloane Avenue, at 36 and 49 Draycott Place, rent for a minimum of three months (see chapter 11). The eight studios and one one-bedroom apartment at 41 Draycott Place, on the other hand, rent for a one-day and one-week minimum, respectively, although a week's stay is less expensive.

These nine flats are in a fully restored redbrick Victorian a block from King's Road and around the corner from the food shops and restaurants of Chelsea Green.

The house was built in 1880 and reflects late-Victorian opulence. Even the hallways are grand with deep-pile carpets, rich window treatments, antique desks, and chairs on the landings.

The deluxe studios are among the largest and most luxurious that we have seen. Those on the first and second floor have high ceilings, tall windows set into alcoves, and area rugs on the light-colored wall-to-wall carpeting. Each studio has a queen bed, side tables with reading lamps, sofa or easy chairs, desk, and fitted wardrobe. Deluxe flats have a larger living area and dining table and chairs, while standards have table and chairs in the kitchen. Although these are all studios, except for flat Number 1, all kitchens are in separate rooms. They are fitted with high-quality Bosch appliances and include refrigerator/freezer, stove with glass door, and microwave. Management provides washing-up liquid and a generous welcome pack on arrival. There is also a laundry that guests may use. Baths are *en suite* with stone vanities, luxurious Floringo bath towels, toiletries, and a choice of tub or tub/shower.

The one-bedroom flat on the lower ground level takes up the entire floor and is very private. It has a full bath with tub and shower. Both the living/dining area and the bedroom are large and furnished in the sumptuous style of the deluxe studios. All flats have entry video phones and security cameras at the doors.

While 41 Draycott Place is excellent for tourists, the flats are fully equipped for the business traveler. There are direct-dial phones with computer connections, answering machines with fax capacity, and secretarial services available through the office.

One caution—there is no elevator. If you take a flat on the third floor (fourth to U.S. travelers), be prepared for a climb.

AMENITIES—Elevator (none), telephone, color satellite TV, radio, computer connection, fax, maid service (once a week), refrigerator/freezer, stove, toaster, tea kettle, teapot, coffee maker, iron, microwave, laundry facilities in basement, hair dryer, toiletries, welcome pack.

RESERVATIONS/PRICES/MISC.—**Minimum stay:** 1 day, studio; 1 week, 1-bdrm flat. **Reservations:** Jane. **Telephone:** 142-866-1831. **Fax:** 142-865-1566. **E-mail:** *sales@theapartments.co.uk*. **Web site:** *www.theapartments.co.uk*. **Prices from:** studios-$171 per night, $999 per week; 1 bdrm-$1,428 per week. **Negotiate price?** no. **Deposit?** yes. **Check in:** flexible. **Check out:** noon. **Credit cards?** 3% charge. **Tube stops:** Sloane Square, South Kensington.

Chelsea Cloisters, Sloane Avenue, London SW3 3DW

Unrated

Chelsea Cloisters must be doing something right. Even though it has 650 flats in a mammoth building that fills an entire city block, each flat was occupied at the time of our mid-August visit. Constructed in 1960 as council flats, Chelsea Cloisters has been completely refurbished and now provides a full range of services and modern conveniences for the tourist or business traveler. The council flat look remains in the long, narrow corridors on each floor

Each of the 650 apartments is individually owned and decorated but placed in Chelsea Cloisters' management's hands for rental. Since management cannot guarantee a visitor a specific apartment, luck determines the amenities, style, and quality of flat a guest is assigned (hence, the "unrated" designation). The three apartments we were able to see (no photographs allowed since all were occupied) clearly showed the wide variation in the quality of apartments.

The Chelsea Cloisters studio that we visited was the smallest of all we have seen in London. It opens directly into the living/dining area with a queen bed immediately ahead and the bath on the left. There are two bedside tables with lamps and a TV but no additional seating. The kitchen is a tiny alcove in the corner of the room. There are two burners, no stove, but a microwave, an under-counter refrigerator, and a washer/dryer. Near the kitchen area is a table with two chairs. China, cutlery, and pots and pans are limited since this kitchen is intended for minimal use. The telephone, on the other hand, provides computer hookup, and all business services are available through the office.

The one-bedroom apartment was more fully equipped and more spacious. We entered into a hallway with the kitchen, a separate room, at the far end. While there is no stove, there is a microwave, a toaster oven, and a washer/dryer. Cooking implements are sufficient for the number of occupants. The living/dining area is pleasantly furnished with a sofa, dining table with four chairs, coffee table, and end tables with reading lamps. Drapes are coordinated with the room's furnishings. The bedroom is also pleasant with matching drapes and bedcovers on the queen bed. In addition to the bed are a wardrobe, dresser, and bedside tables with reading lamps.

The two-bedroom, two-bath apartment is furnished with sofa, easy chair, coffee and end tables, and round dining table with chairs. Both bedrooms are good-sized with queen beds in each. The master bedroom bath is *en suite,* and the second bath is off the hallway.

At Chelsea Cloisters all baths have power showers, and all flats have ample windows since the apartments are all arranged around a center courtyard.

While it is always important to make your wishes known at time of booking, it is essential to do so at Chelsea Cloisters. The wide range of quality and amenities means you pay more for what you get. Be specific to avoid disappointment on arrival.

To put it mildly, the pricing structure at Chelsea Cloisters is complex. There are three types of studio apartments and two types of two-bedroom apartments (with one or two baths). For each additional week's stay, the price of each flat is reduced, as are the extra charges for each period of occupancy. Extra charges include tenancy agreement fee ($114), electricity ($8 to $16 per week), linen change fee ($97 to $130 per week), end-of-tenancy cleaning ($113 to $146), and end-of-tenancy laundry ($113 to $162). The tenancy agreement fee and end-of-tenancy cleaning and laundry are charged only once, so a longer stay is clearly more economical.

Chelsea Cloisters seems most appropriate for the business traveler who has little time to cook, prefers a hotel-like atmosphere (three restaurants on the premises and 24-hour concierge services), and can benefit from corporate discounts.

AMENITIES—Elevator, telephone, color cable TV, radio, computer connection through telephone, fax (through telephone), maid service (Monday–Friday), concierge/housekeeper, refrigerator/freezer, stove (some), toaster, tea kettle, teapot, coffee maker, iron, microwave, washer/dryer, hair dryer (on request), welcome pack (on request for extra charge).

RESERVATIONS/PRICES/MISC.—**Minimum stay:** 1 week. **Reservations:** office staff. **Telephone:** 0207-584-1002. **Fax:** 0207-581-5990. **E-mail:** *lettings@chelsea-cloisters.co.uk*. **Web site:** *www.chelsea-cloisters.co.uk*. **Prices for 1 week from:** studios-$778; 1 bdrm-$1,199; 2 bdrm, 1 bath-$1,580. All plus extra charges as noted above. **Negotiate price?** corporate discounts. **Deposit?** $972 minimum. **Check in:** 2 P.M. **Check out:** 10 A.M. **Credit cards?** all major. **Tube stop:** South Kensington.

The Club Suites, 52 Lower Sloane Street, London SW1W 8BS

photo p. H

The Club Suites at 4 Lower Sloane Street and 11 and 19 Sloane Gardens are unique in the realm of short-term apartments. Not only do they provide plush accommodation in Chelsea, but they also extend to suite patrons all the privileges of membership in the Sloane Club. Once a private association for women military officers, it is now a members-only meeting, dining, and sleeping facility with the look and feel of an old-fashioned gentlemen's club, a setting to tickle the imagination. A guest could enjoy high tea in one of the sitting rooms or dine in candlelit elegance in the club restaurant—all at member prices.

The apartments themselves (studios, one- and two-bedroom, and two-bedroom *maisonette*) are in three locations along a tree-lined avenue just south of Sloane Square. Built in the 1860s, the interiors of these redbrick residences have been reconstructed into modern apartments. With the exception of the two studios, there is never more than one flat to a floor.

The two studios are appealing. Although on the lower ground floor, they are still full of light from above-ground windows, and one has an exterior entrance and a small terrace. It has a fully separate kitchen with breakfast bar that is up a short stairway from the living area. The other studio has a galley kitchen along the far wall and a glass door that opens onto a stone balcony. Both have light-colored walls, high ceilings, and crown moldings. The furnishings in the studios include overstuffed sofas and easy chairs, lamps, tables, and queen-size beds.

Furnishings in the two-bedroom apartments are in a similar style. Living areas have two small sofas, a matching easy chair, and a dining table and chairs at one end. All kitchens are separate rooms. Master bedrooms are a comfortable size with king beds and a trouser press. They have either large windows or glass doors onto an outside terrace. The second bedroom in these flats contains twin beds, each with its own bedside table. The cost of the two-bedroom flats varies with the number of baths and the number of stairs to climb to them, since there are no elevators.

Kitchens are fully equipped with stove, under-counter refrigerator, microwave, washer/dryer, tableware, pots, and pans. Tea and coffee are supplied every day. Bathrooms are modern power shower and tub. Robes, towels, and toiletries are provided, as is an ample welcome pack for those staying a full week. Guests have keyed access to a private garden across the way.

All this and the Sloane Club too!

AMENITIES—Elevator (none), telephone, color satellite TV, computer connection (ISDN), fax (through office), maid service (Monday–Friday), concierge/housekeeper, refrigerator/freezer, stove, toaster, tea kettle, teapot, coffee maker, iron, microwave, washer/dryer (some), hair dryer, bathrobes, toiletries, welcome pack (for a week's stay).

RESERVATIONS/PRICES/MISC.—Minimum stay: 1 night. Reservations: office staff. Telephone: 0207-730-9131. Fax: 0207-730-6146. E-mail: *reservations@ sloaneclub.co.uk*. Web site: *www.sloaneclub.co.uk*. Prices from: studios-$238 per night, $1,668 per week; 1 bdrm-$289 per night, $2,025 per week; 2 bdrm-$289 per night, $2,025 per week; 3-bdrm, 2-bath *maisonette*-$510 per night, $3,571 per week. Negotiate price? yes. Deposit? $810. Check in: 2 P.M. Check out: noon. Credit cards? all major. Tube stop: Sloane Square.

Draycott House, 10 Draycott Avenue, Chelsea, London SW3 3AA

photo p. H

Draycott House, a listed building, is located on a quiet corner in the heart of residential Chelsea. A redbrick Victorian, it has been refreshed on the outside and completely renovated on the inside into 13 one- to three-bedroom apartments and an on-site management office.

The flats are configured in six different layouts and range in size from a small one-bedroom of 367 square feet to four large three-bedroom apartments of 1,100 square feet. Regardless of size, each flat is tastefully furnished in an individual style with decorative touches typical of a family home.

The smallest one-bedroom we visited, Number 12, is on the top floor and has a balcony with wrought-iron table and chairs. Entrance is into a long hallway with the living/dining area to the right and the bedroom and bathroom at the far end of the hall. There are an upholstered sofa, chair, small desk with chair, coffee table, and recessed shelves with knickknacks. A round table with four chairs is in a separate dining area at the end of the living room. The kitchen, which can be closed off, is behind the dining area. The bedroom has a king bed with side tables, dressing table, mirror, and matching drapes and bedcovers.

In the two- and three-bedroom flats, the living area is large with the dining section well set off or in a separate room. There are one or two sofas, additional easy chairs, desk, coffee and side tables. The dining room has a table with six chairs, a server, and a cabinet for glassware and china. The double bedrooms hold king beds, side tables, wall lamps, and dressers. Drapery and bed linens are in matching fabrics. Some third bedrooms are suitable only for a child or one adult.

At Draycott House, bathrooms have power showers (many have tubs and separate showers), large towels, and toiletries.

Kitchens are modern and in separate rooms. They have decorative wall tiles, plenty of cabinet space, stove, full-size refrigerator/freezer, and microwave. Guests may use the laundry facilities in the basement at no charge.

The apartments at Draycott House are large and luxurious. They are expensive but come with many extras. Garage parking and membership in a nearby health club are included in the rent. Each flat has video entry phone, personal safe, DVD, VCR, stereo, telephones with answering and fax machines, and a separate data line.

Draycott is well equipped to meet the needs of the modern businessperson. The well-stocked dining rooms provide an impressive setting for business entertaining. Children are also very welcome. Cribs, high chairs, even safety gates are available on request, free of charge.

AMENITIES—Elevator, telephone (2 lines per flat), color cable TV, radio, computer connection, fax, maid service (Monday–Friday), concierge/housekeeper, refrigerator/freezer, stove, toaster, tea kettle, teapot, coffee maker, iron, microwave, washer/dryer (laundry room in basement), hair dryer, toiletries, welcome pack, daily newspaper.

RESERVATIONS/PRICES/MISC.—**Minimum stay:** 1 night. **Reservations:** office staff. **Telephone:** 0207-584-4659. **Fax:** 0207-225-3694. **E-mail:** *sales@draycotthouse.co.uk*. **Web site:** *www.DraycottHouse.co.uk*. **Prices from:** 1 bdrm-$327 per night, $2,073 per week; 2 bdrm, 1 bath-$607 per night, $3,858 per week; 2 bdrm, 2 bath-$659 per night, $4,216 per week. **Negotiate price?** no. **Deposit?** $810. **Check in:** 2 P.M. **Check out:** noon. **Credit cards?** all major. **Tube stop:** Sloane Square.

Lancaster Apartments, 27 Draycott Place, London SW3 2SH

photo cover

Twenty-seven Draycott was built in the late 19th century in a style derived from 17th-century Flemish and Dutch architecture. A tall townhouse with stone detailing and decorated gables, it is typical of the elegant Victorian structures that line the streets of residential Chelsea.

The location could not be better. It is one block from King's Road, full of boutiques and restaurants. Within two blocks, a traveler can find bakeries, delicatessens, wine stores, and a prize-winning produce market. The Sloane Square tube stop is a five-minute walk.

Although the building dates from the 19th century, the seven flats inside have been completely redecorated and modernized. There are two one-bedroom flats and five two-bedroom flats, including the penthouse with a glassed-in roof terrace. (The one-bedroom flats, unfortunately, are only available for longer stays and have a three-month minimum.) All of the flats got new draperies and carpeting in fall 2000.

The two-bedroom apartments each occupy one floor of the house and are furnished in a traditional style. Except for the penthouse, all of the master bedrooms are in gabled rooms, allowing lots of light. Each has a queen bed, side tables with reading lamps, matching curtains and bed linens, dresser, chair, good-size closet, telephone, and *en suite* bath. Another bath opens off the hallway. The second, smaller bedroom contains either a single bed or twin beds. The living/dining rooms feature high ceilings, crown moldings, cornices, and oriental rugs over wall-to-wall carpeting. Floral fabric covers the sofa and chairs that face the ornate Adams-style fireplace. The period dining table with six matching chairs is at the far end of the room.

The rooms in the penthouse are somewhat smaller than in the other flats, and the master bedroom has a double bed. The compensation for less space is a grand view of Chelsea and an enclosed dining room/conservatory on the rooftop terrace.

All of the kitchens in the Lancaster Apartments are totally modern with glazed tile floors, and fully stocked with cabinet-fronted AEG appliances. Some have full-size refrigerator/freezers while some units have the under-counter type. All have a stove, microwave, and washer/dryer. The bathrooms are also right up-to-date with tile floors, power showers/tubs, ample towels, hair dryers, and Michaelangelo brand fittings. Toiletries are provided.

All in all, the Lancaster Apartments are elegant and welcoming.

AMENITIES—Elevator, telephone, color satellite TV, fax, maid service (Monday–Friday), refrigerator/freezer, stove, toaster, tea kettle, teapot, coffee maker, iron, microwave, washer/dryer, hair dryer, toiletries, welcome pack (at extra charge).

RESERVATIONS/PRICES/MISC.—**Minimum stay:** 2 days. **Reservations:** Anneke D'Arcy. **Telephone:** 0207-225-1928. **Fax:** 0207-225-0570. **Prices from:** 2 bdrm, 2 bath-$334 per night, $1,666 per week; penthouse-$372 per night, $1,999 per week. **Negotiate price?** no. **Deposit?** $486. **Check in:** 2 P.M. **Check out:** 11 A.M. **Credit cards?** only American Express. **Tube stop:** Sloane Square.

Nell Gwynn House, Sloane Avenue, London SW3 2AX

 *photo p. I*

A statue of Nell Gwynn, actress and mistress to Charles II, welcomes visitors to this popular apartment block. The faintly art deco building dates from the late 1930s.

During World War II, it billeted officers stationed in London, but since 1982 the building has served a mixture of permanent residents and travelers. The U-shaped building faces busy (and sometimes noisy) Sloane Avenue, the thoroughfare linking Chelsea and South Kensington, an ideal location for anyone who wants to enjoy the many pleasures of West London. The King's Road scene is three blocks south and the Victoria and Albert museum and Knightsbridge shops, a 15-minute walk in the opposite direction.

The generous lobby entrance is like a traditional hotel, with a concierge on duty 24 hours. The 165 apartments spread through eight floors above. Most are studios and one-bedrooms suitable for two or three people. All are modern, and even the studios are generously proportioned with comfortable wing chairs or sofas, dining tables and kitchenettes.

The apartments vary a great deal in size and amenities. Larger, more recently decorated flats on the quieter back of the building are the most expensive. The differences in quality are reflected in the eight price categories Nell Gwynn House uses, from small studio to superior two-bedroom.

We stayed in the least expensive, smallest one-bedroom. While we were comfortable there (except for street noise some nights), there were some problems. Neither the bathroom nor bedroom doors closed completely, and we had no teapot. Management quickly repaired the doors, and the housekeeper sent up a teapot within the hour. Our living area was furnished with two small nonmatching sofas, a coffee table, an end table, and two lamps. The dining table with four chairs was at the opposite end of the room in front of a wide window. The kitchenette was across from the sofas and behind the dining area. Luckily our kitchen included a full-size refrigerator and a stove with four burners. We did have to unplug the TV to use the microwave and toaster, but managed full dinners for three in the space. Our bedroom was small, as expected, but had a double bed, one side table (we asked for and got a second), a dresser with mirror and chair, and a built-in wardrobe. There was an additional closet in the living room. The bedroom was nicely decorated with chair-rail molding with floral wallpaper below it. The bathroom was modern with a large tub/shower and a heated towel rack.

Our photographer took a standard studio. Her living area was large with two overstuffed wing chairs, a dining table with two chairs, and a double bed with side table. While the kitchen was in an alcove and could be closed off, it provided only minimal cooking facilities—a small microwave with two burners on top. Pots, pans, plates, cups, and glasses were sufficient for two people.

Management told us that it stocks the flats with only basic supplies and relies on guests to ask for what they need. It is essential to make clear at time of booking what you want in your flat.

While we had some small complaints at Nell Gwynn House, on the whole it is very comfortable and a true bargain at Chelsea's prices.

AMENITIES—Elevator, telephone, color satellite TV, computer connection through telephone, fax (through office), maid service (Monday–Friday), concierge/housekeeper, refrigerator/freezer, stove (in some), toaster, tea kettle, teapot, coffee maker, iron, microwave, washer/dryer (in some).

RESERVATIONS/PRICES/MISC.—Minimum stay: 1 week. **Reservations:** office staff. **Telephone:** 0207-589-1105. **Fax:** 0207-589-9433. **E-mail:** *reservations@ ngha apartments.co.uk*. **Web site:** *www.nghapartments.co.uk*. **Prices from:** studios-$795 per week; 1 bdrm-$1,222 per week; 2 bdrm, 1 bath-$1,516 per week; includes additional cleaning charge of $81 to $113 per week. **Negotiate price?** no. **Deposit?** $567–$1,134, depending on size of apartment. **Check in:** 2 P.M. **Check out:** noon. **Credit cards?** all major. **Tube stop:** South Kensington.

Sloane Apartments, 15 and 55 Sloane Gardens, London SW1W 8EB

photo p. I

One block east of Sloane Square, the Sloane Apartments are housed in two large Victorian buildings (15 and 55) along tree-lined Sloane Gardens. The location is ideal for King's Road, the Sloane Square tube stop, and only a few minutes from the Thames and Cheyne Walk.

Sloane Gardens is a fine residential avenue of large redbrick homes built in the 1890s. Although completely modernized and renovated, Sloane Apartments retains its Victorian character with wide hallways and staircases, period furniture, wainscoting, and fancy window treatments. The 15 apartments that make up the group include 7 studios, 3 one-bedroom, and 5 two-bedroom flats. There is a lift in Number 15, but not in Number 55, where management puts families traveling with children.

Studios come in two varieties, small and large. The small studio has a narrow living area with high ceilings and crown molding. There is a small overstuffed sofa that opens into a bed and two additional matching easy chairs, one of which opens into a single bed. A closet runs along over half the length of the interior wall, and a tiled bath is just beyond. Although the room is small, the furnishings are lush, and a full window at the far end creates the impression of space. A short staircase just to the right of the entrance leads to the kitchen, which, in addition to most major appliances, also has a table and two chairs.

The larger studio has more room in the living/dining area, a formal dining table in front of the window, and a china cabinet. The bath is the same as in the smaller studio, but the kitchen is not separate. It is at one end of the room.

The one-bedroom flats open through a small alcove. The reception area is large with two sofas, matching chairs, French doors to the terrace, and a dining table. A separate kitchen is opposite the dining table. The bedroom is comfortably sized with a king bed, side tables with reading lamps, shelves, bureau, cabinets, and a long closet.

In the two-bedroom, the reception space is larger still with the dining table in front of tall windows. The master bedroom is furnished much like the one-bedroom but is much larger. The second bedroom holds twin beds with a table between them.

All of the kitchens have stoves, full-size refrigerator/freezers, and microwaves. The two-bedroom flats have dishwashers.

Baths are beautifully done with striking blue tile on the lower portion of the walls. There is a large tub with power shower, generous towels, and toiletries.

The Sloane Apartments are handsome modernized flats in period houses that were formerly grand private homes.

AMENITIES—Elevator (only in Number 15), telephone, color satellite TV, computer connection through telephone, fax (in flat), maid service (Monday–Friday), resident manager, refrigerator/freezer, stove, toaster, tea kettle, teapot, coffee maker, iron, microwave, dishwasher (only in 2 bdrm), laundry service (at extra charge) hair dryer, toiletries, welcome pack.

RESERVATIONS/PRICES/MISC.—**Minimum stay:** 1 night. **Reservations:** Dianelle. **Telephone:** 0207-730-9400. **Fax:** 0207-581-1922. **E-mail:** *sloane@nygrens.com.* **Prices from:** studios-$219 per night, $1,533 per week; 1 bdrm-$266 per night, $1,865 per week; 2 bdrm, 2 bath-$371 per night, $2,598 per week. **Negotiate price?** yes. **Deposit?** yes. **Check in:** 3 P.M. **Check out:** 11 A.M. **Credit cards?** Visa and MasterCard. **Tube stop:** Sloane Square.

Chelsea: Attractions

The river Thames gave Chelsea life and its name. *Chesil* means gravel bank in Anglo-Saxon. The gravel bank allowed buildings of substance along what was otherwise a tidal plain and wharf for fishermen. They caught "fat sweet salmon" there in the 16th century. The river brought Thomas More in 1520 and his boss, Henry VIII, a few years later. One built an estate; the other, a palace in Chelsea. Both faced the river, which provided an easy commute to the "office" in Westminster. King's Road, the boutique-lined main street of today, was a muddy cattle track.

Neither More's mansion nor Henry's palace survive, but Cheyne Walk, the riverfront settled in the 16th century, remains the prettiest in Chelsea and one of the most historic.

Nineteenth-century Chelsea welcomed a host of literary and artistic celebrities. Thomas Carlyle resided at Cheyne Row from 1834 until his death. Elizabeth Gaskell was born at 93 Cheyne Walk. Rossetti, Swinburne, and George Meredith shared a house on Cheyne Walk. James McNeill Whistler and Oscar Wilde lived on the same street for a time, and painter J. M. W. Turner and novelist George Eliot both died in Chelsea.

Much of old Chelsea has survived. The Royal Hospital (or Chelsea Hospital) is the most distinguished structure in the borough, in both architecture and purpose. Charles II commissioned Christopher Wren to design a hospital for military veterans as the French had recently done. The main building facing the river opened in 1689 with 476 pensioners housed in dormitories that flank either side. It still provides a home and treatment for about that same number today. Their blue uniforms and caps marked with *RH* are prominent in the shops and streets around the neighborhood.

Every spring the Chelsea Flower Show takes over the hospital grounds for a week in May as it has done since 1913 (if you can be in London in May, do take in this spectacular flower show). Next door the National Army Museum illustrates the history of the British army. The museum features a particularly intriguing elaborate scale model of Waterloo battlefield assembled by a participant, and it is free.

The oldest surviving attraction in Chelsea, oddly enough, is a garden. The Apothecaries Company established the Physic Garden in 1676.

The Physic Garden is an unexpected quiet spot in the bustle of the city. Although it is quite beautiful, its purpose is less aesthetic than scientific and academic. It is used extensively for exploring and teaching about the medicinal use of plants. Its location near the river ensures a temperate climate and the survival of a wide range of plants. The garden is open to the public on a very limited basis, so be sure to check for times (summer 2000, it was Sundays, 1 to 6 P.M. and Wednesdays 12 to 5 P.M.). "Friends of the Garden" subscribers can visit all year and during greatly expanded hours. On visiting days, it is well worth catching onto a tour to hear more about the garden's history and unique plants.

— Clare Parmalee

Shops, Restaurants, and Pubs

For most folks, Chelsea means the present not the past, the latest fashions, trendiest restaurants, and chic wine bars. Today's Chelseaite strolls down King's Road sleekly dressed with cell phone handy to catch the latest gossip or appointment. King's Road has been a fashion center since the 1960s. Leading chain stores and one-off boutiques occupy spaces that once provided hardware, groceries, and dry goods to the old neighborhood. Shops, restaurants, and coffee bars run the entire length of the street from Sloane Square to World's End, broken only by the Old Town Hall and library in the middle. We will only mention a few distinctive establishments. Peter Jones, famous for housewares, anchors the east end. Along the way west, you will find a great kids' department store, Daisy and Tom (181); a vintage designer/jewelry store, Steinberg and Tolkien (193); and more women's ware, men's ware, and shoe stores than you can count. Antiquarius at 131–141 houses over 100 antique dealers. They specialize in jewelry, silver, and small items rather than furniture. The most rewarding experience on King's Road is people watching, so grab a latte at a sidewalk table and catch a slice of modern Chelsea life.

If you take Markham Street north off King's Road and walk one block, you will come to the intersections of Cale, Elystan Street, and Elystan Place. The corner is called Chelsea Green, and here you will find a small shopping enclave that will fill the needs of any temporary London apartment dweller. There is Frys, an award-winning greengrocer, Chelsea Fishery (we saw a toddler making friends with a very large crab), the Pie Man with sweet and savory traditional pies, and Maison Blanc, full of too-tempting French breads and pastries made fresh each day with French flour, no less. Finns of Chelsea Green, a delicatessen, adds class to take away. At Finns the emphasis is on foods to go made with high-quality ingredients. What's available varies from day to day, but there are always fish, meat, chicken, and vegetable dishes. Chelsea Green also has a fine butcher, Jago's, and a wine shop, Jeroboams. Convenient for our stay at Nell Gwynn House, we shopped at all of these stores, especially Finns—a lifesaver on a busy day.

In the unique Michelin House (you will see the puffy Michelin tire boy on top) at 81 Fulham Road is the Bibendum Crustacea and Fishmonger. Fresh oysters are the specialty, but a range of shell and fin fish is carried in season. Cooked lobsters are on sale on Saturdays. If you want a snack or light meal, step into the adjacent Bibendum Oyster Bar and enjoy the striking tiles with antique race cars on all the walls.

At 350 King's Road is the Bluebird Foodstore. A former garage and member of the Conran chain, Bluebird has everything—cheeses, fish, organic fruits, vegetables, and meats, cooked items ready to eat at home, wines, breads and pastas made each day, a restaurant (too crowded to get into), and a cafe. An outdoor fruit, vegetable, and flower market decorates the entrance. The huge crimson calla lilies enticed us right into the shop.

Rococo (321 King's Road) is a small shop full of chocolate for baking or eating. It makes its own label candies from the best-quality Valrhona Grand Cru chocolate and sells them as bars or in beautifully made up packages.

If you feel a little homesick and crave a taste of American, head to the Blue Cactus at 86 Fulham Road (0207-823-7858). Comfort yourself with margaritas, chimichangas, and other well-prepared Tex-Mex fare (entrees, $16 to $23). Or try Italian tapas at Riccardo's (0207-370-6656) farther down Fulham Road at 126. Sample salads, pastas, and pizzas, all in appetizer-size servings. For Indian, at 257–259 Fulham Road is Zaika (0207-351-7823; entrees, $16 to $22), selling traditional dishes with an innovative twist in an elegant setting.

Back at Chelsea Green is Elistano at 25–27 Elystan Street (0207-584-5248), an Italian trattoria with good food and good prices (two courses and a drink for $29).

Book early. It's popular. Around the corner at 3 Bray Street, try Creelers (0207-838-0788) for the very freshest Scottish fish and seafood (entrees, $19 to $29).

If you're near the Thames and Thai appeals, there is the Busabong Tree at 112 Cheyne Walk (0207-352-7534; entrees, $12 to $25). Menu choices are many and the setting with a waterfall and carp pool is cool and refreshing.

There are several good food pubs in and around Chelsea. Cooper's Arms (87 Flood Street) is a modern pub with small tables for dining along two walls. Sunday lunch is a good time to go, but get there before all the specials, written on a blackboard, are sold out. If you like spicy, try the Thai fish cakes.

Surprise, a reconstructed older pub at 6 Christ Church, just off Flood Street near the Cooper's Arms, also attracts many locals with food more imaginative than the usual pub grub.

At 35 Church Street is the Front Page. It's a modern pub with interesting and well-prepared food. The soups are especially tasty on a damp and chilly London day.

See also the Admiral Codrington on the north fringe of Chelsea, described in the Kensington chapter.

A Walk in Chelsea

Our walk on a warm and sticky Saturday carefully avoided busy King's Road. First we looked in at a grand and upscale garden shop, the Chelsea Gardener. We knew we couldn't bring plants back to the United States, so it was safe to wander among its glorious flowers, impressive topiaries, and wide array of planters. Garden shops offer a handy education in what you see in public and private gardens around town, and this one carries a fine selection of seeds that you can bring home.

Next we crossed King's Road at Old Church Street to visit Chelsea Old Church. It isn't old now, but it was. A Norman church occupied the site from the 12th century. Its font comes from Thomas More, who rebuilt the south chapel for his family when he lived nearby. The most interesting relics in the church are the chained books given by Hans Sloane. Bombs in World War II destroyed much of the structure, so what you see today is a meticulous reconstruction.

Two blocks and several centuries away stands Thomas Carlyle's House, a typical Queen Anne townhouse that preserves an important chunk of the Victorian age. Thomas Carlyle and his wife lived there from 1834 until his death in 1881. The

National Trust has maintained the house as it was when Dickens, Thackeray, and such visited. From the parlor, where they entertained, to the attic study, where Carlyle wrote, you find the furniture, fixtures, books, and letters of the Carlyles and their era. Even the garden is planted with the trees and flowers they enjoyed. The chatty resident curator will happily elaborate on what you see.

We shed the heavy burden of history over lunch at the King's Head and Eight Bells, a couple of blocks down Cheyne Walk. The pub, built in early Victorian times, doesn't have much history, but its name does. In 1580 two pub licenses merged and with them the names. Then it was a sailor's pub: eight bells is quitting time in naval slang. Now it's a big, comfortable place that does a traditional Sunday lunch (roast beef and all the trimmings).

Following shady Cheyne Walk beside the river, we ended as we began, in a garden, the Physic Garden, and walked off our lunch behind a tour guide who described how to make corks from the massive cork tree on the grounds.

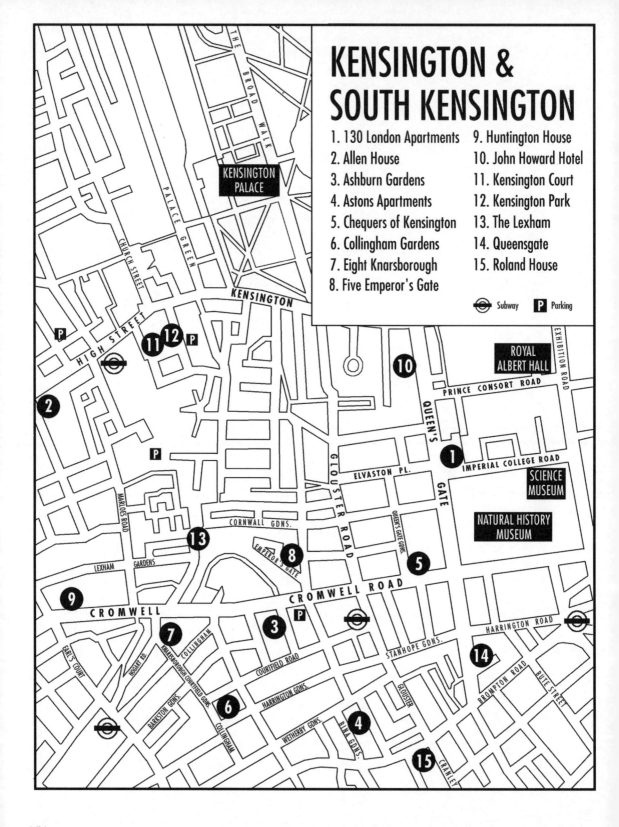

KENSINGTON & SOUTH KENSINGTON

1. 130 London Apartments
2. Allen House
3. Ashburn Gardens
4. Astons Apartments
5. Chequers of Kensington
6. Collingham Gardens
7. Eight Knarsborough
8. Five Emperor's Gate
9. Huntington House
10. John Howard Hotel
11. Kensington Court
12. Kensington Park
13. The Lexham
14. Queensgate
15. Roland House

Subway   P Parking

Chapter 9

Kensington and South Kensington

The borough contains two fashionable shopping streets, Church and the High Street. In adjacent South Kensington, museums are the attraction, most notably the Victoria and Albert (V and A) and the Natural History Museums on Cromwell Road. For music lovers, the Royal Albert Hall and Royal College of Music are here as well, along with a wealth of apartments, small hotels, and B and Bs in a wide range of prices. Two major underground stations provide ready access to the whole of the city and Heathrow. Kensington Palace, just west of Hyde Park, was the birthplace of Queen Victoria, and a handful of royals, including Princess Margaret, still call it home. The gardens and state apartments are open to visitors daily.

Kensington and South Kensington at a Glance

Apartment	Studio	1-Bedroom	2-Bedroom	3-Bedroom	Other
130 Queensgate No minimum stay	$205 n $1,363 w	$270 n $1,891 w	$347–$382 n $2,320–$2,542 w (1 or 2 baths)	$461 n $3,070 w (2 baths)	*Penthouse* $433 n $2,876 w
Allen House No minimum stay		$227–$255 n $1,588–$1,782 w	$324–$347 n $2,268–$2,430 w (2 baths)	$365–$393 n $2,552–$2,754 w (2 baths)	
Ashburn Gardens 1-week minimum		$130–$146 n $907–$1,021 w	$203–$227 n $1,418–$1,588 w (1 bath)		
Astons Apts. No minimum stay	$114–$305 n $760–$2,025 w				
Chequers of Kensington No minimum stay	$295 n $2,065 w	$333 n $2,332 w	$419 n $2,931 w		
Collingham Serviced Apts. No minimum stay refurbished unrefurbished	$146 n $1,021 w	$219 n $1,531 w	$292–$324 n $2,044–$2,268 w (1 or 2 baths)	$397 n $2,778 w	*Penthouse* $348–$421 n $2,436–$2,948 w
Eight Knaresborough Place 2-night minimum	$144–$209 n $1,008–$1,463 w	$160–$258 n $1,120–$1,806 w			
Five Emperor's Gate 2-night minimum	$177–$193 n $1,239–$1,351 w	$177–$258 n $1,239–$1,806 w			

Apartment	Studio	1-Bedroom	2-Bedroom	3-Bedroom	Other
Huntingdon House No minimum stay	$113–$186 n $714–$1,174 w	$154–$348 n $970–$2,194 w	$194–$534 n $1,225–$3,368 w	$308–$713 n $1,939–$4,491 w (2 baths)	*4-bedroom* $567–$851 n $3,572–$5,358 w (4 baths)
John Howard Hotel No minimum stay	$225 n $1,576 w	$274 n $1,916 w	$452 n $3,164 w		
Kensington Court No minimum stay	$135–$219 n $1,223–$1,395 w	$284 n $1,531 w	$389–$422 n $2,236–$2,683 w (2 baths)		
Kensington Park 1-week minimum, high season; 3 nights, low season	$138–$211 n $964–$1,474 w	$243 n $1,701 w	$316–$389 n $2,211–$2,722 w (2 baths)		
The Lexham 1-week minimum	$129 n $904 w	$320 n $2,237 w	$401 n $2,808 w (2 baths)		
Queensgate Apts. No minimum stay		$211–$243 n $1,296–$1,458 w	$389–$486 n $2,471–$3,159 w (2 baths)	$478–$648 n $3,078–$4,374 w (2.5 baths)	$607 n $4,050 w
Roland House No minimum	$296 n $2,065 w	$334 n $2,332 w	$420 n $2,931 w (2 baths)		

NOTES: (1) All prices are in American dollars converted at $1.62 to £1 and include VAT. To convert to the current rate, divide the dollar amount by 1.62 and multiply by the rate listed in today's local paper. (2) n=night; w=week.

Kensington and South Kensington Apartments in Detail

130 Queensgate, 130 Queensgate, London SW7 5LE

photo p. I

One Thirty Queensgate is just north of the intersection of Queensgate Road and Harrington Road. Walk two blocks to the South Kensington tube stop and just a bit farther to the Gloucester Road stop. South Kensington is convenient for the V and A, other museums, and Knightsbridge shopping.

The 54 flats on Queensgate Road occupy a large stone Victorian apartment block. There are 5 studios, 28 one-bedrooms, 13 two-bedrooms (6 small and 7 large), 4 three-bedrooms, and 4 two-bedroom penthouse flats. In each of the six types of flats, the layouts and furnishings are very similar. Kitchens and bathrooms are the same in all types.

The studios (maximum occupancy, two) are spacious with the sleeping area very well set off from the rest of the flat. The living/dining area contains a plush red sofa, coffee table, and chair. A small dining table and cabinet sit near the entrance. The sleeping alcove is large enough to accommodate twin beds with a table and lamp between. The bath is off the sleeping area and the small full kitchen is a separate room.

The one-bedroom sleeps two in the bedroom (double or twin beds—make your preference known at time of booking) and two in the living room, where one of the sofas opens into a double bed. The dining area is set off in a small alcove with the kitchen beside it.

Seven of the two-bedroom flats have sofa beds, so they can accommodate six people. The other six sleep a maximum of five.

The three-bedroom, two-bath apartment has two twin bedrooms. The master has a queen bed and full bath *en suite*. There is an additional bath with just a shower.

Every apartment contains a trouser press, ceiling fan, and safety deposit box, while only the penthouse flats have air conditioning.

Except for the second bath in larger apartments, all baths have tile floors, marblized tile walls, power shower with tub, bidet, sink, hair dryer, and toiletries.

All kitchens, even in studios, have full stoves, microwave ovens, and under-counter refrigerator/freezers. They are also well supplied with cookware, china, and other cooking necessities.

These apartments are a good buy for travelers who are willing to share space to be in a popular and convenient London neighborhood.

AMENITIES—Elevator, telephone (direct line in each bedroom), color satellite TV, radio, computer connection (will provide adapter), fax (through office), maid service (6 days a week), concierge/housekeeper (24 hours), refrigerator/freezer, stove, toaster, tea kettle, teapot, coffee maker, iron (on request), microwave, hair dryer, toiletries, welcome pack.

RESERVATIONS/PRICES/MISC.—**Minimum stay:** 1 night. **Reservations:** office staff. **Telephone:** 0207-581-2322. **Fax:** 0207-823-8488. **E-mail:** *onethirty@compuserve.com*. **Web site:** *www.onethirty.co.uk*. **Prices from:** studios-$205 per night, $1,363 per week; 1 bdrm-$270 per night, $1,891 per week; 2 bdrm, 1 or 2 bath-$347 per night, $2,320 per week; 3 bdrm, 2 bath-$461 per night, $3,070 per week; penthouse-$433 per night, $2,876 per week. **Negotiate price?** yes, corporate and group discounts. **Deposit?** yes. **Check in:** 2 P.M. **Check out:** noon. **Credit cards?** Access, Visa, Amex, Diners. **Tube stop:** Gloucester Road.

Allen House, Allen Street, Kensington, London, W8 6BH

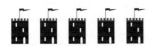

photo p. I

In an ideal location half a block off Kensington High Street, Allen House is an Edwardian mansion block on a charming street of other Edwardian houses. Even in January the palm trees and evergreens in the front garden provide a bright and warm welcome. Guests can also enjoy a larger garden in back. Winner of the RCI's Resort of International Distinction Award again in 2001, Allen House's 44 apartments offer stylish accommodation at a cost that is reasonable in this pricey neighborhood.

Since they were totally occupied, we were able to visit only one of the one-bedroom apartments. Although it was the smallest flat at Allen House, we were impressed with its spaciousness and the restful view of the back garden from windows in each room. Entry is through a hallway with bathroom just to the right. The bedroom, directly opposite the entrance, has a zip-and-link king bed that can be separated into twins on request. There are two bedside tables with reading lamps, a dressing table with chair, and a closet that runs the length of the wall.

The living/dining area is traditionally furnished with two overstuffed sofas, an easy chair, tables, and a cabinet for curios and china. A round dining table with four chairs is at the other end of the room, conveniently next to the kitchen entrance.

In the kitchen, which can be closed off, is a full-size refrigerator/freezer, full-size stove, washer/dryer, dishwasher, and sink that overlooks the garden.

Even on a gloomy winter day, the large windows give plenty of light. Crown molding throughout reinforces the overall impression of Edwardian elegance.

All two- and three-bedroom apartments have a washer/dryer, while only some one-bedrooms do. A few apartments are equipped with dishwashers. Management supplies washing-up liquid, or the maids will do dishes for an extra charge.

These apartments are among the loveliest that we saw in London. It is clear why so many return visitors make Allen House their London home.

AMENITIES—Elevator, telephone, color cable TV, radio, computer connection through telephone, fax (through office), maid service (Monday–Friday), resident porter, refrigerator/freezer, stove, toaster, tea kettle, teapot, coffee maker, iron, microwave, dishwasher (in a few flats), washer/dryer (in larger flats), hair dryer (on request at no charge), toiletries, welcome pack.

RESERVATIONS/PRICES/MISC.—**Minimum stay:** 1 night. **Reservations:** Annie. **Telephone:** 0207-938-1346. **Fax:** 0207-938-4142. **E-mail:** *annie@allenhouse.co.uk*. **Web site:** coming soon. **Prices from:** 1 bdrm-$227 per day, $1,588 per week; 2 bdrm, 2 bath-$324 per day, $2,268 per week; 3 bdrm, 2 bath-$365 per day, $2,552 per week. **Negotiate price?** check with Annie. **Deposit?** credit card information. **Check in:** 2 P.M. **Check out:** 11:30 A.M. **Credit cards?** all major. **Tube stop:** Kensington High Street.

Ashburn Gardens, 3–4 Ashburn Gardens, South Kensington, London SW7 4DG

photo p. I

The 25 one- and two-bedroom apartments of Ashburn Gardens are in an 18th-century brick townhouse. Two blocks to the Gloucester Road subway stop, the flats are also within walking distance of Albert Hall, the Natural History Museum, and the Victoria and Albert Museum.

These 18 one-bedroom and 7 two-bedroom flats have consistently received a "three keys, commended" rating from the British Tourist Authority. All of the kitchens and bathrooms were completely redone in 2000, giving them a three-plus rating from us.

The apartments are comfortably furnished but not fancy. They are scrupulously clean and all are repainted every three years. Susan Coavey, the friendly resident housekeeper, and her husband, Jimmy, work around the clock to keep Ashburn Gardens in tip-top shape and to help guests in all ways possible.

The one-bedroom apartments open into a small hallway with the bath off to the left. The living/dining room has an upholstered sofa and chair in a floral pattern with matching drapes and ceiling border. There are coffee and end tables with reading lamps, and a dining table with four chairs. The kitchen is a separate room behind the dining table. The bedroom has twin beds (all are zip-and-link) with table and reading lamps or wall lamps, dresser with mirror, and color-coordinated spreads and curtains.

Two-bedroom flats also open into a hallway with the kitchen immediately to the left and the bath across from the entrance. The living/dining area is furnished like the one-bedroom. Both bedrooms have twin zip-and-link beds, tables with reading lamps, and a dresser. While the second bedroom is smaller, it is still a comfortable size with large windows.

All of the baths are sparkling clean and shiny new. They are carpeted and have white tile walls, a power shower/tub, and heated towel racks. Bath linens are changed every other day.

Kitchens are also carpeted and have full-size stove, under-counter refrigerator, microwave, and good counter and cabinet space.

Each flat has good storage space and a video entry phone for safety. They do not have washer/dryers, but there is a laundry just across the street. A large supermarket is two blocks away.

Children are very welcome at Ashburn Gardens. According to Susan Coavey, they especially enjoy the lower-level flats, which allow them easy access to the outdoors and neighborhood parks. She also encourages guests to ask for anything they need during their stay.

AMENITIES—Elevator, telephone, color cable TV, radio (on request), computer connection through telephone, fax (through office), maid service (Monday–Friday), resident housekeeper, refrigerator/freezer, stove, toaster, tea kettle, teapot, coffee maker, iron, microwave, hair dryer (on request), welcome pack.

RESERVATIONS/PRICES/MISC.—**Minimum stay:** 1 week. **Reservations:** office staff. **Telephone:** 0207-370-2663. **Fax:** 0207-370-6743. **E-mail:** *info@ashburngardens. co.uk*. **Web site:** *www.ashburngardens.co.uk*. **Prices from:** 1 bdrm-$907 per week; 2 bdrm-$1,418 per week. **Negotiate price?** no. **Deposit?** 50% of total fee. **Check in:** 2 P.M. **Check out:** 11 A.M. **Credit cards?** Visa and MasterCard. **Tube stop:** Gloucester Road.

Astons Apartments, 31 Rosary Gardens, London SW7 4NH

photo p. J

On a quiet residential street off Old Brompton Road in South Kensington, three adjoining Victorian townhouses hold the 54 studios of Astons Apartments. All have been carefully restored, and those in back have a pleasant view of the garden. The Gloucester Road tube is nearby and Kensington's museums but a few blocks away. All of the studios were refurbished and modernized in 1996, so that all now have *en suite* bathrooms and color-coordinated curtains and bedspreads. Prices are determined by number of occupants (from one to four) and how luxurious the studios are. The largest studios with the most amenities are called "designer studios," and are for one or two people.

Maximum occupancy in the least expensive and smallest studio is one person. Two people would feel uncomfortably crowded in these tiny flats. The baths are especially cramped with room for only a toilet, sink, and curtain-enclosed shower, the curtain brushing against the toilet.

More comfortable, but still small, are the studios for two. Number 22, the one we visited, is appealing with its dining table placed in front of floor-to-ceiling bay windows. It has twin beds, tables with reading lamps, a sofa, a kitchen behind doors, and a bath with glass-enclosed shower and heated towel rack. The galley kitchen lacks an oven but has two burners, a microwave, under-counter refrigerator, and the necessary plates, glasses, and cutlery.

The studios for four have twin beds and a sofa bed, dining table with four chairs, bath with enclosed shower, and full separate kitchen that has a stove with four burners.

Designer studios are more luxurious, of course. Number 20 has two windows over the private garden, a queen-size bed, a dining table and chairs, and a complete kitchen. The bath includes a marble shower, a hair dryer, robes, and a trouser press.

Astons Apartments are compact, efficient, newly refurbished, and attractive. They are in a quiet street yet provide easy access to the rest of the city. The young staff are eager to help and enthusiastic about Astons and its plans for expansion.

AMENITIES—Elevator (none), telephone, color satellite TV, radio, computer connection, fax (through office), maid service (7 days a week), office open 8 A.M.–9 P.M. (on call 24 hours), refrigerator/freezer, stove (in some), toaster, tea kettle, teapot, coffee maker, iron, microwave, hair dryer (in some), robes (in some).

RESERVATIONS/PRICES/MISC.—**Minimum stay:** 1 night. **Reservations:** office staff. **Telephone:** from U.S., toll-free, 1-800-525-2810; in UK, 0207-590-6000. **Fax:** 0207-590-6060. **E-mail:** *sales@astons-apartments.com.* **Web site:** *www.astons-apartments.com.* **Prices from:** studios for 1-$114 per night, $760 per week; studios for 2-$162 per night, $1,076 per week; studios for 3-$229 per night, $1,519 per week; studios for 4-$305 per night, $2,025 per week; designer studio-$229 per night, $1,519 per week. **Negotiate price?** 5% for Internet booking and corporate discounts. **Deposit?** yes. **Check in:** noon. **Check out:** 11 A.M. **Credit cards?** all major. **Tube stop:** Gloucester Road.

Chequers of Kensington, 58–66 Cromwell Road, London SW7 5DA

photo p. J

If you've ridden a taxi from Heathrow to central London, you've probably passed by Chequers of Kensington. Its white facade covers half a block of Cromwell Road, which is also the A 4 motorway to the West Country. The new owners, Central Apartments, completely renovated the old Victorian block to make 78 apartments designed especially for the business traveler.

Outside, one finds a typical 19th-century front with pillared doorways and generously detailed bay windows. Inside, the lobby, hallways, and ceilings throughout retain their ornate plaster moldings, yet the apartments themselves are all sleek, streamlined efficiency—hardwood floors, plain white or deep-pastel walls, birch-colored venetian blinds instead of fussy window drapes, and the latest in high-tech fixtures. Most of the flats are studios for two but no more. The smallest measures about 12 by 15 feet. Only the ceiling measurements are large, since the renovation altered neither them nor the strikingly tall bay windows.

Kitchens are fitted efficiently with quality microwave/toaster combinations but not designed for elaborate cooking. When not in use, they are closed off behind folding doors. There are no full ovens, but burner units are available on request.

Bedrooms are small but offer generous queen- or king-size zip-and-link beds that can be separated into twin beds. Reading lamps are wall-mounted and there are bureaus and wooden wardrobes.

Living areas all contain useful office features, including a desk, telephone with fax, and answering machine, and all have full Internet access in the rooms. A keyboard attached to the TV uses the screen as a monitor. Thirty cable channels are available as well. In the smallest studio, in addition to the bed there are an easy chair and a dining table with four chairs. Every flat has a one-person sleep sofa.

All baths have power showers/tubs with marbleized sinks and counters. Housekeeping changes towels and bed linens every three days.

Although Chequers looks first to business travelers, it has one- and two-bedroom flats that would be fine for a family. One particularly appealing design is a two-bedroom in which the loft overlooking the living area becomes the second bedroom. The loft is tiny but cleverly designed and with sufficient privacy for a teenager traveling with parents.

Cromwell Road, which fronts the building, carries a heavy volume of traffic night and day, so the owners have triple-glazed all the front windows to seal out the noise.

Chequers is a good example of the newest type of accommodation styled for the modern visitor: sleek, efficient, and high-tech.

AMENITIES—Elevator, telephone, color satellite TV, radio, computer connection and monitor, fax (in flat), maid service (7 days a week), concierge/housekeeper, refrigerator/freezer, toaster, tea kettle, teapot, coffee maker, iron, microwave, washer/dryer (in basement), hair dryer, welcome pack (at extra charge).

RESERVATIONS/PRICES/MISC.—**Minimum stay:** 1 night. **Reservations:** office staff. **Telephone:** from U.S., toll-free, 1-888-847-5780; in UK, 0207-969-3555. **Fax:** 0207-969-3501. **E-mail:** *reservations@chequershotel.com*. **Web site:** *www.chequers hotel.com*. **Prices from:** studios-$295 per night; 1 bdrm-$333 per night; 2 bdrm-$419 per night. **Negotiate price?** yes, corporate discounts. **Deposit?** from $405. **Check in:** 2 P.M. **Check out:** 11 A.M. **Credit cards?** all major. **Tube stop:** Gloucester Road.

Collingham Serviced Apartments, 26–27 Collingham Gardens, London SW5 0HN

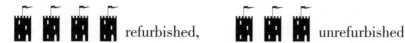 refurbished,  unrefurbished

photo p. J

Collingham Serviced Apartments are within the Kensington Conservation Area. Two adjoining Victorian townhouses with a distinctive tiled entrance and Romanesque double-arch front contain its 25 apartments. Minutes from the Gloucester Road tube stop and busy Cromwell Road, the apartments are on a quiet residential avenue with a large Sainsbury supermarket just around the corner.

New owners bought the property in 1999 and are renovating it from top to bottom. They also hired a new management team headed by John Farrell. Flats range in size from studios to three-bedroom, including two two-bedroom penthouses with balconies. Apartments at the back of the building have terraces. Each flat has a sofa bed.

You enter the one-bedroom via a short hallway with a dining alcove to the left and the kitchen visible through an archway immediately in front. The dining table comes with four chairs. The kitchen, like all kitchens at Collingham Apartments, is well equipped with a large refrigerator and separate freezer, full stove, and microwave. The living room has an upholstered sofa with two matching easy chairs, tables, lamps, and wall-to-wall carpeting. While not large, the master bedroom is comfortable with twin beds, side tables, dresser with mirror, and good closet space. Except for baths and kitchens, rooms have chair-rail and crown moldings.

The two-bedroom flats have one or two baths. In the one we visited, the living area is shaped like an L with the dining table and six chairs at the long end. The kitchen is beside the dining area and can be closed off. The master bedroom with bath *en suite* has zip-and-link twin beds, side tables, dresser, and wardrobe. The second bedroom also has twin beds with table and dresser. If there is a second bath, it is in the hall and is larger than the master bath.

In the three-bedroom flat, the living/dining area is smaller, furnished with sofa, easy chairs, and dining table. The kitchen is a separate room located off the hall. The master bedroom is good-sized with a king bed, table, dresser, and *en suite* bath. The second bedroom has twin beds, while the third is very small with only a single bed and desk. An additional bath is in the hall between the two smaller bedrooms.

All of the baths at Collingham Gardens are fully modern with power shower/tubs. Walls are white and blue tile. Guests receive new towels every other day.

Collingham Serviced Apartments offer very pleasant flats in a quiet residential area in the heart of Kensington.

AMENITIES—Elevator, telephone, color cable TV, radio, fax (through office), maid service (Monday–Saturday), concierge/housekeeper, refrigerator/freezer, stove, toaster, tea kettle, teapot, coffee maker, iron, hair dryer (on request with refundable deposit), welcome pack.

RESERVATIONS/PRICES/MISC.—**Minimum stay:** 1 night. **Reservations:** John Farrell. **Telephone:** 0207-244-8677. **Fax:** 0207-244-7331. **E-mail:** *reservations@collingham apartments.co.uk*. **Web site:** *www.collinghamapartments.com*. **Prices per night from:** studios-$146; 1 bdrm-$219; 2 bdrm, 1 bath-$292; 2 bdrm, 2 bath-$324; 3 bdrm, 2 bath-$397; penthouse-$348. **Negotiate price?** yes. **Deposit?** 25% of total. **Check in:** 2 P.M. **Check out:** noon. **Credit cards?** all major. **Tube stop:** Gloucester Road.

Eight Knaresborough Place, London SW5 0TG

photo p. J

If maid service six days a week at a moderate price is your idea of a dream vacation, then Eight Knaresborough Place is the spot for you. Eleven of the 12 studios sleep at least four, and some can handle five. Since these apartments are priced by the flat rather than number of occupants, they work well for families on a budget who enjoy togetherness. Another benefit for travelers with young children is the washer/dryer in the basement that tenants may use.

Eight Knaresborough Place is a white-stone Victorian converted into apartments. It has no elevator, so if stairs are a problem (and with five levels the upper story is quite a climb), be sure to ask for a flat on the ground floor. On the other hand, prices decrease as one goes up the stairs.

With the exception of one studio, all apartments are equipped with a double bed and a double sleep sofa. In studios, the double bed is concealed in the wall (a Murphy bed) and is easily tucked away during the day for a comfortable living space. As is often the case in a conversion, the apartments have different configurations and vary in size and amenities. The brochure provides helpful details, including dimensions and floor plans.

Although small, the living/dining area of the lower-level one-bedroom is comfortably furnished. There is an upholstered sleep sofa with matching easy chair, side tables with reading lamps, a coffee table, and a tiny round dining table with four chairs at the end of the room near the kitchen alcove. The kitchen has white tile backsplashes, a tile floor, a full stove with four burners, a sink, cabinets, and an under-counter refrigerator. The small bedroom off the hallway holds a double bed with blue headboard and matching spread, a bedside table, and a wardrobe. The reading lights are on the wall above the bed. The bath is opposite the bedroom with white-tiled walls and tub with shower attachment.

The ground floor apartment is larger. The living/dining area is carpeted in blue with coordinated blue sleep sofa and easy chair. There is seating for four at the square dining table. A kitchen alcove with stove, under-counter refrigerator, and cabinets is near the entrance end of the room with the bath behind it.

Furnishings at Eight Knaresborough Place are modest, and some are showing their wear. Unfortunately, some of the lower-level, darker flats also have dark furnishings. Still, it is a welcoming place, and staff are uniformly helpful and friendly.

AMENITIES—Elevator (none), telephone, color TV, computer connection through telephone, fax (through office), maid service (6 days a week), night porter, refrigerator/freezer, stove, toaster, tea kettle, teapot, coffee maker, iron, microwave, washer/dryer (laundry in basement), welcome pack.

RESERVATIONS/PRICES/MISC.—**Minimum stay:** 2 nights. **Reservations:** Polly or Robert Arnold. **Telephone:** 0207-244-8409. **Fax:** 0207-373-6455. **E-mail:** *info@apartment-hotels.com.* **Web site:** *www.apartment-hotels.com.* **Prices from:** studios-$144; 1 bdrm-$160. **Negotiate price?** yes, discount for Internet booking. **Deposit?** 2 nights' rent. **Check in:** 2 P.M. **Check out:** 11 A.M. **Credit cards?** all major. **Tube stop:** Earl's Court.

Five Emperor's Gate, London SW5 0TG

photo p. J

Emperor's Gate is a quiet cul-de-sac off busy Cromwell Road. Number five is a Victorian, former private residence converted to six flats, four studios and two one-bedroom.

There is no elevator in this five-story building, so prices decrease as one goes upstairs. This makes the fifth-floor one-bedroom flat a good buy ($177) for a family of healthy climbers since prices are per flat. The sofa opens into a double bed, true of all the sofas at Five Emperor's Gate. Maid service is six days a week. Minimum stay is two nights.

The most expensive apartment at Emperor's Gate is a one-bedroom on the lower level ($258 per night). It has a separate entrance down the steps behind the wrought-iron fence. Although it is below ground, the apartment gets plenty of light from large windows in the living/dining area. You enter from the outside into a small foyer leading to the small kitchen. Blond cabinets and white tile backsplashes give it a fresh look. It contains a full-size stove with four burners, an under-counter refrigerator/freezer, and sufficient pots, pans, china, and cutlery for four. A microwave is available upon request. The living/dining area opens off the kitchen with a glass dining table next to it. The main room is large with pale-pink walls, ceiling moldings, and two tall wooden closets on either side of a small fireplace. The wall-to-wall carpet is a light blue and the sofa bed a darker blue. There are two additional chairs, end tables with reading lamps, and a coffee table. A tiled bath with tub/shower is off the living room, and the bedroom is off the back. The bedroom disappoints: it is a tiny wedge with barely enough space to hold twin beds at right angles to each other, a table with mirror, a wooden chair, and a window. The bedroom of the apartment on the fifth floor is much larger, with room for twin beds and an easy chair.

The studios on the main level retain the amenities of the original building—tall ceilings and windows, ornate moldings and friezes, and fireplaces. A double bed is concealed in the wall, and there is a double sofa bed, an additional chair, a dining table, and a fireplace. Baths have a tub/shower. In larger studios, the kitchen has a full-size stove with four burners. In smaller studios, all cooking equipment is behind cabinet doors. When opened, the doors reveal a sink, two burners, and an under-counter refrigerator; above this are shelves that hold a microwave and china and glassware for occupants.

Five Emperor's Gate is owned and managed by the Arnolds, who also own Eight Knaresborough Place. They are family-friendly and have many repeat visitors, especially Americans. Daily newspapers are delivered free of charge.

AMENITIES—Elevator (none), telephone, color TV, computer connection through telephone, fax (in office), maid service (6 days a week), refrigerator/freezer, stove (some), toaster, tea kettle, teapot, coffee maker, iron, microwave, welcome pack.

RESERVATIONS/PRICES/MISC.—Minimum stay: 2 nights. **Reservations:** Robert or Polly Arnold. **Telephone:** 0207-373-0323. **Fax:** 0207-373-6455. **E-mail:** *info@ apartment-hotels.com.* **Web site:** *www.apartment-hotels.com.* **Prices per night from:** studios-$177; 1 bdrm-$177 (5th floor), $258 (lower level). **Negotiate price?** yes. **Deposit?** 2 nights' rent. **Check in:** 2 P.M. **Check out:** 11 A.M. **Credit cards?** all major. **Tube stop:** Gloucester Road.

Huntingdon House, 200–222 Cromwell Road, London SW5 0SW

photo p. K

Located on the border between South Kensington and Earl's Court, Huntingdon House has some of the characteristics of both neighborhoods. It is a well-kept and imposing redbrick building on central Cromwell Road typical of Kensington. Its lobby is tall and spacious, yet simple with the plainer decor one might expect in down-to-earth Earl's Court.

Huntingdon House's 52 apartments range from studios beginning at $113 per night ($714 per week) to a five-bedroom, five-bath, air-conditioned penthouse ($567 per night; $3,572 per week). Prices for the one-, two-, and three-bedroom apartments in between vary according to location and amenities; flats on the upper floors and in the back are more expensive.

Studios are large and provide good separation between the living and sleeping area. Entry is into a small foyer with the L-shaped kitchen immediately to the right, a half wall with closet ahead, and a sitting area with two easy chairs and table. The room also contains a double bed, a small dining table next to the window, and, in their own alcove, a sofa and coffee table. Wall-to-wall carpeting, sofa, bedcovers, and drapes are in blues and reds. A large bath with tub and shower attachment, bidet, and hair dryer are off the alcove. The kitchen has an under-counter refrigerator, a stove with four burners, and basic pots, pans, china, and cutlery.

In the one-bedroom apartment, in addition to the sofa and three chairs, a dark-glass dining table for four stands in the corner near the door. Two floor-to-ceiling windows give plenty of light. The large kitchen comes with full-size refrigerator/freezer (under-counters are only in studios), stove, microwave, washer/dryer, and lots of good-quality pots, pans, and tableware. Tiled in dramatic black, the bath has a beige tub/shower, pedestal sink, and heated towel racks. The bedroom with double bed has two wardrobes and a dressing table with mirror.

The penthouse apartments, like Huntingdon House itself, are a combination of elegant spaces (high ceilings, mahogany trim, graceful stairways, intricate moldings) and dormitory-style sleeping arrangements in the "lesser" bedrooms. They are fine for families with kids or work groups where status is clearly defined or some do not mind being in a back room.

Best of all, Huntingdon House backs onto a one-acre garden. Guests may stroll there or enjoy the conservatory, a welcome respite from the clatter of Cromwell Road. Huntingdon House is also popular for its proximity to the Earl's Court Exhibition Center, especially during the January boat show.

AMENITIES—Elevator, telephone, color TV, radio, computer connection (through office), fax (through reception), maid service (Monday–Saturday), concierge/housekeeper, refrigerator/freezer, stove, toaster, tea kettle, teapot, coffee maker, iron, microwave, dishwasher (in penthouse), washer/dryer (all flats second floor and up), hair dryer, toiletries, welcome pack.

RESERVATIONS/PRICES/MISC.—**Minimum stay:** 1 night. **Reservations:** Mimi Bevins. **Telephone:** 0207-373-4525. **Fax:** 0207-373-6676. **Prices from:** studios-$113 per night, $714 per week; 1 bdrm-$154 per night, $970 per week; 2 bdrm-$194 per night, $1,225 per week; 3 bdrm, 2 bath-$308 per night, $1,939 per week; 4 bdrm, 4 bath-$567 per night, $3,572 per week; penthouse (5 bdrm, 5 bath)-$709 per night, $4,466 per week. **Negotiate price?** yes, 10% discount for 7 nights. **Deposit?** 50% of total. **Check in:** 2 P.M. **Check out:** noon. **Credit cards?** all major. **Tube stop:** Earl's Court. **Garage parking:** $32 per day, $194 per week.

John Howard Hotel, 4 Queens Gate, Kensington, London SW7 5EH

photo p. K

Three converted Victorian townhouses make up John Howard's 40 hotel rooms and 12 self-contained studios and apartments. Located on a tree-lined boulevard, it is within an easy walk of Kensington High Street's department stores and just a half block south of Kensington Gardens and Palace. Royal Albert Hall, the Natural History Museum, and the Victoria and Albert are all within a 10-minute stroll.

If you stay at John Howard, you may enjoy the privacy of your own apartment plus the benefits of a full-service hotel: a restaurant and bar off the lobby, 24-hour room service, maid service seven days a week, a full-time concierge, and catering for up to 45 guests. Apartments in the front of the building, some of which have balconies, overlook the trees of Queens Gate, while those in back have a view of a reconstructed stable mews with a restored Victorian pub. Each of the 12 flats is different.

The studio apartments have a sofa and an easy chair and a small dining table with two chairs. Against the wall beside the table is a desk. Opposite the sofa is a queen bed with headboard and cover in light floral pattern that matches the curtains on the two windows. The kitchen is a separate room, very attractive with glass-and-wood cabinets, under-counter refrigerator/freezer, stove, microwave, high-quality pots and pans, china and glassware for four, and ample counter space.

The two one-bedroom apartments we visited are quite different from each other. In one, the bedroom and kitchen are in a loft with the living room below. The loft with dining bar is decorated in a rustic style with oiled wooden beams. The bedroom has a queen bed.

The other one-bedroom is in the basement. (Don't automatically reject basement flats in Victorian buildings. They are often sunny with broad window wells, have private entrances, and are separated from the street by about four or five feet. Usually they are cheaper.) This flat has three floor-to-ceiling windows and two French doors—excellent light even on a rainy January day. It is comfortably furnished with sofa and easy chair, desk, dining table, and full kitchen at the far end of the living room. A plus for the flat is the patio just off the French doors.

The two-bedroom apartment opens from a small foyer with the bathroom at the far end, bedrooms to the right, and the living/dining room on the left. The master bedroom has a king bed, chair, dresser, double closet, and TV. The second bedroom has twin beds and two small closets. The living/dining area has sofa and matching chair with dining table near the kitchen.

Baths at John Howard have power shower/tubs, bidets, soaps, heated towel racks, and facecloths.

While the flats we saw are not as glamorous as the ones in John Howard's brochure, they are comfortable and complete. John Howard is a Best Western property and so offers discounts to AARP members and some American corporations. Book through Best Western for these discounts.

AMENITIES—Elevator, telephone, color satellite TV, radio, computer connection through telephone, fax (through office), maid service (7 days a week), concierge/housekeeper, refrigerator/freezer, stove, toaster, tea kettle, teapot, coffee maker, iron, microwave, dishwasher, hair dryer, toiletries, welcome pack (replenished daily).

RESERVATIONS/PRICES/MISC.—Minimum stay: 1 night. **Reservations:** Best Western in U.S. **Telephone:** 0207-581-3011. **Fax:** 0207-589-8403. **E-mail:** *johnhoward hotel@btinternet.com.* **Web site:** *www.johnhowardhotel.co.uk, www.bestwestern.com.* **Prices per night from:** studios-$225; 1 bdrm-$274; 2 bdrm-$452. **Negotiate price?** yes. **Deposit?** credit card information. **Check in:** 2 P.M. **Check out:** noon. **Credit cards?** all major. **Tube stop:** Gloucester Road.

Kensington Court, 51 Kensington Court, London W8 5DB

photo p. K

If you have the taste of an Oriental potentate, then Kensington Court may be just for you, because it was once a residence of the Aga Khan. This elegant brick Victorian townhouse with wrought-iron balconies stands on a tree-lined street near Kensington Gardens and Palace, and one block off Kensington High Street.

The house was converted to 11 apartments, from studios to two-bedrooms, and the present owners refurbished each one in the summer of 2001. Although modernized, the building retains the decorative details it originally held—high ceilings, crown moldings, cornices, and bay windows.

Three large windows light the studio we saw on the first floor. The room accommodates a double bed, sofa, and dining set for three. The kitchen is a separate room with an under-counter refrigerator, two burners, and a microwave that serves as both an oven and a grill. Pots and pans are plentiful and of good quality, as are china and cutlery. Decor is appropriate for the period of the building with fancy window treatments and coordinated colors and patterns.

The two-bedroom apartment opens onto a landing overlooking the flat. Down a short flight of steps is the living/dining room with the master bedroom off to the right, the kitchen, second bedroom, and bath down the hall. Three floor-to-ceiling windows, in a bay set off by full-length drapes, add drama and make the room feel spacious. A dining table with six chairs is in this area with a chest of drawers and an intricately plastered fireplace with marble inset along the wall. The sofa, which opens into a double bed, is opposite the fireplace. There are a matching easy chair and coffee table. The master bedroom has a queen bed, tables and reading lamps, and a closet. The kitchen is between the two bedrooms and has a full stove, wooden cabinets, and tiled counters. The smaller second bedroom holds twin beds, table, lamp, tiny dresser, and closet.

Baths are tiled and fully modern with a power shower/tub. Bath towels are large, and toiletries are supplied by management.

AMENITIES—Elevator, telephone, color satellite TV, radio, computer connection through telephone, fax (through office), maid service (Monday–Friday), concierge/housekeeper (on duty 8 A.M.–10 P.M.), refrigerator/freezer, stove (except in studios), toaster, tea kettle, teapot, coffee maker, iron, microwave, washer/dryer (in larger flats, laundry room in basement), hair dryer, toiletries, welcome pack.

RESERVATIONS/PRICES/MISC.—**Minimum stay:** 1 night. **Reservations:** office staff. **Telephone:** 0207-937-2030. **Fax:** 0207-938-5312. **E-mail:** *kencourt@btinternet.com*. **Web site:** *www.demon.co.uk/hotel-net/kcl.html*. **Prices from:** studios-$135 per night, $1,248 per week; 1 bdrm-$284 per night, $1,531 per week; 2 bdrm, 2 bath-$389 per night, $2,236 per week. **Negotiate price?** no. **Deposit?** credit card information and 25% of total. **Check in:** 2 P.M. **Check out:** 11 A.M. **Credit cards?** all major. **Tube stop:** Kensington High Street.

Kensington Park, 58 Kensington Court, London W8 5DG

photo p. K

You'll find Kensington Park on the same block as Kensington Court in a similar period building. Although the building is Victorian, its interior was constructed in a Georgian style replete with tall windows, wide hallways, high ceilings, crown and chair-rail moldings, wainscoting, and elaborate plasterwork in fireplaces and some ceilings.

The 14 flats include 8 studios, 1 one-bedroom, 4 two-bedroom, and 1 three-bedroom. The studio features three bay windows overlooking the garden square; these are treated with sheers and full-length red-velvet drapes with gold floral accents. The room is amply furnished with a double bed, dining set for four, sofa, and matching easy chair, but is rather small, so that the chair obscures the handsome fireplace. A separate room, the kitchen is well stocked with under-counter refrigerator, full stove, microwave, and washer/dryer.

The two-bedroom apartments open into a hallway. The living room is to the left and a long dining table is set in front of the three windows, with a desk immediately to its left and a sofa to its right. An elaborate fireplace is next to the desk. There are a TV and a CD player with CDs supplied. The kitchen separates the bedrooms from the living area, and has a large refrigerator and freezer (some two-bedrooms have only an under-counter refrigerator), stove, microwave, washer/dryer, and dishwasher. The master bedroom has a queen bed, lamp tables, dresser, and its own TV. The second bedroom also has a queen bed, as well as an *en suite* bath with shower. The other bath with tub and shower is in the hallway. All two-bedroom apartments have two baths.

As is typical for buildings of this period, the higher you go, the lower the ceilings and the smaller the windows. For more spacious and generously proportioned rooms, ask for an apartment on the first or second floor. Check on amenities, also, since they vary from flat to flat. All do have fireplaces.

AMENITIES—Elevator, telephone, color satellite TV, radio (on request), computer connection through telephone, fax (through office), maid service (Monday–Friday), concierge/housekeeper (9:30 A.M.–6:30 P.M.), refrigerator/freezer, stove, toaster, tea kettle, teapot, coffee maker, iron, microwave, washer/dryer, hair dryer, toiletries.

RESERVATIONS/PRICES/MISC.—**Minimum stay:** 3 nights, 7 in high season. **Reservations:** Bass. **Telephone:** 0207-937-2469. **Fax:** 0207-795-6215. **E-mail:** *info@ kensingtonparkapartments.com.* **Web site:** *www.kensingtonparkapartments.com.* **Prices from:** studios-$138 per night, $964 per week; 1 bdrm-$243 per night, $1,701 per week; 2 bdrm, 2 bath-$316 per night, $2,211 per week. **Negotiate price?** yes. **Deposit?** credit card information. **Check in:** 2 P.M. **Check out:** 11 A.M. **Credit cards?** all but Diners. **Tube stop:** Kensington High Street.

The Lexham, 32–38 Lexham Gardens, Kensington, London W8 5JE

   *photo p. K*

Two stately, stone-columned Victorian mansion houses make up the Lexham. On a quiet garden square, the Lexham is a short walk to the Gloucester Road tube and a few minutes more to the fashionable Kensington High Street.

All of the public areas of the Lexham are decorated with care and elegance in light, warm colors and wallpapers appropriate to the style of the building. The apartments themselves are spacious and feel more like private homes than flats. This impression is enhanced by views of the formal back garden with benches and chairs amid the greenery. Guests have exclusive use of the garden.

With space and garden, the Lexham's 30 one- and two-bedroom apartments are excellent for families, and they also provide up-to-the-minute services for the business traveler. Within each flat are a fax machine, computer connection, laser printer, voice mail, LCD with caller's number, and conference call facilities for five people.

While the flats are individually decorated, they are all in a traditional English country style. Entrance to each apartment is into a hallway. In Number 11, a one-bedroom, the living/dining area is to the left off the hall with the bedroom directly ahead. All bedrooms at the Lexham have an *en suite* bath, a king bed, bedside tables with reading lamps, matching drapes and bedcovers, and a large double window overlooking the garden. The living/dining room has two sofas, matching easy chair, mirror over an ornately plastered fireplace, and French doors onto a wrought-iron balcony. An oval dining table seating four is to the left of the fireplace. The kitchen contains a double sink, stove, microwave, large refrigerator/freezer, dishwasher, washer/dryer, and plenty of cabinet space.

Apartment Number 20, a two-bedroom at the front of the building, is especially appealing because of its large bay windows. A dining table sits in front of these windows with a view onto the square. The living area has two sofas, matching chair, and fireplace with topiary planting on either side. Bedrooms are at one end of the apartment with living/dining and kitchen at the other. The second bedroom has a double bed. There is a half bath in the hall.

All in all, these are elegant flats, beautifully furnished in an appropriate period style.

AMENITIES—Elevator (two), telephone (2 lines), color cable TV, computer connection through telephone, fax (in apartment), maid service (Monday–Friday), concierge/housekeeper, refrigerator/freezer, stove, toaster, tea kettle, teapot, coffee maker, iron, microwave, dishwasher, washer/dryer, hair dryer, welcome pack (replenished daily).

RESERVATIONS/PRICES/MISC.—**Minimum stay:** 1 week. **Reservations:** office staff. **Telephone:** 0207-559-4444. **Fax:** 0207-559-4400. **E-mail:** *reservations@lexham.com*. **Web site:** *www.lexham.com*. **Prices per week from:** studio-$904 (tiny, but with garden view); 1 bdrm-$2,237; 2 bdrm, 2 bath-$2,808. **Negotiate price?** yes. **Deposit?** yes. **Check in:** 2 P.M. **Check out:** 11 A.M. **Credit cards?** all major. **Tube stop:** Gloucester Road.

Queensgate Apartments, 115 Queensgate and 5 Manson Place, London SW7

   *photo p. K*

The two properties that make up the Queensgate Apartments are located on the fringe of South Kensington within easy walking distance of the shops and restaurants of Chelsea and Knightsbridge. The South Kensington tube stop is two blocks away. At 115 Queensgate, there are 15 one- to three-bedroom apartments, and at 5 Manson Place, there are 6.

Number 5 Manson Place is a stone and beige brick townhouse with balcony terraces for the apartments on the first floor (second floor for U.S. visitors). All of the Queensgate Apartments are quite large, but the ones on Manson Place, a quiet cul-de-sac around the corner, are slightly smaller. Even so, the flats on the first and second level are grand indeed. The living room of the two-bedroom apartment on the first has three floor-to-ceiling French doors that open onto the terrace. The walls are cream-colored with crown and chair-rail moldings. Persian rugs decorate the wall-to-wall beige carpeting. Two sofas, coffee tables, lamps, and a large dining table with six chairs complete the room. The master bedroom, bath *en suite,* runs the width of the flat and has two windows, queen bed, and ample closet space. A second bedroom is smaller but has windows, twin beds with table between them, and, again, plenty of closet space. A bathroom is across the hall.

Although it is on the lower level, the one-bedroom is well lit and comfortable. The living area has crown and chair-rail moldings, two small sofas, coffee table, and cabinet. The bedroom has a queen bed, two windows, a wardrobe, and an *en suite* bath.

All baths at Number 5 are completely modern with marbleized tile floor, power shower/tubs, tiled backsplashes, and large sinks with cabinets.

The kitchens are remarkable, more like American "country kitchens" than those in most flats. Cream-colored wooden cabinets line the walls and full ovens are built in. All have a full-size refrigerator/freezer, washer/dryer, and microwave. Each kitchen has a family-size breakfast table and chairs. Three-bedroom apartments have a dishwasher.

Number 115 is an impeccable white stone Regency mansion on a tree-lined boulevard with other similar houses. The refurbished apartments kept the high ceilings, tall windows, and some fireplaces of the original structure. The living/dining area is unusually large, open, and airy, providing elegant space for entertaining or just relaxing.

Even though the one-bedroom is again on the lower level, there are enough windows to provide good light. A leather sofa bed with matching easy chair furnish the living room. Down the hall, the bedroom has a queen bed with tables, lamps, and good closet space.

Two- and three-bedroom apartments are more lavishly decorated with elegant window treatments and crown, chair-rail, and other moldings. Living/dining areas have two upholstered sofas with matching chair, coffee table, and glass dining table for eight. The master bedrooms, bath *en suite,* have king beds, while second bedrooms have doubles. The two-bedroom has one full bath and a powder room.

The three-bedroom apartments all have two baths with an additional half bath and a dishwasher. The three-bedroom penthouse has a roof terrace.

The kitchens at 115 match the quality of those at 5 Manson Place and are even larger.

Baths are large with dark blue tiled floors, gray tiled walls, tubs with power showers, and hair dryers.

The Queensgate Apartments are spacious and elegant in the style of gracious times past. They provide an excellent and impressive setting for entertaining business clients or guests.

AMENITIES—Elevator, telephone, color satellite TV, computer connection, fax, maid service (Monday–Friday), resident housekeeper, refrigerator/freezer, stove, toaster, tea kettle, teapot, coffee maker, iron, microwave, washer/dryer, hair dryer, toiletries, welcome pack (at extra charge).

RESERVATIONS/PRICES/MISC.—**Minimum stay:** 1 night. **Reservations:** Manors and Co. **Telephone:** toll-free from U.S., 1-800-454-4385; in UK, 0207-486-5982. **Fax:** 0207-486-6770. **E-mail:** *enquiry@manors.co.uk.* **Web site:** *www.manors.co.uk.* **Prices from:** 1 bdrm-$211 per night, $1,296 per week; 2 bdrm, 2 bath-$389 per night, $2,471 per week; 3 bdrm, 2.5 bath-$478 per night, $3,078 per week; penthouse-$607 per night, $4,050 per week. **Negotiate price?** yes. **Deposit?** yes. **Check in:** 2 P.M. **Check out:** noon. **Credit cards?** all major. **Tube stops:** South Kensington, Gloucester Road.

Roland House, 121 Old Brompton Road, Kensington, London SW7

Central Apartments bought Roland House in 1999. Since then, the building has been completely gutted and reconstructed into 95 studio, one-, and two-bedroom apartments. Roland House is a listed building so changes to the exterior could only be cosmetic, while the inside, like other properties taken over by Central Apartments, is totally modern and high-tech. The new Roland House opened in summer 2001.

There are 78 executive studios, each one cleverly and efficiently constructed and each one just like all the others. Entry into the studio is into a small hallway. Built into the left side of the hall is the kitchenette with under-counter refrigerator/freezer, stove, microwave, and blond wood cabinets. At the end of the hall is the bath with gray tile floor, white tile walls, power shower/tub, heated towel rack, and hair dryer. The entrance to the main living area contains a built-in L-shaped desk with a TV suspended above. The desk holds a fax machine and telephone with modem and programable answering service. In the other corner on the same side of the room is a beige leather sofa that opens into a double bed. A cleverly designed dining table that can be raised for dining or lowered to become a coffee table centers the room. A wardrobe on one wall and a dresser on the other separate the living from the sleeping portion of the studio. Beyond the dresser is a queen-size bed with reading lamps on either side.

The one-bedroom is similarly furnished. The small bedroom has a queen bed, bedside tables with reading lamps, dresser, and closet. The living room is next off the hall and has a leather sofa, gray velvet easy chair, two desks, and an étagère with TV and stereo/CD player. A glass dining table for four faces the kitchen with its built-in oven, blond cabinets, under-counter refrigerator, microwave, and dramatic black extractor fan.

Standard in every apartment in Roland are a ceiling fan and a sofa bed in the living area, two desks, Venetian blinds rather than drapes, wooden floors with area rugs, and a computer modem. Some flats have a washer/dryer, but for those without one, there is a laundry room for guest use.

Roland House is just a five-minute walk from the Gloucester Road tube, and it is around the corner from many pubs, restaurants, and shops. Chelsea's boutiques and cafes are but a short walk to the east, and the Museum of Natural History and the Victoria and Albert are just a few blocks north.

If you prefer modern to traditional, and sleek suits you better than fussy, you will be very comfortable at Roland House. The location is great and the electronic facilities a boon for business travelers.

AMENITIES—Elevator, telephone, color satellite TV, radio, computer connection, fax (in flat), maid service (6 days a week), concierge/housekeeper, refrigerator/freezer, stove, toaster, tea kettle, teapot, coffee maker, iron, microwave, washer/dryer (in some; otherwise, laundry room available), hair dryer, toiletries, welcome pack (for extra charge).

RESERVATIONS/PRICES/MISC.—**Minimum stay:** 1 night. **Reservations:** office staff. **Telephone:** 0207-608-9111. **Fax:** 0207-608-9223. **E-mail:** *citypav@central-apartments.com.* **Web site:** *www.central-apartments.com.* **Prices per night from:** studios-$296; 1 bdrm-$334; 2 bdrm, 2 bath-$420. **Negotiate price?** yes. **Deposit?** credit card information. **Check in:** 2 P.M. **Check out:** 11 A.M. **Credit cards?** all major. **Tube stop:** Gloucester Road.

Kensington and South Kensington: Attractions

Kensington occupies a ridge of ground that rises above West London. Its slight altitude gave the area a healthful reputation, while the fertile soil in the vicinity made it an ideal market garden and orchard for the city to the east. William III, an avid gardener and asthma sufferer, purchased a local estate here in 1689 and had the ever-busy Christopher Wren reconstruct the house. Within a few years, the entire court moved to Kensington Palace, and by the mid-18th century, the village of Kensington was a thriving London suburb. Streets of new houses replaced the farms and market gardens in the 19th century, and in 1901 Kensington won the status of a "Royal Borough," owing to the fact that Queen Victoria was born and grew up in Kensington Palace.

Kensington Palace still contains apartments for various members of the royal family, but both the palace and its gardens are open to the public. Kensington itself prospers as a respectable residential and commercial center. Kensington High Street contains branches of most major London retail shops, while Kensington Church Street, which intersects it, runs more to antiques (Alfie's Antique Market) and bargain designer clothing.

On Holland Park Road, just off Kensington High Street, is one of the most unusual houses and museums in the borough, Leighton House. Lord Leighton built it as a showplace for his collection of Victorian and Islamic art. The fantastic Arab Hall re-creates a Moorish courtyard. Patterned tiles from Damascus and Cairo cover the walls, and a fountain rises from its mosaic floor. It's a unique treasure and free (11 A.M. to 5:30 P.M., Monday through Saturday).

South Kensington, an unofficial neighborhood between Cromwell Road and Fulham Road, is a solid middle-class residential area in the main with a distinctive cosmopolitan flair. The section around Harrington Road, for example, has a French flavor with a French-language school, patisserie, and French butcher nearby.

Museums dominate the eastern end of South Kensington, where it joins Knightsbridge. The Natural History Museum, Science Museum, and Victoria and Albert Museum share the neighborhood just north of the South Kensington tube station. Each is a day trip of its own, and all charge admission. The Victoria and Albert just opened 30,000 square feet of new British galleries devoted to British design from 1500 to 1900.

> **Hint:** Admission is free at the Victoria and Albert, Natural History, and Science museums an hour before closing.

Shops, Restaurants, and Pubs

"& Clarke's," 122 Kensington Church Street, should be your first stop for breads. It makes 35 kinds daily, including rosemary, rye, fennel, and its own shortbreads. The "&" refers to Sally Clarke's restaurant next door. The restaurant wins awards for its carefully prepared modern European food, but not for selection. At lunch there are a few choices, but at dinner there is one set menu. You can call ahead to see if it suits (0207-229-2190).

Aside from Sally Clarke's, your best choices in Kensington for price and quality are ethnic restaurants. On Kensington High Street (284), the Blue Lagoon's owner/chef prepares superb Thai cuisine in a pretty dining room complete with waterfall (0207-603-1231). Farther east at 20 Gloucester Road, Jacob's serves Armenian dishes (stuffed cabbage, tabouleh, poached chicken) in a rustic setting. If you, like us, haven't a clue about Armenian food, the dishes are on display at the entrance. Just point and it's yours at a modest price (entree, $8 to $11; 0207-581-9292). There is an updated Polish menu (venison, smoked salmon, beef with noodles) at Wodka, 12 Saint Alban's Grove near Jacob's and Gloucester Road. Meals are served in a wood-paneled dining room at $14 to $21 per entree (0207-937-6513).

We've enjoyed the French brasserie menu at Francofill, especially its steak frites and daily stew. Nothing fancy here, either in food or decor, but satisfying, moderately priced, and handy for the museums. It is just opposite the South Kensington tube at 1 Old Brompton Road.

Farther down Old Brompton Road, we can recommend a modern Belgian brasserie, Abbaye Brasserie, for both its *moule frites* (try the mussels with wine, shallots, and cream; $16 per kilo with frites) and the distinctive Belgian beers, Laffe Blond and Brun, or the fruity Krick.

There are plenty of pubs in the neighborhood but few that are worth going out of your way for. In Kensington proper, Scarsdale at Edward Square retains its 19th-century glass windows and fine old bar. It's also handy for Leighton House and close to Kensington High Street. The Churchill Arms (119 Kensington Church Street) displays memorabilia of the great leader in a traditional setting, but the dining room specializes in Thai food. The combination tells you a lot about contemporary London. South Kensington has a good neighborhood local, Blenheim at 27 Cale Street. You come for the beer here, brews from the small Dorset Badger Brewery, and to escape the trendy. Cale Street is on the edge of Chelsea, between the South Kensington tube and King's Road.

Much older than Blenheim and a few blocks west (above Fulham Road), find Anglesea Arms. It's been here since 1835, but, like many old pubs, the original separate rooms, or snugs, have been combined into one. Still, one snug survives, and there are no annoying game machines, jukeboxes, or even television to distract you from the varied ales on offer. It is one of the few "free houses" in the district (meaning it can sell any brew it likes, often from small, independent brewers). The Anglesea also serves excellent full meals in its restaurant downstairs.

Admiral Codrington borders three jurisdictions, South Kensington, Chelsea, and Knightsbridge, at 17 Mossop Street. It's both a convenient stop for a drink and a good choice for dinner. Codrington commanded the *Orion* at the battle of Trafalgar and lived in the neighborhood. The affluent 30-something clientele visit "Admiral Cod" more for its food and wine than the beer. It's a gastropub with excellent house wines selected by Berry Brothers and Rudd and with good modern cooking. Try the roasted cod specialty.

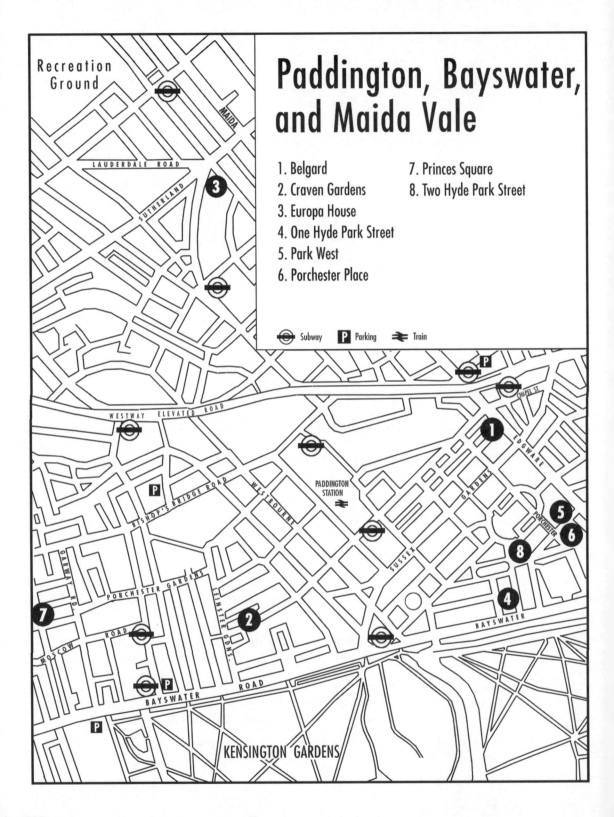

Paddington, Bayswater, and Maida Vale

1. Belgard
2. Craven Gardens
3. Europa House
4. One Hyde Park Street
5. Park West
6. Porchester Place

7. Princes Square
8. Two Hyde Park Street

Subway   P Parking   Train

Chapter 10

❧❧❧

Paddington, Bayswater, and Maida Vale

T his area covers three adjacent but very different neighborhoods. Paddington Station, famous for its intricate iron roof, links London to the West country and to Heathrow Airport with connections to major underground lines. Paddington serves commercial travelers and students with budget hotels and cafes, but little else. Bayswater, on the other hand, offers a mixture of apartment blocks, Victorian terraces, and elegant flats overlooking Hyde Park. It borders London's most famous antique market, Portobello Road in Notting Hill, where on Saturdays a mile of stalls sells everything from fine antiques and jewelry to junk.

Regent's Canal and the Westway (A 40 highway) separated Maida Vale from Paddington some time ago. It has blossomed into a prime residential neighborhood of Edwardian homes, well-kept apartment buildings, and shady streets. Lord's Cricket Ground and a lovely canal walk are nearby.

The differences in the three neighborhoods are reflected in the variety of apartments available. The least expensive are in Paddington near Edgware Road. Bayswater offers more and a good range of prices. Maida Vale has a stately apartment building especially suited for families. On the whole, this section of London is more residential and less expensive than other central areas, yet convenient to popular attractions.

Paddington, Bayswater, and Maida Vale at a Glance

Apartment	Studio	1-Bedroom	2-Bedroom	3-Bedroom	Other
Belgard 1-week minimum		$93–$150 n $648–$1,053 w			
Craven Garden Lodge 1-week minimum	$87–$104 n $608–$729 w	$127 n $892 w	$220–$255 n $1,539–$1,782 w (1 and 2 baths)		
Europa House No minimum stay		$194–$272 n $1,361–$1,905 w	$324–$395 n $2,268–$2,767 w		
One Hyde Park Street 1-week minimum			$200–$250 n $1,400–$1,750 w (2 baths)		
Park West 1-week minimum (Unrated)	$65–$94 n $455–$658 w	$94–$138 n $658–$966 w	$122–$219 n $854–$1,533 w	$178–$275 n $1,246–$1,928 w	
Porchester Place Indurrah Apts. No minimum stay			$251–$421 n $1,717–$2,916 w (2 baths)	$340–$583 n $2,349–$3,726 w (2 baths)	
Princes Square Apts. No minimum stay	$295 n $2,065 w	$333 n $2,332 w	$419 n $2,931 w		
Two Hyde Park Square 1-week minimum	$134–$156 n $941–$1,111 w	$167–$194 n $1,168–$1,355 w			

NOTES: (1) All prices are in American dollars converted at $1.62 to £1 and include VAT. To convert to the current rate, divide the dollar amount by 1.62 and multiply by the rate listed in today's local paper. (2) n=night; w=week.

Paddington, Bayswater, and Maida Vale Apartments in Detail

Belgard, P.O. Box 1026, London, W2 1QE

photo p. L

The Belgard, a brick, Victorian terraced house just off Edgware Road, contains four one-bedroom apartments. The flat we visited on the ground floor opens into a small foyer. The bedroom is in the rear of the flat and down a few steps. It's a small room but holds a queen-size bed, two bedside tables with lamps, and a radio. The room opens out onto a small terrace, neatly enclosed by the rest of the house.

Across the hall is the living/dining area, very comfortably furnished with a leather sofa with matching leather chair, several side tables, TV with satellite reception, VCR, and modern fireplace. Under a large window along the wall are a dining table and three chairs. All is carpeted except the hallway.

The kitchen, across from the living room, has light wood cabinets and white tile walls. The sink overlooks the terrace and provides a pleasant workspace. There is a convection oven with a stove-top, microwave, refrigerator, dishwasher, and washer/dryer.

Between the kitchen and living room is the bathroom. It is small but well designed with avocado-colored sink and tub with power shower.

While this flat is modest in size and in a neighborhood that is not glamorous, it is nicely furnished, sparkling clean, and freshly painted throughout. A folding bed is provided if a third person stays in the flat.

The Belgard is convenient to the Edgware Road tube and the many buses that run up and down Edgware Road. There is a bank on the corner, a Boots pharmacy next to it, and a large Safeway nearby.

The Belgard is one of the least expensive flats we found in London. The dishwasher and washer/dryer are unexpected luxuries at this price.

AMENITIES—Elevator (none), telephone, color TV, radio, refrigerator, freezer (small), stove, toaster, tea kettle, teapot, coffee maker, iron, microwave.

Reservations/Prices/Misc.—Minimum stay: 1 week. **Reservations:** Nili Reynish. **Telephone:** 0207-262-5273. **Fax:** 0207-402-7173. **E-mail:** *Nil.rey.apt@bigfoot.com.* **Price per week from:** 1 bdrm-$648 to $1,053 (max. occupancy, 3). **Negotiate price?** no. **Deposit?** yes. **Check in:** 2 P.M. **Check out:** 12 noon. **Credit cards?** yes. **Tube stops:** Edgware Road, Marylebone.

Craven Garden Lodge, Lero Properties, 24 Leinster Terrace, London W2 3ET

photo cover

Three short blocks from Bayswater Road, Hyde Park, and Kensington Gardens, Craven Garden Lodge provides a convenient location in a quiet residential neighborhood. Five minutes away is the Queensway tube stop, a direct line to Oxford Circus and the rest of London.

The 153 studios, one-, and two-bedroom apartments of Craven Garden Lodge are in a block of handsome white-stone townhouses constructed around 1900.

Each type of apartment comes in two price ranges—standard and superior. Superior apartments are larger, on lower floors, and the two-bedroom has two baths. Prices start at a low of $567 for a standard studio and go to $1,788 per week for a two-bedroom, two-bath apartment with patio. Each flat has a sofa bed for additional guests. All are bargains in the Bayswater area of London.

The rooms in the one-bedroom apartment are quite small but tastefully decorated in a traditional style. The living room, about 12 feet by 12 feet, contains a green sofa and two cushioned chairs in front of floor-to-ceiling windows. Across from the sofa is a dresser that holds the TV. A dining table with four chairs is in the corner. Carpeting is the same green as the sofa and chair cushions. Pink-and-white accent colors in the living room are carried over into the bedroom, which uses the same colors for drapes and bedcovers on the double bed. There are bedside tables with reading lamps and a closet. Although the room has little walking-around space, the tall window and light fabrics make it feel less confining. The tiny kitchen is equipped with a small four-burner stove, under-counter refrigerator, ample plates, cups, and saucers, and basic pots and pans. Some one-bedroom apartments have a washer/dryer. The bath has a beige tub with shower attachment and a heated towel rack.

The two-bedroom, one-bath apartment has a slightly larger living room with bigger sofa and chairs in a green floral fabric and a round dining table with six chairs. A narrow second bedroom has room for only twin beds on each wall and a table with lamp between them. Again, the tall windows and pleasant decor help to make up for the lack of space. A small but modern and sparkling clean bath separate the second bedroom from the master bedroom. The master bedroom has a double bed, side tables, wide windows, and a lovely marble fireplace. The kitchen is larger but still compact and has a full-size stove, and a washer/dryer—standard in all two-bedroom flats.

All two-bedroom, two-bath apartments are on the lower level. Even so, they are bright and each has its own patio off the living room in an inner courtyard. All rooms are larger. These flats have a separate entrance for more privacy and run the length of the building. Bedrooms are separated from the living area by a hallway.

Under the eagle eye of manager Hazim Shabout, the public areas and flats are kept shipshape with constant touch-ups and repairs as needed. Craven Garden Lodge apartments are small but a good buy in a good neighborhood.

AMENITIES—Elevator (none), telephone, color TV, computer connection through telephone, fax (through office), maid service (once a week), staff on duty (10 A.M.–6 P.M., Monday–Saturday), refrigerator/freezer, stove, toaster, tea kettle, teapot, coffee maker, iron, microwave, washer/dryer (in all 2-bedroom, some 1-bedroom).

RESERVATIONS/PRICES/MISC.—**Minimum stay:** 1 week. **Reservations:** Hazim Shabout. **Telephone:** 0207-402-7402. **Fax:** 0207-262-7179. **E-mail:** *lero@ cravenlodge.swinternet.co.uk.* **Web site:** *www.lero.co.uk.* **Prices per week from:** budget studios-$608; standard studio-$729; 1 bdrm-$892; 2 bdrm, 1 bath-$1,539; 2 bdrm, 2 bath-$1,782. **Negotiate price?** no. **Deposit?** $324 and up, depending on size of flat. **Check in:** 2 P.M. **Check out:** 11 A.M. **Credit cards?** none honored—payment by traveler's checks or cash. **Tube stop:** Queensway.

Europa House, 79a Randolph Avenue, London W9 1DW

photo p. L

Europa House sits beside a landscaped, three-acre garden in Little Venice, ideal for families whose children have energy to burn. It is a fashionable neighborhood interesting in and of itself. Regent's Canal, with its rows and rows of houseboats, is fun to explore and provides a lovely walk that can take you directly to Regent's Park, another wonderful place for children, and the site of the London Zoo. A five-minute walk from Europa House is the Maida Vale tube stop on the Bakerloo line, a direct route to Piccadilly Circus and West End theaters.

Europa House is a stately, white, marbled building in a row of similar elegant city houses. It was built as an apartment complex in 1990. To check in, guests go first to a sister property, Jerome House, near the Marylebone train station, where they are then transported by management staff to Europa House. Entry to the building is secured via a video phone system.

Europa House contains 2 one-bedroom and 12 two-bedroom flats within its four stories. Three flats on the ground level and two flats on the top floor have patios. All flats are equipped with at least one TV with satellite reception, VCR, stereo, clock-radio, direct-dial telephone, hair dryer, and trouser press.

All of the main rooms in the flats have a spacious, airy feel with garden views. Furnishings are modern. Since it was built as an apartment complex, all of the flats are decorated and equipped to the same high standard.

One-bedroom apartments enter into the living/dining area, some with floor-to-ceiling windows that overlook the garden. A comfortable sofa opens up into a double bed. Matching easy chairs, coordinated drapes, a coffee table, and a dining table for four complete the room. The kitchen, while smaller than in the two-bedroom, is well supplied and quite functional. The bedroom has a queen-size bed with built-in side tables. The marbled bathroom has a sink and tub with power shower.

The two-bedroom apartment is furnished in much the same way as the one-bedroom, but the kitchen is very large with a breakfast table at one end. All of the kitchens contain a convection oven, microwave, good-size refrigerator/freezer, dishwasher, and washer/dryer. All of the two-bedrooms have two baths. The second bedroom has twin beds.

Near Europa House are two of our favorite pubs. Crocker's Folly, a lovely spot for a traditional English Sunday lunch, and the Warrington, an elegant Victorian hotel and pub next door.

While Europa House is represented by several booking agencies, the best chance for a break in the rates is directly through the manager. That, of course, would depend on time of year and availability.

AMENITIES—Elevator, telephone, color TV with satellite, radio, maid service (Monday–Friday), concierge (live-in housekeeper), refrigerator, freezer (large), stove, toaster, tea kettle, teapot, coffee maker, iron, microwave, dishwasher, washer/dryer, hair dryer, toiletries, welcome pack.

RESERVATIONS/PRICES/MISC.—**Minimum stay:** 1 night. **Reservations:** Joanne Joyce. **Telephone:** 0207-221-1400. **Fax:** 0207-229-3917. **E-mail:** *westminsterapartments@ vienna-group.co.uk*. **Web site:** *www.vienna-group.co.uk*. **Prices per night:** 1 bdrm-$194–$272 (max. occupancy, 4); 2 bdrm-$324–$395 (max. occupancy, 6). **Negotiate price?** yes. **Deposit?** yes. **Check in:** 2 P.M. **Check out:** 11 A.M. **Credit cards?** yes. **Tube stops:** Maida Vale, Warwick Avenue.

One Hyde Park Street, London W2 3PF

photo p. L

The London Connection, based in Ogden, Utah, rents apartments and houses vacated by their owners. This two-bedroom, two-bath flat in the Georgian building at One Hyde Park Street is one of its exclusive properties. It is the London pied-à-terre of an owner who lives outside the city and only comes to town for special occasions.

One Hyde Park Street is an excellent location in a stylish neighborhood. It is near the shops of Oxford Street and yet just across the way from Hyde Park. A brisk walk across the park will take one to Knightsbridge.

Located on the ground floor, the apartment includes a glass conservatory and a terrace with seating. The entrance, equipped with a video entry phone for security, opens into the small end of a tiled, L-shaped hallway that runs the length of the flat. The master bath and bedroom are off one side of the L, with the living room off the other side. At the bottom of the hall, separated by the conservatory, is the second bedroom with bath, and the kitchen.

The living room is bright with windows, and cozy with comfortable seating and a working fireplace. It has two sofas, one of which becomes a double bed; an ottoman; shelves with decorative objects; and a TV with satellite reception, plus a radio and VCR.

The dining room is in the conservatory with a view through glass doors onto the terrace. It is a small space, sparsely furnished with two small, round, marble tables and three folding chairs—suitable for breakfast but not for more formal dining.

One of the pleasures of staying in a flat that is actually lived in is that the kitchens are usually very well stocked. This is certainly the case at One Hyde Park Street. China, glasses, and cookware are ample. Spices are in the spice rack! There are a refrigerator/freezer, gas oven, microwave, dishwasher, disposal, and washer/dryer.

The bedroom off the conservatory is small but quite suitable for one person. It has a single bed, bedside table, large wardrobe, telephone, window with a terrace view, and a startling painting on the wall. A small bath with mirror, sink, and shower is opposite the bedroom. The area can be closed off for privacy.

On the other side of the conservatory and up the hallway is the master bedroom. It is decorated in a Chinese motif with an ornately carved wardrobe, oriental prints on the wall, a queen-size bed with side tables and reading lamps, and a telephone. Next door is the master bath with sink, mirror, and tub with power shower.

AMENITIES—Elevator, telephone, color TV with satellite, radio, refrigerator, freezer, stove, toaster, tea kettle, teapot, coffee maker, iron, microwave, dishwasher, washer/dryer.

RESERVATIONS/PRICES/MISC.—**Minimum stay:** 1 week. **Reservations:** office staff. **Telephone:** toll-free from U.S., 888-393-4530, ext. 10. **Fax:** 801-621-4933. **E-mail:** *Sales@LondonConnection.com.* **Web site:** *www.londonconn.com.* **Price per week:** 2 bdrm, 2 bath-$1,400–$1,750 (max. occupancy, 5). **Negotiate price?** no **Deposit?** by credit card. **Check in:** 2 P.M. or by arrangement. **Check out:** 10 A.M. **Credit cards?** yes. **Tube stops:** Marble Arch, Baker Street.

Park West, London, W2 2QL

Unrated

There are more than 600 apartments in the eight-building complex that makes up Park West. Two hundred sixteen of them are available for short-term rental. When built in 1935, Park West was the height of fashion. Today it is somewhat faded but retains a luxurious lobby in red and gold and a uniformed doorman of earlier years.

All of the Park West apartments are owned and decorated by different individuals. That is the potential problem with Park West (hence, the "unrated" designation). Beyond a certain bare minimum of requirements (number of beds, plates, cups, glasses per occupant), management exerts little influence on the owners' choices. In some flats, economy seems to be the overriding principle. Since management cannot guarantee you a particular flat (it tries but cannot always accommodate), the flat you get is a matter of chance and availability. This is a shame, because Park West has some of the most reasonably priced flats that we found in London. They are clean with maid service twice a week. While their location is convenient, the area, lower Edgware Road, has become somewhat seedy.

The three apartments we visited are typical of the range of quality.

The studio flat is pleasant, comfortable, and modestly furnished. Entrance is into a small hallway with the kitchen on the left and the living/sleeping area in front. At one end, away from immediate view behind the kitchen, is a queen-size bed with bedside table and lamp. Built-in glass shelves run along one wall. A satellite TV sits on a mobile stand. The kitchen holds a small dining table with two chairs, a sink, an electric stove, and an under-counter refrigerator. The walls are nicely decorated with blue tiles, and there is a window overlooking the courtyard. For a studio, this is an efficient and agreeable use of space.

One enters the two-bedroom through a foyer. The living/dining area can be closed off by a glass door. The furniture is comfortable but old-fashioned, a dowdy purplish upholstered sofa, two matching easy chairs, an ottoman, a TV, and a coffee table. A modern glass dining table with seating for four is along the wall. The two bedrooms, both with twin beds, are minimally furnished. Beds have duvets but no bedskirts. In the master bedroom, there is one table with a small lamp between the two beds. The kitchen is a workable space with the sink in front of a window. There are an electric stove, counters, and an upright refrigerator/freezer.

The second two-bedroom we saw is more carefully furnished with matching chair and sofa, and three windows that give the room a cheery light. The dining table in front of a window has seating for six. The master bedroom has twin beds with a table with lamp between the beds, and a dresser. The other bedroom also has twin beds and a dresser with mirror. The kitchen is fitted much like the one-bedroom, simple but adequate.

All of the baths in the Park West are similar with a sink and tub/shower.

Concierge and check-in services are available 24 hours a day. Closed circuit television provides security. Safety deposit boxes are available in the office.

AMENITIES—Elevator, telephone, color TV with satellite (extra), fax (in office), concierge, refrigerator, freezer (small), stove with oven, toaster, tea kettle, teapot, coffee maker, iron, microwave.

RESERVATIONS/PRICES/MISC.—**Minimum stay:** 1 week. **Reservations:** Lesley. **Telephone:** 0207-724-1001. **Fax:** 0207-724-7592. **E-mail:** *info@parkwest.demon. co.uk.* **Prices per week:** studios-$455–$658 (max. occupancy, 2); 1 bdrm-$658–$966 (max. occupancy, 4); 2 bdrm: $854–$1,533 (max. occupancy, 6); 3 bdrm-$1,246–$1,928 (max. occupancy, 8). **Negotiate price?** no. **Deposit?** $486–$972, depending on flat size. **Check in:** 2 P.M. **Check out:** before noon. **Credit cards?** at 4% service charge. **Tube stops:** Edgware Road, Marble Arch.

Porchester Place Indurrah Apartments, 20 Porchester Place, London W1Y 7DA

photo p. L

The Indurrah apartments at Porchester Place are in a modern, purpose-built building in Connaught Village, two blocks west of Edgware Road. The Marble Arch tube stop is a short walk away, and Hyde Park is just across Bayswater Road. The department stores of Oxford Street, Marks and Spencer and Selfridges, are just beyond Marble Arch.

There are eight two- and three-bedroom flats at Porchester Place, all of which have two baths. While the exterior is modern, the decor, typical of Indurrah, is traditional and elaborate.

Each apartment opens into a wide foyer with wallpaper in a yellow-bordered, pink and white stripe, the same pattern on the walls of the living/dining area. In the living room, very large, especially by London standards, are two overstuffed sofas in a rich red, gold, and black fabric; brass and glass coffee and end tables; and a built-in white wooden seat running the length of the wide window. Drapes match the fabric of the sofas. The dining room is separate with a large table and six chairs upholstered in the same pattern as the blue and white wall-to-wall carpet. An art deco brass chandelier lights the table. Two wide windows brighten the room. The kitchen is tiled in gray with bright pink cabinets, and well equipped with full-size refrigerator/ freezer, double wall oven, four burners, microwave, and washer/dryer. One apartment, Number 7, also has a dishwasher. There are plenty of new pots, pans, tableware, and utensils.

The decor in the master bedroom is quieter. The wallpaper, white with a small blue flower above chair-rail molding, has a blue and white stripe below. The king-size bed has a brass and white metal headboard and matching bedside tables. There are an upholstered chair and an additional small table.

Second and third bedrooms are spacious and also more subdued with simple wallpaper with ceiling border. Twin beds are separated with brass lamps (more like minichandeliers) suspended from the wall above them.

Both baths are off the hallway, and here elaborate decor returns. Sink, tub, toilet, and bidet are in pale pink. Wall tiles are a gray and white floral pattern with a different design around the tub/shower. All towels and linens are changed every four days.

The decor at Porchester Place may be too rich for some, but the apartments are unusually spacious and light. Families are welcome and can enjoy casual dining nearby or cook almost anything in the well-stocked kitchen.

AMENITIES—Elevator, telephone, color cable TV, computer connection, fax (through office), maid service (Monday–Friday), concierge/housekeeper, refrigerator/freezer, stove, toaster, tea kettle, teapot, coffee maker, iron, microwave, dishwasher (in some), washer/dryer, hair dryer (on request).

RESERVATIONS/PRICES/MISC.—**Minimum stay:** 1 night. **Reservations:** office staff. **Telephone:** 0207-629-3946. **Fax:** 0207-629-3690. **E-mail:** *admin@indurrah apartment.freeserve.co.uk.* **Web site:** *www.indurrahapartment.freeserve.co.uk.* **Prices per night from:** 2 bdrm, 2 bath-$251; 3 bdrm, 2 bath-$340. **Negotiate price?** yes. **Deposit?** one night's rental. **Check in:** 3 P.M. **Check out:** noon. **Credit cards?** Amex, Visa, MasterCard, debit cards. **Tube stop:** Marble Arch.

Princes Square Apartments, Prince's Square, London

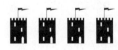   *photo p. L*

The Princes Square Apartments are located in a white stone, vintage-1900 mansion block on a quiet garden square in Bayswater. Central Apartments recently purchased the property, and, as is its norm, it has completely modernized the interior. All appliances are the very latest model and its computer connections are state-of-the-art. In each flat, a TV screen is attached to a keyboard on the desk that allows access to the Internet, e-mail connections, and even video games.

They rent 5 studios, 32 one-bedroom, 1 two-bedroom, and 1 three-bedroom apartments here. All furnishings are modern, and each flat has a sofa that opens into a double bed.

The test of a good studio is separation between living and sleeping areas, and these pass the test. A pillar, now painted white, preserved from the reconstruction, emphasizes the division. The sleeping section contains a double bed, side tables with reading lamps and drawers, and a lingerie chest against the far wall. A glass dining table with three chairs separates the bed and the kitchenette. The kitchenette squeezes a full set of appliances in a small space: small refrigerator/freezer, full stove with four burners and extractor hood, microwave, and cooking utensils of good quality. The living area contains a leather sofa, easy chair, tables, and TV/keyboard. A desk is in the corner. Floors are pine.

The one-bedroom is similar but everything is larger. The bathroom is off the right of the small foyer. It has power shower/tub, gray tiled floor, and a green tile backsplash around the tub. The sink is built into a black tile counter with cabinet beneath. A closet is off the hallway and there is an additional closet in the bedroom. Small, about 9 by 12 feet, the bedroom has a queen bed, side tables with reading lamps, and a chest of drawers. In keeping with the contemporary decor, there are blinds on the windows rather than drapes. The living room is next to the bedroom and has a leather sofa, a velvet easy chair, and a wooden desk. The étagère holds a TV and stereo/CD player. A glass table and chairs are opposite the sofa in the kitchen area. The kitchen is the same as in the studio.

While these apartments attract many corporate clients, families are certainly welcome. Management provides cribs and high chairs free of charge and puts them in apartments before the family arrives. Kensington Park, a great place for kids, is four blocks away, and the whole family can enjoy a visit to the Kensington Palace court dress collection. A quiet pub, the Prince Edward, occupies an adjacent corner, and the Bayswater tube stop is three blocks away.

These flats are convenient to London attractions but in a peaceful residential neighborhood. If use of the Internet is part of your daily routine, they are an especially good choice.

AMENITIES—Elevator, telephone (2 lines), color satellite TV, radio, computer connection, fax (in flat), maid service (Monday–Friday), concierge/housekeeper (on duty 8 A.M.–8 P.M.), refrigerator/freezer, stove, toaster, tea kettle, teapot, coffee maker, iron, microwave, washer/dryer (in 2-bdrm), hair dryer, toiletries, welcome pack (on request at extra charge).

RESERVATIONS/PRICES/MISC.—**Minimum stay:** 1 night. **Reservations:** office staff. **Telephone:** 0207-313-7888. **Fax:** 0207-313-7889. **E-mail:** *citypav@central-apartments.com*. **Web site:** *www.central-apartments.com*. **Prices from:** studios-$295 per night, $2,065 per week; 1 bdrm-$333 per night, $2,332 per week; 2 bdrm-$419 per night, $2,931 per week. **Negotiate price?** yes. **Deposit?** yes. **Check in:** 2 P.M. **Check out:** 12 noon. **Credit cards?** yes. **Tube stop:** Bayswater.

Two Hyde Park Square, London W2 2JY

photo p. L

Two Hyde Park Square, a modern block of 74 studio and one-bedroom apartments, is located three streets north of Hyde Park, and a five-minute walk from Marble Arch in a residential area known as Connaught Village. The gated park opposite is available to guests.

Management classifies each studio as either standard or superior, and one-bedroom apartments as superior or senior. Superior studios and senior one-bedrooms are simply the largest and most recently refurbished, but the terminology can be confusing.

Regardless of the category, the studio flats are appealing and designed for maximum privacy and efficient use of living area. Both types are L-shaped with twin beds in the alcove formed at the bottom of the L. In the superior studio, you gain a table with a lamp between the beds, while the standard makes do with two reading lights on the wall. Both have a sofa, easy chair, coffee table, and TV. A dining table with seating for four is at the top of the L. The superior studio also has a sofa table/cupboard and a small desk with telephone and lamp in front of a window. Rightfully called a kitchenette, the cooking area is tiny, almost a closet. While some studios have no ovens, they do have a stove top and a microwave, refrigerator, sink, dishwasher, and coffee maker. Bathrooms are also small but adequate with a sink and tub with power shower.

The one-bedroom apartments come with larger kitchens and have a full-size convection oven. All of the senior one-bedrooms occupy the corners of the building, giving them more floor space and light. They contain the same furnishings as the studios but also have a bookcase and an additional cupboard in the dining area.

All of the flats have tiny, tiny balconies (room for one person standing), direct-dial telephones, satellite television, underground car parking, secured entrance, and maid service five days a week. A concierge is on duty round the clock. For the business traveler, fax, photocopying, and message services are available through the office. Additional guests may stay in each flat at a cost of £10 ($16) per person per night.

AMENITIES—Elevator, telephone, color TV with satellite, fax (in office), maid service (5 days), concierge, refrigerator, freezer (small), stove (except some studios), toaster, tea kettle, teapot, coffee maker, iron, microwave, dishwasher.

RESERVATIONS/PRICES/MISC.—**Minimum stay:** 7 nights. **Reservations:** Salim Hansa. **Telephone:** 0207-262-8271. **Fax:** 0207-262-7628. **E-mail:** none. **Web site:** *www. apartments-hps-london-paris.co.uk*. **Prices per week:** standard studio-$941, superior studio-$1,111; superior 1 bdrm-$1,168, senior 1 bdrm-$1,355. **Negotiate price?** no. **Deposit?** by credit card. **Check in:** 4 P.M. **Check out:** 12 noon. **Credit cards?** yes. **Tube stops:** Marble Arch, Lancaster Gate.

Paddington, Bayswater, and Maida Vale: Attractions

What once was simply Paddington evolved into three distinct neighborhoods. Paddington Station dominates the area and links London to the West country and Heathrow Airport. The surrounding streets serve commercial travelers and students with budget hotels, cafes, and little else. The multistory Hilton Hotel that recently broke the skyline on Edgware Road may change the neighborhood somewhat, but for now it's a busy, ethnic, and commercial place with a surprisingly rich past.

Paddington began as an Anglo-Saxon chieftain's village and in the 18th century became a haven for French Huguenots fleeing persecution. Regent's Canal bisected the area in 1812 and established a direct trade link with the industrial midlands. Paddington Station followed in 1838, and the first underground line, the Metropolitan, in 1863. As a major hub of transportation, Paddington and Bayswater acquired the cosmopolitan character that they retain today. French, Greek, and Jewish settlers have now given way to Asian and Arab communities.

Bayswater is really the southern part of Paddington, but developers under the influence of architect John Nash adopted it for upper-middle-class housing in the 1830s. Four- and five-story mansions arranged around a series of garden squares attracted merchants and successful professionals. Although it would never rival Mayfair or Belgravia, Bayswater's finer streets (Gloucester Square, Lancaster Gate, and Porchester Gardens) compare favorably. Proximity to Hyde Park and the Italian Fountains of Kensington gardens adds to the attraction.

The part of Paddington north of Regent's Canal took its name from the Battle of Maida, a British victory in 1806. Large, white, stucco mansions and terraces set on wide streets make this one of the most desirable addresses in London. The section by the canal called Little Venice is particularly attractive. Gaily painted canal boats still ply the waters from Camden Town to Kensal Green, and a shady path alongside provides an easy walk all the way to Regent's Park.

Shops, Restaurants, and Pubs

Whiteleys of Bayswater on Queensway is a modern shopping mall, and the only one of its type in the area. It has more than 75 stores, cafes, and restaurants, anchored by Marks and Spencer. Many London chain stores have branches here.

The Portobello Road Market from Penbridge Road to Westbourne Grove is one of the biggest open-air markets in London. You either love it or hate it (it gets one *yes* and one *no* in our family). The market is divided into three sections: antiques, foods (see below), and a flea market with used (sometimes very used) clothing and all sorts of odds and ends. It's open from 6 A.M. to 5 P.M. on Saturdays and is very crowded.

Saturday is a great day for foods in the Portobello Market. Food stalls run along one side of the road from Colville Terrace to Lancaster Road. Fresh produce (some of it organic), breads, cakes, pies, pastries, bagels, and muffins tempt every step of the way.

Otherwise the whole area is a gold mine of ethnic groceries that reflect the make-up of the neighborhood.

In addition to the market on Portobello Road are the Breadstall at 172 with outstanding French and Italian breads, pastries, and croissants, and R. Garcia and Sons at 248–250, a Spanish delicatessen and grocery. R. Garcia and Sons features Serrano ham, cheese, olives, and a huge selection of olive oils. Not ethnic, but also on Portobello Road, is Kingsland Master Butchers (140). Kingsland is an old-fashioned butcher shop and the only accredited Rare Breed Survival Trust outlet in London. You will find exceptional quality pork, beef, and lamb plus sausages, game, pâtés, and pies.

Two Portuguese shops are worth a special visit. Lisboa Delicatessen at 54 Golborne Road is a large and friendly shop with olive oils, figs, herbs, salt cod, cured meats, and other Portuguese specialities. The Lisboa Patisserie across the way is a bakery and coffee shop. The coffee is Sical and the pastries, cream-filled cakes and pumpkin-filled pillow cakes, are the best tastes of Portugal. You may take out or have with coffee in the shop.

Also on Golborne Road at 94 is an outstanding Moroccan grocery, Le Maroc. Here you will find Moroccan meats, cheeses, olives, dried fruits, and several barrels of different types of couscous.

For Belgian chocolates and a chance to say the zippiest shop name in town, go to Choccywoccydoodah (47 Harrowby Street) off Edgware Road. While it specializes in wedding cakes that are fun to see, you can also buy truffles to take home or munch as you walk along.

Those in search of food and beverage in Paddington and Bayswater are best served by the many Middle Eastern and oriental restaurants in the area. Three fine Chinese restaurants cluster near the Queensway tube. Mandarin Kitchen (14–16 Queensway, 0207-727-9012; entrees, $10 to $40) specializes in Scottish lobster served on noodles, while the Royal China (13 Queensway, 0207-221-2535; entrees, $14 to $16) gets high marks for its dim sum, the steamed pork dumplings especially. Neither is cheap but the rooms are spacious, comfortable, and tastefully decorated. Four Seasons at 84 Queensway (0207-229-4320; entrees, $7 to $40) prepares authentic Cantonese dishes. The most popular is the Cantonese roast duck. All of these restaurants are popular and have loyal advocates. Reserve early.

Near the Portobello Market at 95–97 is Portobello Gold, a pleasant brasserie with a glass-roofed conservatory and wall-to-wall plants. The food is tasty and reasonably priced (0207-460-4918; entrees, $12 to $19). For inexpensive but high-quality Polish food, there is Anthony's at 54 Porchester Road. Try the potato pancakes or the herring (0207-243-8743; entrees, $12 to $22). Meson Bilbao at 33 Malvern Road (0207-328-1744; entrees, $14 to $22) serves Basque seafood dishes of outstanding quality.

There are lots of pubs in Paddington and Bayswater, but few to go out of the way for. The Westbourne, 101 Westbourne Park Villas, may be the best for food (it's considered by *Time Out* to be one of the best gastropubs in London). Good roasts, fish and fish soups, a sound wine list, and a range of beers combine to create crowds at peak hours, especially dinner hour. Come early or for lunch. The Prince Edward on Prince's Square (just opposite Princes Square Apartments) fits the bill if you want a quiet drink in a local. Between Paddington Station and Lancaster Gate, the Mitre (24 Craven Terrace) serves traditional food in an Edwardian setting to a largely local crowd. It has a no-smoking area and patio tables in summer. My first choice in Bayswater would be The Archery Tavern, the first building in the development, dating from 1839. At 4 Bathhurst Road, it is just a bow shot north of Hyde Park and serves hard-to-find Dorset beers like Tanglefoot. The wood-paneled interior has a rural feel and the owners have resisted the temptation to remodel it. There is even a bit of a garden.

For public establishments in the grand manner, go north to Maida Vale. The Warrington (round the corner from Europa House, above) dominates Warrington Crescent and was once a hotel and, some say, brothel. It exemplifies the Edwardian extravagance of its heyday, from the carved columns and etched glass outside to the marble bar and floral ceiling inside. Order a pint of Marston Pedigree, sit on one of the velvet plush sofas, and take in the opulence. It is a fitting neighbor to Crocker's Folly, which we praised in the chapter on Marylebone. Both are described in detail by Mark Girouard in his classic *Victorian Pubs* (1984). Nearby, in the Little Venice section of Maida Vale, The Warwick Castle on Warwick Place deserves mention as a charming, unspoiled local serving this classy neighborhood.

Chapter 11

❧❧❧

Longer Short-Term Stays

The Apartments, Sloane Square, 1 Sloane Avenue, Chelsea, London SW3 2SH

The longer-stay apartments of Sloane Square are at three locations: 1 Sloane Avenue, and 36 and 49 Draycott Place. They include a variety of sizes from bedsitting rooms to two-bedroom apartments. All are in lovely redbrick Victorian buildings with public spaces decorated in period style. Floors and doors are highly polished wood, stairways are wide, and walls are papered with floral prints. Numbers 6 and 49 Draycott Place have just been renovated and converted to flats; they opened for business in the winter of 2000.

Apartments at the oldest of the three, 1 Sloane Avenue, owned by Panorama Property Services since 1998, retained the high ceilings of the original lower floors and reproduced the cornices, chair-rail, and crown moldings that once adorned the walls. Three of the five one-bedroom apartments at Number 1 have sitting areas in the gabled portion of the building, giving them three large bay windows. The dining table and chairs are in front of the windows, nicely set off from the rest of the large room. A sofa bed and matching easy chair are along one wall. Bedrooms have five-foot double beds and bedside tables with reading lamps. Baths are modern with either tub/shower combinations or showers. Kitchens have tiled floors, white cabinets, full stoves, microwaves, and washer/dryers. Some have a breakfast table and chairs. Every apartment has a fax machine, TV with VCR, and ministereo. Alarm clocks, radios, and hair dryers are standard.

The other two buildings have been completely reconstructed and modernized inside. While the high ceilings are gone, gabled windows remain in flats on the lower floors. With one exception, the one- and two-bedroom apartments occupy an entire floor. All of the flats, including the one studio and four bedsitting rooms have an upholstered sofa bed and matching easy chair in blue or white, coffee and occasional tables, dining table and chairs, five-foot double beds, baths with showers or tub/showers, and complete kitchens with white cabinets, stoves, full refrigerators, microwaves, and washer/dryers. One of the fourth-floor bedsitting rooms has French doors leading to a tiled terrace.

The prices below include VAT at 17.5 percent, which reduces to 3.5 percent after 28 days.

AMENITIES—Elevator (none), telephone, color satellite TV, radio, computer connection, fax (in apartment), maid service (once a week), housekeeper, refrigerator/freezer, stove, toaster, tea kettle, teapot, coffee maker, iron, microwave, washer/dryer, hair dryer, toiletries, welcome pack.

RESERVATIONS/PRICES/MISC.—**Minimum stay:** 3 months. **Reservations:** Panorama Property Services, Ltd. **Telephone:** 0142-866-1831. **Fax:** 0142-865-1566. **E-mail:** *sales@theapartments.co.uk*. **Web site:** *www.theapartments.co.uk*. **Prices per week from:** studios-$1,066; 1 bdrm-$1,142; bedsitting rooms-$809; 2 bdrm, 2 bath-$1,704. **Negotiate price?** depends on length of stay. **Deposit?** varies with property. **Check in:** 2 P.M. **Check out:** noon. **Credit cards?** at 3% surcharge. **Tube stop:** Sloane Avenue and South Kensington.

NOTE: "The Apartments" just opened a fifth building at 49 Hans Place. Even though just behind Harrods, the six-story Victorian is on a quiet street and faces a private garden. The flats are studios, one-, and two-bedrooms, and prices start at $1,900 per week.

Arlington House

During the summer high season, Arlington House rents for a minimum stay of 21 days. Please see chapter 6, page 101, for a full description of Arlington House.

Elliott House, 1 Molyneux Street, London W1H 6BY

Built in 1939, this corner art deco building served briefly as a police station before it was fully renovated as a block of luxury flats in 1995. These stylish apartments provide abundant space and elegance at a price lower than comparable properties, perhaps because Marylebone is less expensive than Mayfair or Knightsbridge. On a small street a block off Old Marylebone Road and two short blocks from Edgware Road, Elliott House seems a special treasure hidden in a quiet nook in this busy city.

There are 17 flats in Elliott House, all but three are two-bedroom apartments that range in size from "small" to "deluxe business." There are two three-bedroom apartments and a mews house that is larger still. Furnishings are traditional with art deco touches throughout. Many flats have either a patio or a terrace. Most have two and a half baths, and each flat is equipped with convection oven, microwave, large refrigerator and freezer, dishwasher, and washer/dryer. All kitchens have ample cupboards well supplied with fine china, crystal, glassware, and coordinated linens. The reception desk in the lobby is managed 24 hours a day for service and security. Flats have color televisions, independent telephone and fax lines, video entry phone, and five-day maid service. Conference facilities are available at an additional fee.

We did not find the "small" apartment to be small at all. Entered through an alcove, the living/dining area is large enough to hold two easy chairs, coffee and side tables, a television set, and a dining table seating four. The master bedroom with *en suite* bath can be closed off from the rest of the flat for optimum privacy and quiet. It has a queen-size bed, lamp tables, and a dressing table. The second bedroom, also with *en suite* bath, has twin beds, side tables, and a dressing table. Both baths have tubs with power showers. The kitchen is bright with white wall tiles and a window. The "small" apartment we visited had its own exit to the street.

The standard two-bedroom apartment is large. There is a long hall that opens into a spacious living/dining area with large windows. There are two sofas, two easy chairs, side tables with lamps, a TV, and a dining table for six. The kitchen is separate and roomy with designer-coordinated appliances and cabinets. The bedrooms, down a short flight of stairs, are furnished and stocked with the same amenities as those in the smaller apartment. In the "family two-bedroom," the floor plan is reversed. The bedrooms are on the upper level and the kitchen with breakfast table is on the lower level.

Elliott House is conveniently located near the Edgware Road. A large Safeway is two blocks away. Across the street is the Duke of Windsor Pub, serving fine Thai food to eat in or take away, and down the road is the Wargrave Arms, a Young's Brewery pub.

AMENITIES—Elevator, telephone, color TV with satellite, radio, computer connection, fax (in flat), maid service (5 days), concierge, refrigerator, freezer (large), stove with oven, toaster, tea kettle, teapot, coffee maker, iron, microwave, dishwasher, washer/dryer, hair dryer, toiletries, welcome pack.

RESERVATIONS/PRICES/MISC.—**Minimum stay:** 1 month. **Reservations:** HPS Apartment Rentals. **Telephone:** 0207-262-8271. **Fax:** 0207-262-7628. **E-mail:** *reservations@apartments-hps-london-paris.co.uk*. **Web site:** *www.apartments-hps-london-paris.co.uk*. **Prices per week:** 2 bdrm (small)-$1,173–$1,759, 2 bdrm (standard)-$1,265–$1,852, 2 bdrm (family)-$1,665–$2,398, 2 bdrm (deluxe business)-$1,933–$2,731; 3 bdrm-$2,132–$3,331; mews house-$1,999–$2,798. **Negotiate price?** no. **Deposit?** yes. **Check in:** 2 P.M. **Check out:** 11 A.M. **Credit cards?** Yes. **Tube stops:** Edgware Road, Marylebone, Marble Arch.

Gloucester Park Apartments, Ashburn Place, Kensington, London SW7 4LL

Situated in its own gardens off Cromwell Road, Gloucester Park's 100 apartments offer modern luxury in a parklike but convenient location. Managed by the Cheval Group, these one-, two-, and three-bedroom flats have the style and amenities typical of Cheval Apartments.

Each apartment at Gloucester Park has large picture windows in the living room that open onto a balcony with a view of the gardens and of London itself on the higher floors. Provided with table and chairs, the balconies make a delightful setting for breakfast coffee or an evening cocktail. Each bedroom in Gloucester Park has its own *en suite* bath, and every apartment has an additional powder room. There is an on-site fitness center with saunas, free for guest use. Secured parking in its underground garage is available for a charge of $124 per week.

The one-bedroom apartment, about 800 square feet in total size, opens into a foyer with a powder room immediately to the right and the kitchen just beyond. The kitchen is complete with ample cabinets, high-quality china and glassware, and Miele appliances: full stove, microwave, dishwasher, and washer/dryer. The living/ dining area is next to the kitchen. It is a large room full of light from the floor-to-ceiling windows leading to the balcony that runs the length of the exterior wall. Decorated in coordinated neutral colors and fabrics, the sectional sofa and easy chair give the apartment a comfortable, homey feel. A dining table with four chairs is across from the windows near the foyer. Allowing maximum privacy, the bedroom is at the far end of the apartment. Entry is into a short hallway with bath and bedroom behind it. The bed is king size and the room is spacious enough for a reading corner with two upholstered chairs. A bureau with mirror above it is along one wall, while a walk-in closet runs the length of another. The tiled bath has a power shower/ tub and lots of plushy towels.

In the three-bedroom apartment, 1,700 square feet, each of the bedrooms also enters into a hallway with bath and bedroom beyond. All bedrooms have king-size beds, bedside tables, bureau with mirror, and reading corner. Curtains, bedcovers, and walls are in coordinated pastel shades. The master bathroom has a tub with a separate power shower, while the other *en suite* baths have power shower/tubs combined. The living/dining room (very large at 332 square feet) is to the right of the apartment entrance. Furnishings are similar to the one-bedroom flat except for the dining table with eight chairs. The powder room is behind this main room, off the hallway. In addition to the balcony off the living room, there is one off the smaller third bedroom.

Business equipment, such as computers, printers, and fax machines, is available for rent. In fact, in the two- and three-bedroom apartments, Gloucester Park staff will convert one room into a full office complete with desk.

Concierge services are available 24 hours a day. Towels are changed twice a week and linen once.

AMENITIES—Elevator, telephone, color multilanguage satellite TV, radio, computer connection, fax (at extra charge), maid service (Monday–Friday), concierge/ housekeeper, refrigerator/freezer, stove, toaster, tea kettle, teapot, coffee maker, iron, microwave, dishwasher, washer/dryer, hair dryer, toiletries.

RESERVATIONS/PRICES/MISC.—**Minimum stay:** 90 days. **Reservations:** office staff. **Telephone:** 0207-373-1444. **Fax:** 0207-244-5050. **E-mail:** *gpa@chevalgroup.com.* **Web site:** *www.chevalgroup.com.* **Prices from:** 1 bdrm, 1.5 bath-$1,799 per week; 2 bdrm, 2.5 bath-$2,836 per week; 3 bdrm, 3.5 bath-$3,797 (after 28 days, VAT reduces from 17.5% to 14%). **Negotiate price?** for longer stay. **Deposit?** yes. **Credit cards?** all major. **Tube stop:** Gloucester Road.

Hyde Park Gate, 2, 3, and 4 Hyde Park Gate, Kensington, London W8 5EW

All of the properties of the Cheval Group are luxurious, but the baronial apartments of Hyde Park Gate are the most imposing of all. With very large living and dining rooms, they are an excellent choice for the statesperson or CEO who wants to entertain in the grand style. Just off Kensington High Street, many of the apartments have sweeping views of Kensington Palace Gardens. Guests themselves could feel like royalty in these handsomely done apartments.

The three fine Georgian mansions that comprise these flats were carefully restored over four years, so that many structural details of the original homes remain. Ceilings are high, sashed windows are tall, and wide-arched doorways separate living rooms from dining rooms. Consistent with the exterior, the interior design of the apartments is Georgian. Walls are pale in color with wainscoting above and below, chair-rail moldings, neoclassical plasterwork on some walls, and ornate, rococo work with cherubs, roses, and garlands on others.

The living room, more properly called the drawing room since it is designed for public rather than family use, has two upholstered sofas with additional easy chairs. Reproduction side tables and candlestick table and floor lamps continue the Georgian motif, as does the marble fireplace with intricate carvings and the mantlepiece with symmetrically placed decorative objects. The wooden archway into the dining room is a combination of Roman columns on the bottom and carved flowers on the top. The dining room also has a marble fireplace with a gilt-framed portrait above it. There is a triple-crown molding with frieze. Windows are treated dramatically with drapes and sconces. The long dining table seats 10 comfortably.

Each bedroom has its own *en suite* bath, and many have separate walk-in showers and whirlpool baths. Every apartment has an additional powder room. Beds are queen size with covers and drapes in the same fabric. The bedrooms have large dressers with gilded mirrors, bedside tables with reading lamps, and easy chairs.

Luxury kitchens contain Miele appliances—stove, full-size refrigerator, microwave, washer/dryer, and dishwasher. China and crystal are Villeroy and Boch.

The 10 three-bedroom and 5 two-bedroom apartments vary somewhat in size and configuration. Be sure to ask for a complete description at time of booking.

AMENITIES—Elevator, telephone, color TV, radio, computer connection, fax, maid service (Monday–Friday), concierge/housekeeper, refrigerator/freezer, stove, toaster, tea kettle, teapot, coffee maker, iron, microwave, dishwasher, washer/dryer, hair dryer, toiletries.

RESERVATIONS/PRICES/MISC.—**Minimum stay:** 13 weeks. **Reservations:** Sharon Plowman. **Telephone:** 0207-581-5324. **Fax:** 0207-584-1659. **E-mail:** *sharon. plowman@chevalgroup.com.* **Web site:** *www.chevalgroup.com.* **Prices:** 2 bdrm, 2.5 bath-$2,285–$3,046 (after 28 days, $2,012–$2,683) per week; 3 bdrm, 3.5 bath-$5,330–$7,234 (after 28 days, $4,695–$6,372). **Negotiate price?** yes. **Deposit?** yes. **Check in:** by arrangement. **Check out:** by arrangement. **Credit cards?** yes. **Tube stop:** High Street Kensington.

Hyde Park Residence, 55 Park Lane, London W1Y 3AE

At 55 Park Lane, the Hyde Park Residence keeps company with the Dorchester and Four Seasons, two of the most elegant and expensive hotels in London. Like them, it exudes luxury from its spacious lobby to the fine fabrics, high-quality wall coverings, and antique-style furnishings in its lavish and roomy flats.

Built as an apartment block in the 1930s, Hyde Park Residence has an art deco exterior, but a traditional interior. The lobby is grand with a concierge staff on duty 24 hours.

The 109 flats range in size from one-bedroom to four-bedroom penthouses. Every bedroom has its own bath. Some flats have balconies overlooking Hyde Park.

Each flat opens on a marble-tiled foyer with a silk flower arrangement, sculpture, and prints or paintings on the walls. The living room is just off the foyer. The bedrooms are down a generous hallway.

The flats are all individually decorated and continually refurbished. Those most recently redone in each category are more expensive. Decorated in typical English-country-manor style, the living rooms have sofas in floral fabrics, matching easy chairs, other comfortable chairs, fireplace, VCR, CD player, stereo, and large 28-channel satellite TV. There is a separate dining room with large table, chairs, side tables, and chandelier. The china is Wedgewood and the goblets and wine glasses are crystal. Some dining rooms have fireplaces.

All bedrooms have either king-size or twin beds, bedside tables, and coordinated comforters and drapes. Many master bedrooms have a seating alcove just off the bedroom with an easy chair, a lamp, and a dressing table.

Bathrooms are equally generous and have Italian marble counters and walls. Towels are plentiful, and bathrobes and toiletries are supplied.

The kitchens are among the largest we saw and stocked with a complete range of cooking and serving implements. There are a convection stove, microwave, refrigerator/ freezer, dishwasher, washing machine, and every appliance a homemaker might want. For those who don't want, catering services are available.

Hyde Park Residence provides equally well for the business executive, with fax lines, modems, two telephone lines, voice mail in each apartment, and optional typing and secretarial services. It also welcomes families and can arrange for babysitting. The rooms are certainly large enough for energetic children, and Hyde Park is right across the street.

Maid service is twice weekly but can be daily for an additional cost. Staff will shop at Harrods or Marks and Spencer's food halls for a 10 percent service charge.

Security is top-notch with a computerized Guestkey system, video surveillance of corridors, and 24-hour security staff.

AMENITIES—Elevator, telephone (2 lines with voice mail), color TV with satellite, radio, computer connection with modem, fax (for extra charge), maid service (2 days), concierge, refrigerator, freezer, stove, toaster, tea kettle, teapot, coffee maker, iron, microwave, dishwasher, washer/dryer, hair dryer, toiletries, welcome pack.

RESERVATIONS/PRICES/MISC.—**Minimum stay:** 13 weeks. **Reservations:** office staff. **Telephone:** 0207-409-9000. **Fax:** 0207-493-4041. **E-mail:** *internet@hpr.co.uk*. **Web site:** *www.hpr.co.uk*. **Prices per week:** 1 bdrm-$2,094–$2,950; 2 bdrm, 2 bath-$3,426–$4,283; 3 bdrm, 3 bath-$5,520–$6,853; 4 bdrm, 4 bath-$7,614. **Negotiate price?** no. **Deposit?** 1 week's rent. **Check in:** 12 noon. **Check out:** by arrangement. **Credit cards?** yes. **Tube stop:** Hyde Park Corner.

Lancaster Apartments, 27 Draycott Place, Chelsea, London SW3 2SH

Although most of the flats at Lancaster Apartments rent for a one-week minimum, the two one-bedroom apartments in this stone townhouse will rent for a 90-day minimum stay. (Please see chapter 8, p. 143, for a complete description of the exterior of Lancaster Apartments.) Both of these apartments are on the basement level, but don't let this stop you from considering them. Each has a private entrance and a large window in the living room to provide plenty of light. Even though they are the smallest flats in the building, they are surprisingly spacious and well equipped for a long stay.

Entry to each flat is down a small stairway by the side of the building and into a foyer. In Flat 1 to the left of the foyer are a storage area, kitchen, and tiny dining area (six feet by six feet). To the right are the bedroom with another window and *en suite* bath, and the living room. Flat 2, the rear basement flat, is somewhat larger. To the right of the foyer is a shower room. On the left is a short hallway, with the bedroom and *en suite* bath to the right and the living room to the left. Through the living room at the far end are the kitchen and dining alcove.

Both living rooms are furnished with a sofa and two matching easy chairs beside a nonworking fireplace. There are side tables, a mirror, lamps, pictures, and area rugs over the wall-to-wall carpeting. A TV with satellite reception and a VCR are in one corner. In Flat 1, the dining area is separate, while in Flat 2, it is set off in the main room. Each has an ample supply of china, crystal, silver, table linens, and dining tables with four chairs. Kitchens have a large refrigerator/freezer, full stove, microwave, washer/dryer, and good cabinet space. The bedrooms have double beds, side tables with reading lamps, dresser, and closet.

AMENITIES—Elevator, telephone, color satellite TV, radio, computer connection through phone, fax (available for rent), maid service (Monday–Friday), refrigerator/freezer, stove, toaster, tea kettle, teapot, coffee maker, iron, microwave, washer/dryer, hair dryer.

RESERVATIONS/PRICES/MISC.—**Minimum stay:** 90 days. **Reservations:** Annek D'Arcy. **Telephone:** 0207-225-0928. **Fax:** 0207-225-0570. **Prices from:** 1 bdrm-$1,047 per week. **Negotiate price?** yes. **Deposit?** $570. **Check in:** 2 P.M. **Check out:** 11 A.M. **Credit cards?** only American Express. **Tube stop:** Sloane Avenue.

Nell Gwynn House, Sloane Avenue, Chelsea, London SW3 3AX

Nell Gwynn House rents short-term and longer-term apartments, and the two types of rentals are under separate management. The Accommodation Office of Nell Gwynn House handles longer-term rentals, a minimum stay of 22 nights, for 200 individual owners. There are three classes of studios: small (one or two people), standard (two occupants), and superior (large studios, some of which have a sofa bed for two additional people). There are small one-bedroom apartments for two to three, and large one-bedrooms that can accommodate four. Size and amenities increase as the price goes up.

Nell Gwynn House is in an excellent location with a large Safeway just down the block, greengrocer, baker, butcher, and pie shop at Chelsea Green two blocks east; the shops of King's Road are nearby, and Harrods is a 10-minute walk. Prices at Nell Gwynn House are modest for the neighborhood. For a full description of the exterior and lobby, please see chapter 8, pp. 144 and 145.

Since the apartments are individually owned, style of furnishing and decor differ from traditional to modern, depending on the choice of the owner. A plus is that owners do stay in them from time to time, so they tend to be well equipped with cooking utensils, tableware, and glasses. Studios have a sofa and an easy chair, a coffee table, a dining table with the appropriate number of chairs for number of occupants, and a cabinet or dresser. Beds range from singles through doubles to queen size. Smaller studios may have only a microwave and two burners without an oven. Larger studios have full stoves with four burners and microwaves. All have at least an under-counter refrigerator and some have full-size refrigerator/freezers.

One-bedroom apartments have a sofa and an easy chair or two sofas, dining table with chairs, and occasional tables. Bedrooms have double, twin, or queen-size beds. A few have washer/dryers and/or dishwashers.

All baths at Nell Gwynn House are good-size, tiled, with sink, mirror, shower/bath combinations, and heated towel racks. Fixtures range from simple to gilded. Towels and linens are changed once a week.

Since the apartments vary, it is essential to ask for what you want at time of booking. Flats at the back are quieter and more expensive. They also tend to be better decorated with more complete kitchens.

The longer you stay, the lower the weekly rental is. After 28 days, the VAT, included in the prices listed below, decreases from 17.5 percent to 3.5 percent.

AMENITIES—Elevator, telephone (metered), color TV, maid service (Monday–Friday), concierge/housekeeper (24 hours a day), refrigerator, stove (in some), toaster, tea kettle, teapot, iron, microwave, dishwasher (in larger one-bedrooms), washer/dryer (in larger one-bedrooms).

RESERVATIONS/PRICES/MISC.—**Minimum stay:** 22 nights. **Reservations:** Christiane Ewing or Sue Hawke, The Accommodation Office. **Telephone:** 0207-584-8317. **Fax:** 0207-823-7133. **Prices from:** studios (small)-$640 per week, (large)-$794 per week; 1 bdrm (small)-$956 per week, (large)-$1,280 per week. **Negotiate price?** depends on length of stay. **Deposit?** 1 week's rent. **Check in:** noon. **Check out:** noon. **Credit cards?** all major. **Tube stop:** Sloane Square.

Priory House, The City, London

Go Native manages rentals for a block of one-bedroom apartments in a newly renovated period building in The City. The apartments are small and suitable for no more than two adults.

While compact, they are comfortable with an uncluttered, open, and airy feel. Each apartment enters into a living/dining area with the kitchen off one end and the bedroom off the other. The room has two wide windows and is a good size, with a blue sofa and matching easy chair on wall-to-wall beige carpeting. There are end tables with reading lamps and a small dining table with two chairs. The TV and VCR are tucked into a corner. The galley kitchen is attractive and well equipped with a full-size stove, microwave, under-counter refrigerator freezer, washer/dryer, and white cabinets on three sides. Counter space is ample. In the bedroom, there are plenty of closet space, a double bed, and blond wood bedside tables with reading lamps. The tiled bath has a power shower but no tub.

These apartments are well located. The Blackfriars subway stop is a five-minute walk, and St. Paul's Cathedral is nearby. A short stroll across Blackfriars Bridge takes you to Jubilee Walk and the South Bank Centre with many art galleries, theaters, restaurants, markets, and bars. A popular pub, the Blackfriar, is close to the tube stop. It has good food, excellent beers (Marston's Pedigree is a favorite of ours), and fanciful decor.

AMENITIES—Elevator, telephone, color TV, radio, computer connection through telephone, fax (available at extra charge), refrigerator/freezer, stove, toaster, tea kettle, teapot, coffee maker, iron, microwave, washer/dryer, hair dryer.

RESERVATIONS/PRICES/MISC.—**Minimum stay:** 4 weeks. **Reservations:** Katy, at Go Native. **Telephone:** 0207-221-2028. **Fax:** 0207-221-2088. **E-mail:** *katy@gonative.*

co.uk. **Web site:** *www.gonative.co.uk*. **Prices from:** 1 bdrm–$1,047 (VAT included). **Negotiate price?** yes. **Deposit?** 1 week's rent. **Check in:** 2 P.M. **Check out:** noon. **Credit cards?** all major. **Tube stop:** Blackfriars.

Thorney Court, Palace Gate, Kensington, London W8 5NJ

Thorney Court is a modern brick building across Kensington High Street from Kensington Palace Gardens. Each of the 60 two- and three-bedroom apartments has a large picture window off the living room that provides a lovely view of the palace and gardens. Penthouse vistas are even more spectacular.

All apartments are decorated in traditional English style with comfortable, overstuffed furniture, elaborate window treatments, fireplaces, fine wallpapers, and color-coordinated furnishings throughout. Each also has a leather-topped desk with two telephone lines for fax/modem and an answering machine. Every bedroom has an *en suite* bath with an extra powder room in each flat.

Flats are large. Two-bedrooms range from 1,450 to 2,200 square feet, while three-bedrooms run from 2,200 to 2,500 square feet. Living rooms have bay windows that enhance the feeling of spaciousness. While all kitchens are galley type, each has a window and is fitted with fine Miele appliances. Floors are black and white tile, and counter surfaces are granite. There is room for a breakfast table and chairs. Baths are in marble and have power shower/tub combinations, heated mirror and towel racks, and fine toiletries.

The smaller two-bedroom apartment opens into a foyer with kitchen to the right and master bedroom to the left. The bedroom has a king-size bed, tables with reading lamps, a chaise lounge, a dressing table and chair, and a small balcony. To the right of the bedroom is the dining room with table and six chairs and a cabinet with an ample supply of china and crystal. Through the dining room is the living room with two sofas in different but coordinated fabrics, easy chairs, tables, and a hassock. The powder room is behind the dining room, and the second bedroom is beyond it, next to the kitchen.

The largest three-bedroom apartment enters into a hallway with powder room to the right and a large square foyer directly ahead. Off the left of the foyer are the two smaller bedrooms, then the dining room leading to the living room, then the kitchen, and finally the master bedroom. Furnishings are similar to the two-bedroom apartment. The master bath has a separate dressing room. A small balcony is off the dining room. The smaller three-bedroom apartment has balconies off two bedrooms.

AMENITIES—Elevator, telephone, color TV, radio, computer connection, fax, maid service, concierge/housekeeper, refrigerator/freezer, stove, toaster, tea kettle, teapot, coffee maker, iron, microwave, dishwasher, washer/dryer, hair dryer, toiletries, welcome pack.

RESERVATIONS/PRICES/MISC.—**Minimum stay:** 22 days. **Reservations:** office staff. **Telephone:** 0207-581-5324. **Fax:** 0207-594-1659. **E-mail:** *sharonplowman@ chevalgroup.com*. **Web site:** *www.chevalgroup.com*. **Prices per week from:** 2 bdrm, 2 bath-$2,284; 3 bdrm, 3 bath-$3,807; penthouse-$3,427 (2 bdrm). **Negotiate price?** yes. **Deposit?** yes. **Check in:** by arrangement. **Check out:** by arrangement. **Credit cards?** all major. **Tube stop:** High Street Kensington.

Appendix

Agencies

This first group of agencies are those we have worked with in writing *How to Stay in London for Less.* We have found them helpful, responsive, and we can recommend them to you. The second and third groups are agencies listed in other sources. We have had no personal contact with them but list them here to broaden your choices. Those ending with an [A] accept rentals through other travel agents.

Agencies We Know

Avanti Apartments, Brookfield, 11 Penshurst Close, New Barn, Kent DA3 7LN
    Telephone: 0147-470-8701   **Fax:** 0147-470-8702
    E-mail: *avanti@avanti-london-demon.co.uk*

    Apartments from budget to luxury, from studio to four-bedroom. Rentals available throughout UK, France, Italy, and U.S., as well as London. Represent Red Lion Square and Soho Square exclusively. [A]

Barclay International, 3 School Street, Glen Cove, NY 11542
    Telephone: toll-free, 800-845-6636 or 516-759-5100
    E-mail: *barcint@ix.network.com*   **Web site:** *www.barclayweb.com*

    The Barclay London Collection includes more than 3,500 apartments throughout London from studios to four-bedroom, from moderate to luxury. Other rentals available in UK and Europe. [A]

British Travel International, P.O. Box 299, Elkton, VA 22827

Telephone: toll-free, 800-327-6097

Web site: *www.britishtravel.com*

A range of apartments in London, UK, France, Italy, and Spain. Catalog descriptions are accurate. Specialist in English country cottages of high quality at reasonable prices.

Cheval Group of Serviced Apartments Limited, 140 Brompton Road, Knightsbridge, London SW3 lHY

Telephone: 0207-225-3325   **Fax:** 0207-581-2869

E-mail: *cheval@chevalgroup.com*   **Web site:** *www.chevalgroup.com*

Manages and rents apartments and townhouses in mansion blocks in central London. Range from superior to luxury. One-week to long-term stays. *See* Cheval Apartments and others in chapter 8, Longer Short-Term Stays. [A]

Globe Apartments, 36 James Street, London W1M 5HS

Telephone: 0207-935-9512   **Fax:** 0207-935-7531

E-mail: *lettings@globeapt.com*   **Web site:** *www.globeapts.com*

A range of well-priced apartments, most in central London. Globe manages most of its rental apartments with good oversight of quality. One-week minimum. *See* Barrett Street, James Street, and St. Christopher's in Marylebone (chapter 2) and others. [A]

Go Native, 26 Westbourne Grove, London W2 5RH

Telephone: 0207-221-2028   **Fax:** 0207-221-2088

E-mail: *enquiries@gonative.co.uk*   **Web site:** *www.gonative.co.uk*

Private apartments and homes of Londoners away from the city temporarily. Each is individually decorated. Now moving toward longer-term rentals, but short-term still available. *See* New Cavendish Street (chapter 2), St. John's (chapter 6), and Priory House (chapter 11).

HPS Apartment Rentals, 2 Hyde Park Square, London W2 2JY

Telephone: 0207-262-8271   **Fax:** 0207-262-7628

E-mail: *reservation@apartments-hps-london-paris.co.uk*

Web site: *www.apartments-hps-london-paris.co.uk*

Represents a range of apartment blocks in central London from moderate to luxury. Manages Two Hyde Park Square. Apartments in U.S., France, and Italy. *See* Two Hyde Park Square (chapter 10).

London Connection, P.O. Box 427, Ogden, UT 84402

Telephone: toll-free, 888-393-9120   **Fax:** 801-393-3024

E-mail: *Sales@LondonConnection.com*   **Web site:** *www.londonconnection.com*

A U.S.-based company renting apartments owned by Londoners. Works closely with a staff team based in London. Apartment rentals from moderate to luxury. One-week minimum. *See* Hill Street (chapter 5) and One Hyde Park Street (chapter 10).

Manors and Co., 1 Baker Street, London W1M 1AA

Telephone: toll-free, 800-454-4385   **Fax:** 0207-486-6770

E-mail: *reservations@manors.co.uk*   **Web site:** *www.manors.co.uk*

Manager and rental agent for five apartment blocks in central London. All properties superior to luxury, with especially roomy flats in Kensington. *See* Portman Square (chapter 2), Basils and Cheshams (chapter 7), and Queensgate Apartments (chapter 9). [A]

Park Lane Apartments, 119/121 Park Lane, Mayfair, London W1Y 3AE

Telephone: 0207-629-0763   **Fax:** 0207-493-1308

E-mail: *parklane@cpd.co.uk*   **Web site:** *www.parklane.co.uk*

Represents superior to luxury apartments throughout central London. Offers one complimentary pass and bus service for each flat. *See* 92 Middlesex (chapter 4), and Barlow Mews and Shaw House (chapter 5). [A]

Westminster Apartment Services Ltd., 28 Ruth Road, Cortlandt Manor, NY 10566

Telephone: 914-736-6168   **Fax:** 914-736-5977

U.S.-based firm associated with the Vienna Group of Companies. Represents blocks of serviced flats in central London. Studios to two-bedroom. Budget to luxury. *See* Jerome House (chapter 2) and Europa House (chapter 10).

Other Agencies in U.S.

Beau Nash International, 164 Greenmeadow Avenue, Thousand Oaks, CA 91320

    Telephone: 800-700-6316   **Fax:** 805-375-9957

British Breaks Ltd., P.O. Box 1176, Middleburg, VA 20118

    Telephone: 540-687-6971   **Fax:** 540-687-6291
    Web site: *www.britishbreaks.net*

British Network Ltd., "The Mews," 594 Valley Road, Upper Montclair, NJ 07043

    Telephone: 800-274-8583   **Fax:** 973-744-0531
    Web site: *www.BritishNetworkLtd.com*

Castles Cottages and Flats Ltd., 70 Walnut Street, Arlington, MA 02476

    Telephone: 800-742-6030   **Fax:** 781-641-1125
    E-mail: *cca@paiera.com*   **Web site:** *www.castlescottages-flats.com.*

Farnum and Christ, 12 Bank Street, Bristol, TN 37620

    Telephone: 800-366-2048   **Fax:** 423-652-2478
    E-mail: *info@farnum-christ.com*   **Web site:** *www.farnum-christ.com*

Global Home Network Inc., 1110-D Elden Street, #205, Herndon, VA 20170-5527

    Telephone: 800-528-3549   **Fax:** 703-318-2086
    E-mail: *ghn@globalhomenetwork.com*   **Web site:** *www.globalhomenetwork.com*

Grant Reid Communications, Inc., P.O. Box 810216, Dallas, TX 75381

    Telephone: 800-327-1849   **Fax:** 972-484-5778

Hometowntours International, P.O. Box 11503, Knoxville, TN 37939

    Telephone: 800-367-4668   **Fax:** 423-690-8484
    E-mail: *hometours@aol.com*

Interhome Vacation Rentals, 124 Little Falls Road, Fairfield, NJ 07004

    Telephone: 800-882-6864   **Fax:** 973-808-1742

In the English Manner, 515 South Figueroa, #1000, Los Angeles, CA 90071

    Telephone: 800-422-0799   **Fax:** 213-629-4759

    Web site: *www.intheenglish-manner.com.*

Keith Prowse and Co., 234 West 44th Street, New York, NY 10036

    Telephone: 800-669-8687   **Fax:** 212-302-4251

London Lodgings Travel, 3483 Golden Gate Way, #211, Lafayette, CA 94549

    Telephone: 800-366-8748   **Fax:** 510-283-1154

Prestige Villas, P.O. Box 1046, Southport, CT 06490

    Telephone: 800-336-0080   **Fax:** 203-254-7261

    E-mail: *prestigevillas@compuserve.com*   **Web site:** *www.villaliving.com*

Villas International, 950 Northgate Drive, #206, San Raphael, CA 94903

    Telephone: 800-221-2660   **Fax:** 415-499-9491

    Web site: *www.villanet.com*

Other Agencies in UK

Apartment Services London, 2 Sandwich Street, London WC1H 9PL

    Telephone: 0207-388-3558   **Fax:** 0207-383-7255

    E-mail: *aptserltd@aol.com*

Capital City Apartments, 40 Buckingham Palace Road, London SW1W 0RE

    Telephone: 0207-828-7724   **Fax:** 0207-931-7126

Central Estates Lettings, 75 Wigmore Street, London W1H 9LH

    Telephone: 0207-224-3773   **Fax:** 0207-224-0033

    E-mail: *lettings@centralestates.demon.co.uk*

Euracom, 52–53 Margaret Street, London W1N 7FF

    Telephone: 0207-436-3201   **Fax:** 0207-436-3203

E-mail: *info@euracom.co.uk*   **Web site:** *www.euracom.co.uk*

Holiday Serviced Apartments, 2nd floor, 140 Cromwell Road, London SW7 4HA

Telephone: 0207-373-4477   **Fax:** 0207-373-4282
E-mail: *reservations@holidayapartments.co.uk*
Web site: *www.holidayapartments.co.uk*

Kay and Co., 45 Chiltern Street, London W1M 1HN

Telephone: 0207-486-6338   **Fax:** 0207-487-3953
E-mail: *kayco@globalnet.co.uk*

Londonettes, 76 Old Brompton Road, South Kensington, London SW7 3LQ

Telephone: 0207-584-3334   **Fax:** 0207-581-0688
E-mail: *londonettes@dial.pipex.com*

Perfect Match, 53 Margravine Gardens, London W6 8RN

Telephone: 0208-748-6095   **Fax:** 0208-741-4213
E-mail: *permatch@netcomuk.co.uk*

Bibliography

Ackroyd, Peter. *London: The Biography.* London: Chatto and Windus, 2000.

Bruning, Ted. *Historic Pubs of London.* Lincolnwood, Ill.: Passport Books, NTC/Contemporary Publishing, 2000.

Girouard, Mark. *Victorian Pubs.* New Haven and London: Yale University Press, 1984.

Gustafson, Sandra. *Sandra Gustafson's Cheap Eats in London.* 4th ed. San Francisco: Chronicle Books, 2000.

————. *Sandra Gustafson's Cheap Sleeps in London.* 4th ed. San Francisco: Chronicle Books, 2000.

Kettler, Sarah, and Carole Trimble. *The Amateur Historian's Guide to Medieval and Tudor London.* Sterling, Va.: Capital Books, 2001.

Messner, Nancy, and Damian Sherlock. *Your Key to Vacation Apartments in London.* Bedford, Mass.: Mills & Sanderson, 1991.

Porter, Darwin, and Danforth Prince. *Frommer's 2000 London.* New York: Macmillan, 2000.

Rista, Christine, ed. *The Essential Guide to London's Best Food Shops.* London: New Holland, 2000.

Time Out Eating and Drinking Guide 2001. 18th ed. London: Time Out Guides, 2001.

Time Out Guide London. 8th ed. London: Time Out Guides, 2000.

Time Out Guide Pubs and Bars. London: Time Out Guides, 2000.

Weinreb, Ben, and Christopher Hibbert, eds. *The London Encyclopaedia.* London: Macmillan, 1995.

Index